INVERNESS, OUR STORY

"*Mind thon time*"

Compiled by

SHEILA S. MACKAY OBE.

FOR

INVERNESS LOCAL HISTORY FORUM

I.L.H.F.

First published in 2004 by
Inverness Local History Forum
Suite 161
24 Station Square
Inverness
IV1 1LD

ISBN 0-9548206-0-6

Printed by,
Highland Printers
Henderson Road
Longman North
Inverness, IV1 1SP

Index

Foreword

This book is an unashamedly nostalgic look back in time at the 'Town' and the lives of its people during the first fifty years of the 20th Century. While you read, imagine yourself listening to the voices of people talking of their own memories of the areas they lived in, the schools they attended, the way they worked, lived and played in an era, which was very different to the Inverness we know in the 21st Century.

Over the last few years we, the Inverness Local History Forum, have recorded on tape many of the stories an older generation of Invernessians had to tell. They shared with us their own personal memories of life in a much smaller and compact Town where families grew up, lived, worked and played together in communities which each had their own special character. Extended families often lived close to each other, everyone knew their neighbours and helped out when hard times came and children formed friendships, which were often forged in the years of the two World Wars and the poverty, which came to many homes during those times.

We have tried to paint a word picture of each of those communities which made up the Town of Inverness, from the rural suburbs of the farming lands at Culduthel, Drummond, Culcabock, the Leachkin, to the Town Centre with its densely populated tenement flats and closes, and the Shore and Merkinch areas. Later as the 20th Century moved on, the farm fields of Dalneigh and Tomnahurich became the streets of new houses at Bruce Gardens, Park Road and Dalneigh. The suburban villages of Culcabock and Clachnaharry became absorbed within the Town boundaries as Inverness expanded outwards in all directions.

History is seldom an exact science. Perhaps as you read through the book you will find slightly differing accounts of an event or descriptions of an area of the Town which you, the reader, may recall differently. We have simply recorded the words of the person relating the story and how they remember it looking back over the years. It is the memory, which is personal to that particular individual and their version of how events were shaped as they saw it. So, as you read, try to imagine you are sitting listening to the person relating their story.

You may recall many of the places, people and events referred to and have a slightly different memory of them, but you will also see that a common thread runs through many of the reminiscences. It is the bond of close communities, shared childhoods and schooldays, which is the thread, which links people from generation to generation. Through these stories we have tried to keep the link from past to present so that it might be passed on to the Invernessians of the future.

The Town of Inverness almost certainly saw its earliest inhabitants in settlements close to the river and to this day our river is still a very clear boundary in the minds of Invernessians. The question, "Do you live on this side or the other side of the river?" has been tacitly understood by many generations of townsfolk and needs no translation. Perhaps the other well-known Invernessian statement of intent, "I'm going over the Town", or "I'm going up the Town", or "I'm going down the Town" signifies to a local exactly where the speaker lives in relation to the river but might well confuse a stranger. However it does highlight what an important part the river has in the local psyche.

This is by no means a comprehensive social history of the people of Inverness. There are many, many more fascinating stories still out there, which are waiting to be told. We are very aware that we have only scratched the surface of the available material and, hopefully as our 'Inverness Remembered' project continues, we will be able to add to the information on the stories of the people of Inverness in the 20th Century, the century, which saw so many changes in the lives and lifestyles of its citizens. It is only through the voices and memories of those who lived throughout these changing times when Inverness was growing, changing and expanding that we can recapture for posterity the story of the people at first hand.

We hope you will enjoy this look back over the years at the lives of the people of the Town, which is now a City. There are funny stories, happy stories and sad stories, but above all it is the peoples' stories.

If you, the reader, have a tale to tell, or if you know of someone, perhaps a relative or friend who does, do please get in touch with us at the address below, but please – don't leave it too long!

Inverness Local History Forum
Suite 161
24 Station Square
Inverness
IV1 1LD

Special Thanks

Our special thanks are also due to those who did some of the interviewing over the years.

John Barnes and Alan Michael in particular.

Burnside Residential Home Art Class for the artwork.

The staff of Inverness Museum, Highland Archives and Reference Library.

The committee members of Inverness Local History Forum who transcribed and typed some of the tape recordings and gave so much support to the project over the years.

Vi Murray for her meticulous proof reading.

Gillian Simpson and Margaret Macleod who dealt so willingly and patiently with typing the manuscripts.

The printing of this book was funded by a Grant from the Lottery "Awards For All".

Grateful Thanks

Our grateful thanks are due to all the following Inverness people who so kindly agreed to share their memories with us over the last few years. Each of them has made a lasting and valuable contribution to the social history of Inverness in the first half of the 20th Century. We apologise if there are any omissions.

Harry Abbott	George MacDonald
Dorothy Ahearn	Hector MacDonald
Helen Barron	Janetta MacDonald
Mary Bain	Joyce MacDonald
James Breakey	Stanley MacDonald
C Burns	Lorna MacEchern
Alexander Chisholm	Robin McEwen
Ron Chisholm	Duncan MacFarlane
Iain Cochrane (New Zealand)	George & Florence MacGillivray
Frank Critchley	Catherine MacKay
Hugh Crout	Eric MacKay
Jack Cummings	Sheila MacKay OBE
Bette Davies	Rev Wm MacKay
Alastair Dunnett	Connie MacKenzie
Grace Fairbairn	Donald (Syd) MacKenzie
Alex (Scoop) Fraser	Donald MacKenzie
Olive Fraser	(Cummings Hotel)
Tommy Fraser	Mona MacKenzie
W Godsman	John Wilson MacKintosh

Menzies Graham	Jean MacLeman
Rita Graham	Jackie & Kay MacLennan
Alastair Grewar	Margaret MacLennan
Bob Jamieson	Helen MacLeod
Ann Fraser	Ian & Grace MacLeod
Flora Jenner	Jean MacNeil
Fred Kelly	Nancy Scott
Catherine Krenz & Wm Hay	Ruth Sharp
Isobel Lindsay & Chris	Robert Sim
Shaw	Ray Skinner MBE
A M Lawrie	James Smith
Mr & Mrs Maxwell	Alastair Sutherland
Alan Michael (Snr)	Alex Sutherland
Ian Michie	Gregor Urquhart
Robert Milne	Louis Urquhart
Chris Morrison	John MacPherson
Louise Munro	Roy Reid
Chris Munro	Murdo Shand
M McAllister	Dugald MacRae
Ann McArthur	John & Daisy Watson
Betty MacDonald	

Lastly, the present Chairman George Christie for his successful application for a grant from 'Awards for All' and his editing in the final stages.

You Must Remember This

Perhaps some of this miscellany of old memories and snippets from the Past (in no particular order but just as they come to mind) will bring back some memories.

The Foundry Hooter at 12.25 every weekday morning

The old Horse Trough at Chapel Street

The horses' hooves clopping on the cobbled streets especially on a frosty day

The old lady and her dog in the little room at the top of the old Museum beside the Police Station on Castle Wynd

Open air dancing and concerts in the Islands, and the little café on the right when you crossed the bridge from Island Bank Road

The sheep and cattle going along Southside Road and down Stephen's Brae to the Mart – it wasn't just their tails they left behind them!

The Saturday matinée at the 'pictures'

The temperature of the water in the 'Baths' during
the war years – Brrr

The lamplighter with his pole in the late afternoon
when the nights started
to draw in

The Invernessians' first sign of approaching winter
"There's snow on the Ben today"

Playing at 'The Stonies' and the 'Lions' Gate' (did
anyone ever see
the lions changing places?)

The fields and farms which are now Hilton, Dalneigh
– and even earlier Bruce Gardens, Dochfour Drive,
Columba Road

The tenement blocks of Castle Street and Bridge
Street and the hundreds of Invernessians who grew
up in them

Taking home a bag of cinders from the gas works in
your hurley or
the bar of your bike

The smell of the gasometer

Scraping the frost off the INSIDE of your bedroom
window in the winter

The old wifie who came round the doors selling
Kessock herrings

The pocket for your hankie in your navy blue school
knickers – and
your liberty bodice

The porpoises which swam alongside the boat when
you were crossing the
Ferry to the Black Isle

The 'tattie' holidays in October and the chapped
fingers that went with the work

The model lodging house in Chapel Street - an early
version of
'Care in the Community'

'Aleckie Duff' following the music wherever it went

The Old High Church curfew bell at 8pm

The farm workers using an old tattie sack over their
heads and shoulders to
keep out the rain and snow

Invernessians referring to the local authority as 'The
Town'

The rush to get out of the 'pictures' before the
National Anthem was played and you might miss the
last bus home

The home-made hurley that was every young lad's pride and joy

The games seasons – marbles, steelack, clayack, glassack, skipping, skeetchie, rounders and by the time autumn came collecting conkers.

Keeping your balance while doing the 'cock-a-doogie' on an icy slide.

The boys wearing short grey flannel trousers, even into secondary school, the girls' hair tortured into ringlets with rags and topped off by a big bow for special occasions.

The dancing days – Wednesday night at the 'Caley', Thursday the Meeting Rooms, Friday off to the Country dances by the bus load to 'Drum', 'The Strath' even Elgin and then back to the Caley on a Saturday night – or perhaps the Empire if a good show was on – Will Starr or the White Heather Club.

The long queues at the Playhouse or La Scala or Palace Cinemas when a popular film was showing and the queue being firmly controlled by a uniformed commissionaire and of course 'snogging' in the back row, but nobody could see through the blue haze of cigarette smoke which permeated the whole cinema.

The Playhouse at Christmas where James Nairn created a magical world of Disney characters which had children staring round-eyed and in even earlier years the display in Fraser's store, Union Street which the older Invernessians remember.

The sixpence halfpenny bazaar, Walkers Toy Shop, the first American style post-war snack bar on Queensgate which sold ice cream sundaes in tall glasses and long spoons and sitting on a high stool just like the 'movies'. The special treat of going out to the Fish and Chip shop for a 'sit down' fish supper with bread, butter and cups of tea or even better 'High Tea' at the Carlton Restaurant in Inglis Street – that was really living it up.

Afternoon Tea in Burnets Tearooms on Academy Street with waitresses in black dresses and little white frilly 'pinnies' serving teas and loaded three storey plates of cakes and scones.

Coopers the grocers in Union Street with the smell of ground coffee scenting the whole street, while MacDonald and MacKintosh's did the same for High Street.

Camerons on High Street and Church Street with the overhead wires and little containers to transport the money from the counter to the cash desk and back with your change when the assistant pulled the wire.

'Wet' batteries for the wireless, sticking your finger on them and tasting the acid.

Listening to children's hour – Uncle Mac and Auntie Kathleen – waiting for the wireless to 'warm up' before the sound came through. Then there was the first TV's, Ernie Mason's shop on Eastgate doing a roaring trade because he sold them cheaper.

Waiting for the TV to 'warm up' before the signal came through.

Street photographers (1950's) snapping you as you shopped in town.

'Faith, Hope and Charity' above Grant's Clan Tartan Warehouse.

Mind Thon Place

Towards the end of the 19th Century and the first half of the 20th Century a lot of the old streets and closes and shops disappeared from the landscape of the Town Centre. Many of those were knocked down to make way for new buildings as the town grew, or were demolished in the clearance of poor and derelict housing. But they were where many Invernessians grew up and spent their early years, despite the lack of any of the amenities we take for granted nowadays.

Here are a few of the names of some of these long lost corners of our history.

Albion Square	Off King Street (rear of British Legion)
The Black 'Closie'	King Street
The Klondyke	Queensgate - a shop to the right of the GPO.
Washington Court	The top of Hamilton Street where the BB's Hall was, earlier, a Synagogue.
Dempster Gardens	The old Back Station – now Safeway's store.

Beaton's Lane	Off Friars Street
Noble's Close	Between King Street and Fairfield Lane
Factory Close	Off King Street
Dyer's Court	Lane off the riverside to King Street/Huntly Street
Bissett's Close	Off Muirtown Street
Cameron's Close	Off Muirtown Street
MacIntosh's Close	Off Muirtown Street
MacRae's Buildings	The Haugh
Loch Ness Buildings	The Haugh
Princes Place	Huntly Street/Queen Street
Victoria Square	Off Rose Street
Milne's Buildings	Rose Street
Albert Place	Former Glebe Street Baths site

Culduthel and Drummond

There was one severe winter and the roads were blocked right up to Culduthel. They were OK up as far as the Hospital (Culduthel) but then the cars got stuck. There used to be old high dykes going up the brae and it was a twisting, winding road, not the straight road now past the Academy. We tried getting up the school brae in my car, my husband had an old mat and cardboard in the boot and he put them under the wheels and eventually we got to the top of the brae, but Leys often got snowed in then. There was an old lady who lived at No 6 on the left as you go up the brae where Balmore Farm is on the right. Years after, she moved down to Culduthel and her old fireplace – an old range – was taken out of the house and I believe it's now in the Museum.

The house we lived in was an old County Council one, but it was great, because for the first time we had an inside toilet and bathroom. When my father was away during the war we were still in the farm cottage, my mother milked the cows just to keep the job open for him and also the cottage. She used to get up at four or five in the morning to do the milking. It was a hard life. Part of the perks of working on the farm was free milk, tatties and free firewood.

Culduthel Smithy was next to us. It was owned by Jock MacDonald, we called him 'Jock the Smith'. They knocked down the Smithy when 'Jock' sold it. You wonder how they got permission for that – to knock down a building like the Smithy. There was actually a burn that ran right under it and I remember the sound of the anvil when we were going to school in the morning.

Och the flooding problems are going to get worse and worse as the trees come down. You see the three burns coming in there down near Balloan Farm, quite near the Undertaker's place, would be flooded as well. It used to be known as St Mary's Loch – I don't know why. And then on the Moor, which used to be between Green Drive and Lodge Road (now Lochardil housing estate) there was a loch there as well called the Black Loch. I used to catch newts there. There was a lot of newts and we used to catch them and keep them as pets but they didn't last very long although we had them in water.

On Sunday then the young men went out for walks and they got all dressed up, and sometimes even wore spats on top of their shoes and some of them carried canes. Some of them used to have a gambling school up in the woods at the end of Green Drive beside Lochardil Hall. They used to go into the woods and play cards, and as a small boy I found out that on a Monday, if I had a walk around, I would find where they were gambling and find some of the pennies they'd lost. If they saw me around on a Sunday, they gave me pennies to keep me quiet so I wouldn't tell my father I'd seen them gambling. It was quite a lucrative way of making a penny or two.

There were severe winters, which we don't get now, drifts in the fields and the roadsides. From our house up Culduthel right down to the main road to the bus-stop it would be blocked with snow and all the men had was a spade to make a pathway. The sheep and cattle were fed by the farm workers, they had to take a tractor but they weren't modern tractors with hoods and things. They would just go and feed the sheep by throwing the turnips off the tractor with spades. The cattle were kept inside and the pigs. The hens were let out but it wasn't long before they all came back into the henhouse. But our mother went and fed the hens, irrespective of how much snow there was the hens always got fed.

The MacFarlane's croft was very much the focal point of our area. I remember they used to keep cows and they used to graze in the summer in what we then called Brackens Park. That was a big field on

Culduthel Road where three houses (approximately numbers 96, 98, 100) now stand. I believe up until the late 20's there were two farm cottages semi-detached, stood there, which were called Burnside cottages – they were 66 and 68. They had fallen down by the time I used to play there, but I recall seeing the foundations, which were still sticking up through the ground, and there was the remains of an old orchard. It was my job on the summer nights when I came home from school at milking time to go and take the cows through the gate, which was just about where number 98 Culduthel Road stands now. I used to get on the back of the old red cow, I can't remember how I got on because she was a big cow, and she just led the way along Culduthel Road, down Burn Road and in the back into the byres where they were milked. Then the milk was taken fresh and put into a great big vat and then all the pails were filled. Everybody in the neighbourhood had a little churn, or two, or three, depending on the size of their family, and once they were filled I would take them round, collecting the empty ones. There were eight or nine houses that used to get their milk every night that way. That was a job I liked very much. I used to muck out the hen house as well, because they also kept hens. I was never so keen on that because I didn't like the hens flapping down on top of my head.

But we had a wonderful childhood really in that particular place, because the MacFarlanes were always there, they never seemed to get fed up with all of us kids who ran around in the yard. Most of us played there for a large part of the day and of course their own two sons who were a bit older than I was. They were all very much part of our family and we had wonderful times together.

The big field at the back where Burnside Home stands now, that used to be cropped some years, and I recall all the men in the area used to turn up with their scythes and all the corn was cut by hand, and the kids used to come along and stook it. They used to have as well, the old dung heap in the middle of the field. I remember when my sister was about three she fell in and they had to drag her out of it, and she was bobbing about in all the liquid matter. So I had to take her home and I think it was me that got into trouble for letting her get near it. But most of the houses on Burn Road were there at that time – with a few exceptions. Where Delnies Road is now, that was a big market garden, owned by a man called Ben Barclay. He supplied a lot of the local fruit and vegetable shops.

On the other side of Delnies Road was a Mr & Mrs MacDougall and they kept turkeys in a big field at the back of their garden and then a little bit round on Drummond Road, just about where Beech Avenue is, again that was a field, a chicken farm, and the old man that kept it was known as 'Willie the Hen'. He didn't used to speak to anybody much, but he had lots of free-range chickens. I suppose he sold the eggs to the shops. But it was a very rural area. There was one bus a day would come down, I think it was a Greig's bus. Before that I think there was only one or two buses a week that came down and picked folk up. There was only one person at that time who had a car. That was the people who lived at number 9, an old couple called MacPhail. He was an ex Station Master. They were a very nice old couple. They had an old Austin 7 and occasionally they would go into town with the car. I don't think it was very often. I thought they were very old then, maybe in their 80's. The old lady, she looked like a female version of Churchill. She was a very small dumpy lady and she always wore full-length black dresses and her hair in a bun. Half the neighbourhood used to cram into the car and off we would set to town, probably about 20 miles per hour. I remember it was a very slow progress, but it was so exciting going in a car.

It was a very close community, because I suppose it was quite isolated. Hilton hadn't been built at all. There was Hilton Farm but that was a good way away, over the fields. I remember in the very bad winter, I think probably the winter of 1947, there was very, very heavy snow and we all had a sledge in those days. We used to sledge down the field of what's now Daviot Drive and Cauldeen Road and then straight over Culduthel Road and down Burn Road on the sledges. You could get a tremendous distance because there was no traffic on the roads then and no gritters. So the snow just lay and packed. It was in the late 40's when they started building the first houses on what's now Daviot Drive and Hilton Avenue, post war. I think they were the first ones because we used to go and play on the building site and get chased by the watchman. But we didn't really do anything very dangerous.

The men in the area, once a year in the autumn, they all used to go up to the Gulls Moor, up Old Edinburgh Road above Druidh Temple where there's a moor and take the gulls' eggs. They took them home and they used to be pickled to keep the supplies going over the winter. Of course we always went to pick brambles. That was a major event. You packed a picnic for the day and we went up by Essich Road and Torbreck. There was a little place in there by a burn we called the Dell. It had a lovely little burn running through it, and so many brambles you could never pick them all. But we all took a picnic and all the mothers would come as well. By the time we got home at night we were pretty exhausted but it was always one of those memorable days. Usually the October holiday Monday seemed to be the day everybody went out for brambles. Then there was a major jam-making exercise after that because nearly all our food was homemade. There was very little bought. You either grew it yourself or made it yourself. Every cupboard in the area was well stocked with homemade jams and pickles, and you always had your potatoes in and grew vegetables. There really wasn't a lot of buying of food. A lot of people had hens, so they could have a chicken. I think a pig used to be slaughtered at the MacFarlane's once a year but that was all kept very much away from us children because the farm animals were all pets. We had names for them all.

We were very much a self-sufficient community, going into town was a major adventure.

One of the other things we used to have a lot of problems with was the Aultnaskiach burn at the bottom of the garden on Burn Road. It regularly flooded. It appears, from what I can recall the folk around the area saying, that up till the time of the war there was very little problem with flooding. But then through the war all the trees on the hills up at the top had all been cut down and of course the trees took up a tremendous amount of water. So when they were taken away the water rose considerably, so every year for many years the burn flooded. One of my memories is the MacFarlanes who had the wee farm beside us – they used to preserve eggs in stuff called 'waterglass' which used to be dissolved in big pottery jars. At one flood the MacFarlane's house, which was quite low lying – the whole ground floor was flooded. I can recall seeing the eggs, which had floated out of the waterglass jars, floating about in the kitchen. Another time, we used to keep hens, and we had a little hen coop at the bottom of our garden which also lay close to the water level, and the hen had obviously been trying to save the chickens when the burn came over. I remember howling the next morning because we found the hen and all the chickens on her back – drowned. So it wasn't easy and the mess it left behind, there was no central heating or anything then to dry off the house and furnishings. So it certainly didn't make life too easy for the women who had to clean up the mess.

On the other side from us was a little cottage – Arch Cottage – which still exists although it's been modernised. That also stood in the middle of a field and at one time after a flood there was thousands of eels left in the field after the water went down – all slithering about in the mud trying to make their way back to the water. But as the years went on the burn went from being quite a broad clean watercourse and it got narrower and dirtier and muddier. We used to paddle as children, I don't think you could do that now, and indeed it dries up often now. They did put in a culvert after the war to divert it from the wee bridge on Burn Road, which couldn't cope with the flow of water, and to bypass the bridge and take it through to the other side. I think that was something the folk in Burn Road used to make great representations to the old Town Council about in those days.

I remember when Drummond Stores opened first, it was owned by Peggy MacKintosh, who had lived in the Laundry in Burn Road. I think I was the first person to get a cake of toffee out of the shop. We used to go there delivering the milk. It was a community then, everybody knew everybody else and it was like a little village.

When I got married first we stayed in Arch Cottage (now 94 Culduthel Road). It was sitting in a big field, and next up the road was another field which had once had cottages in it. One of the things that was very bad was the burn flooding at our croft on Burn Road, it didn't flood so much when I was young but then they started cutting down the trees up at Leys so there was nothing to hold the water.

There was also a pond up by Broom Drive, which used to be a moor and there was a nursery where Drummond School is now that belonged to Urquhart the Seed Merchant and behind that was another pond called the Black Loch. We used to go and collect frogspawn there. It was all heather and woodland at Broom Drive and Green Drive. It was an old wooden bridge on Burn Road when I was young, then they heightened the road to take the steepness away from the brae and built a new waterway to stop the burn flooding right across the road. One time in 1948 the neighbours had to dig a trench across Burn Road to let the flood water run away and the Fire Brigade were out pumping the floodwater. There was a croft Jock Ross had at Upper Drummond, they've built houses on it now but I mind we used to call it the ' stinking croft'. Then where the Michies lived just past Lodge Road there was a wee shop, a Miss Adams had it, the only shop in the district (before Drummond Stores opened) and she sold everything.

In the Drummond area there was a lot of big houses around. We used to go and play in their gardens but nobody every bothered us, we used to have a super play place at Drummond, it was the front part of the big house 'Oaklands' which is actually on Merlewood Road. There's houses built in front of it now but there must have been at some point gardens there, because there were old raspberry bushes, and we all played in there during the summer. We would play hide and seek. It was a wonderful place for children and you couldn't really come to any harm. Then if you went right down by the side of it you came through into an orchard and there was an old building which must have been an old fruit store or granary, which really was in quite dangerous condition but we used to play in it as well. Then we used to slide on our bottoms through the leaves down all the terracing, which took us down on to Island Bank Road, and there was a little green door, just as it comes off Drummond Circus and there you're opposite the Islands and we would go in there and play as well. We would be away all day playing and probably go back home when we were hungry.

I was born at 102 Culduthel Road (now 132) and it was the last house within the Burgh boundary then. We all lived there, it was a rented house and there was no electricity, we had paraffin lamps and a gas supply downstairs only. If you looked at these gas mantles sideways they broke. There were no houses at all on the opposite side of Culduthel Road, the side the Highland Orphanage was on was all fields belonging to Davy Rose of Hilton Farm.

I mind on Burn Road, at the bridge, in those days it was a wooden bridge and the locals used to have dances on it. There was a fellow with a melodeon playing on the bridge at night and they would dance there. The burn itself isn't very big but it was good for fishing but I don't think there's anything much in it now.

DANCING ON the BURN ROAD BRIDGE

The locals used to play football on the bridge as well, there was a chap John MacDonald and he was a cripple, he had crutches and he would use them when he was the goalkeeper and if you went too close to him he would hit you over the head.

And then there was Lodge Road; there was five houses on the one side and nothing on the other side except the fields and the burn. From Beech Avenue right round to the burn on Lodge Road there was a big field, and then there was a piggery belonging to a chap MacDonald and he also had a market garden. He used to have a stall in the Market where he sold fruit and vegetables and his piggery was right beside the burn. On Lodge Road there was very often flooding, and there was a flood one time and I asked this man MacKintosh who grew very good chrysanthemums what had happened to them and he says, "I last saw them hanging on fences at Drummond". Mrs MacKenzie, Stratton, also lived beside the burn on Lodge Road, she had goldfish and I asked her what happened to them and she said they were seen swimming towards Beauly.

On Burn Road there were about five houses on the one side and just a couple on the other side. There was a laundry run by a family MacKintosh next to where Burnside Home is now.

They used to have dances in the Laundry with an accordion or melodeon and they were a great feature in the neighbourhood. Then just up from the Laundry there was a croft run by Bob MacFarlane. He used to go round before the war selling his milk and Bob knew everything that was going on, and when he was doing his rounds he told all the folk the local news. Then at the top of Burn Road on the Brae was a little cottage (No 13) and when I was young, it was occupied by a Mrs MacKenzie, who was a widow with six children. She was put out of her house up in Farr and she walked from there down to the cottage on Burn Road carrying her youngest child, and on foot all the way from Farr. That was about 1920 and she was living on a widow's pension – it must have been very hard for her.

There were things called Glenfield taps or Glenfield fountains and there was two of them on Culduthel Road – one near Drummond Stores and the other one towards Burn Road, and the local people drew their water from them in buckets. None of the houses had hot water at that time, it had to be heated up on the range in buckets. We were just about the top of Lodge Road next to a field and before I was born the field was the site of a military post because it was a special security area and they had soldiers there during the First World War and during the last war. You had to have passes to get through. The farm workers from further up got a special dispensation. When I was a wee boy some of the soldiers came back to see my mother, I think she used to give them tea and plates of soup. But they were there to stop strangers coming in over the hills into a military area. They had a sentry post and a big shed for the guardroom.

Hilton, Muirfield, Culcabock, Drakies and the Crown/Hill

Hilton
(This is old Hilton Village on Old Edinburgh Road)

I was born at No 16 Hilton Village. The old Hilton Village was from Hilton Hospital to Hilton Avenue. There were few other houses in the area at that time and on the left hand side of Old Edinburgh Road was open fields which MacDonald and Fraser Auction Marts used to graze the animals between the sales. There were five fields they used for grazing. There was a shop at No 2, that was the Hilton Village shop. Next door to that was the Robertsons who used to have a Wine Lodge on Castle Street but after the landslide in 1934 they moved their shop to Grant Street. Next to the Robertsons was a little yard we used to call the Laundry. There was a shed at the end of the yard which was used as a laundry at one time but I don't remember it being used.

There was a little croft at the end of the lane. That was the old village and it was a great community in its day. I remember before the war the boys would come to play football at the 'Hollow'. When the dark nights came in they would all sit on the wall under the lamp-post and they would all have an instrument of some sort, a fiddle or an accordion, a mouth organ, a Jew's harp, they had everything, pipes the lot. We used to have great entertainment sitting at the roadside on the wall under the lamppost. It was amazing the number of people who would gather there and they came from all over. Holm Mills, Culcabock, the Town, from all round the town for a game of football, entertainment and no doubt there was a bit of courting going on there too.

Muirfield

In 1906 when I was four we moved to No 2 Muirfield Road and we lived in this house for a year. It was an ancient house, very, very old and it hadn't been occupied for years. Then we moved to No 26 Old Edinburgh Road, it was a funny old house, two steps at the front door and three steps at the back. It was built on a slope on Old Edinburgh Road and why it was I don't know because the houses round about were built on the level. It was No 26 in the old days and then it became No 56.

In the 1920's we lived in Muirfield House on Muirfield Road. The grounds extended as far as Hedgefield and Sunnybank Road and there were few other buildings around then. MacKenzie the Builders put up the new houses on Muirfield Road, semi-detached houses using breeze blocks which he made himself. People thought these blocks wouldn't last but the houses are better than a lot of modern ones.

There was a sawmill there where wood was cut up into faggots, bound into bundles with wire and sold by the Poor House inmates. There was a seat at the corner of Muirfield Road and Muirfield Lane and some of the inmates would sit there in the sun.

About 1918 near Old Edinburgh Road there was a Sentry Box and a Sentry and people were not supposed to go beyond that point. Hedgefield was the hostel for pupils of the Royal Academy and in charge was a Mr Robson, the Latin Master at the Academy. He would 'adjust' exam marks to the level he thought was appropriate.

Mayfield Road didn't have a name at that time, it was just a track with grass and nettles and donkeys grazed there – it was called 'Donkey's Lane'. In Muirfield Road there was a sand pit and all the rubbish was dumped there. Then it was covered up and houses built on it. The sand pit was also called a quarry and it was where the children preferred to play, more fun than in their own gardens.

Well Craigmonie Hotel was originally a Maternity Home, the Ida Merry Nursing Home. I remember the late Willie MacKay the solicitor telling me he was born there. I remember it changing to a hotel but so many different people have had it. And there's the

Kingsmills Hotel, it used to be Kingsmills House. I remember there was a group of people from Culcabock Golf Club who thought it would make a good Club House. They were badly in need of one at the time and I think some of them regretted that they didn't take it on. It would have meant a different approach to the golf course because the first hole would have been there at Kingsmills House. Then there were a lot of houses in Culcabock Avenue where the wee school was – it was very thickly populated. Small cottages but a lot of people in them, it was quite an important community then and of course the Golf Course took a lot of business into the area.

There was a big change years ago at the junction where Damfield Road and Kingsmills Road met. That was completely changed. There used to be a wee cottage right in the middle of the intersection. It wasn't all that dangerous getting by it because there was very little traffic then. That part flooded badly every year. I remember 'Lemon Cottage' at Diriebught, the MacIntyres, was one of the houses that flooded and it still stands there.

Annfield, Culcabock and Drakies

Our house at 5 Darnaway Road was the last house in the road then, the rest was all fields from there to the back of what's now Southside Place. In those days

house in Leys Drive was No 7 and from there
s fields to Craigmonie and Annfield Road and
in the 1920's houses started to be built along
Leys Drive to what is now Walker Park. At a nearby
house 'Lethington' on Annfield Road, every Autumn
a threshing mill came up to the back of the house and
threshed the crops of the surrounding farm land.
Fields of oats and barley were threshed and
harvested. The cattle were brought along Southside
Road. There were fields on the other side of Annfield
Road down to Damfield Road.

There was a pond where Kingsmills Gardens are now
situated, often used for skating in the winter. In those
days Kingsmills House was owned by the Hon Mrs
Walker and she granted to the Town the ground
opposite so that houses wouldn't be built there. It
was to be used as a park – the reason it's called
Walker Park. Fraser Park nearby was given to the
Town by the Frasers of Fraser & Co Furnishers.
Their store is now Arnotts in Union Street.

The Crown and The Hill

Back in my boyhood there was no electricity up here,
it was all gas lighting. All those big flats on Reay
Street, there was no electricity until it was converted

after the War. Trying to do your homework in that light was no joke. I can't mind when we got electric streetlights, they were still going round with the pole up here. It was gas lamps till well after the War.

In the War Time at the back of us was an A.T.S. Camp. That was in the grounds of Porterfield House. The huts and the ATS lassies were still here in 1949, where the retirement flats are now (Hanover Housing). The lower half of it was a market garden, a mannie MacDonald had it for tatties and vegetables. There was a dairy (Eldad Dairy) and a byre down there as well at one time and then Bowman built a bakery there. At the Kingdom Hall down at Bale's Buildings, the bakery was in there and before that it was part of the Eldad Dairy. We used to get our milk from down there in a tin pail.

There was a shop on every corner up here. The only ones that haven't got a shop now are the Hill Street/Denny Street corner and the Reay Street/Hill Street corner. That's where all the spinster wifies lived and they were half blind even when I was a boy. We used to try and give them halfpennies wrapped in silver paper to pretend it was a shilling.

In those days there was no such thing as transport to your school. We walked to the Crown School and we would either go down Old Edinburgh Road and along Southside Road or down Damfield Road and through what we called the 'twirly birlys'. This was a little path with a 'twirly birly' (revolving gate) at either end and there was also a big gate for letting the cattle in and out of the fields. The fields belonged to Mr Munro 'Eldad' who had a dairy at the end of Southside Road and Argyle Street where the surgery is now. It was quite a big dairy and the fields for the cattle were on both sides of Old Mill Road and down to the boundary fence of the Kingsmills Hotel where Harris Road and Uist Road are now.

We had good and bad times at school. One of my mates used to come up Stephen's Brae with Skinner's the Bakers message bike. It was a little three-wheeled bike with a box on it and he used to sell the cakes and pies and doughnuts out of the box, for a penny or a half penny. As often as not we used to go over to what we called 'The Bog' at Josie Grant's, which was another piggery. We'd take jam jars and we'd get a penny or halfpenny for them and that would get us a pie or a bun.

There was another wee shop on the corner of Hill Street called 'Sophie's' and we used to go in there for gob stoppers. You got big sweets for a penny. Bowman the Bakers was there too and when the bakers would be taking the stuff from the bakehouse, which was on Argyle Street, they would have the buns and pies on trays carried on their heads. If you knew the baker he would bend down and we would help ourselves off the tray. Bowman's lost a few coppers there I think.

Then there was a post office on the corner of Union Road. A Miss Yeudall had it. If you didn't stand to attention when you went into the shop or you started talking she would say "Boy, you're in my shop, just be quiet". She was an awful character and she was there for years and years.

There was a BB's football pitch at Kingsmills Road and there were fields where MacEwen Drive is now. It was all fields and in the summer they were hayfields and there were corncrakes in them. At the Kingsmills shops there was Mr Ross the Chemist and a Post Office run by a Miss Yeudall, a 'funny old thing', she had a kettle behind her glass screen and her sister helped her. Next was MacGregor Frasers and a shoe shop run by Alan MacGillivray who sold Tottenham Hotspurs football boots which were much admired by the local youngsters.

There were a lot of very nice folk in Ardconnel Terrace in those days, very nice indeed. The Chief Constable of the day lived at the far end of the Terrace – Charlie MacNaughton – a well known character. I remember getting a post card from him – I was only a kid at the time – saying "Would L.U. please refrain from throwing stones onto the top of the buildings on Eastgate" signed Chas MacNaughton Chief Constable.

About the early 30's the new houses were going up in MacEwen Drive. The sad thing I remember about that was that where the building materials were collected by the workmen there was a huge mound of sand which was a great attraction for the young boys. There were two boys playing there, twins from Broadstone Park, they were just playing when the sand came down and killed one – he choked to death. The other twin was killed in the War. That happened at the first building stage of MacEwen Drive, it took place in two stages. I think the side the Fraser Park Bowling Green is on came later.

We were lucky getting a house in Reay Street, Seaforth Mansions. It was large after living in a couple of attic rooms. It really was a mansion, there were bells in every room in the house. You pressed a bell and in the kitchen there was a sign above the door with Bedroom 1, Bedroom 2, Parlour etc and a flag waved at the room sign which was calling. It wasn't working when we moved there, but my brother was an electrician and he got the bells working. We were the only people on the stair with the bells working. The building is now privately owned but it hasn't changed much. I think the interior has been modernised but they were lovely houses. There was a huge, what we called the Parlour, a huge room with a bed recess. Then there was a front bedroom, a back bedroom and a toilet. There was a place for a bath and every family on the stair had a bath in their bathroom except us. Apparently when they were doing the plumbing they couldn't get access to our bit at the time. The house was just being built and eventually it was just forgotten about so the place for the bath was there, but we never had a bath. However, we got a big zinc bath, a long one which we fitted in and we heated the water and carried it through in a pail. I tell you we didn't have all that many baths. By the time the whole lot of us had a bath on a Friday night there wasn't much water left. Eventually when we got a bit older, we went down to the public baths at the swimming pool (Glebe Street). We had a swim as well, but we got our bath and that's the way we lived then.

Drakies and Culcabock Village

From the oldest houses Wee Drakies and its neighbour up to King Duncan's Well, it was once known as Front Street. From King Duncan's Well up to Old Drakies Farm was known as Back Street.

They are now called Culcabock Road and Culcabock Avenue. Culcabock was once a village in its own right. In the County of Inverness, the County boundary was the little burn down by Kingsmills, at the foot of the Golf Course. The Toll House that stood on the Perth Road was taken down some years ago.

There is still a village community in Culcabock. People who have come to live in the village have become part of the community. There are several shops nearby which serve the village. Drakies House, the Farm House, is still there as part of the village. People lived there for many years, in the same houses and tending their own gardens. There are only three or four original villagers left in the village now.

There was a school in Culcabock and the local children gave concerts. At Hallowe'en all the children went up to Drakies and sang, danced or performed to earn their 'Hallowe'en'. People went 'down town' through the golf course and down Stephen's Brae. Never down Midmills Road and Eastgate. The village was like a separate part. The flat 'Wee Drakies West' was the original village shop, probably built about 1900's.

Viewfield Farm was a mixed dairy and sheep farm, owned by MacIver who had a butcher's shop on Castle Street. Drakies Farm supplied most of the village people with milk and also made their own cheese. The name Culcabock may translate from Gaelic as 'The Neuk of the Cheese'.

The exact age of Drakies Farm House is unknown but pre-dates Culloden. A legend says that there was a secret passage between Drakies and Culloden – probably not true.

The old water pump meant water came to Culcabock in 1905. An old lady would put her wooden buckets at the pump and pump up and down to get water for washing blankets.

The main road which runs past Culcabock Village used to be the old road from Nairn. The east road used to come in that way and turn down Castle Street.

Beside the Fluke Inn there used to be an old cottage called the 'Mission House' – possibly for holding prayer meetings. The story goes that the name 'Fluke' was because the fisher wives from Nairn used to come in with their creels. They would have a band round their head and they would stand in front of the pub and sell their fish locally, and walk up and down the street selling the 'flukes' – haddies.

Culcabock Avenue used to be known as Back Street. There is a block – now flats – which used to be called Smith Buildings. The old Police Station building for The County Police still stands. Then comes the site of the old threshing mill which was owned by a Mr Stewart. The local grain harvest would be done by this mill. Many of the local cottages were named after flowers and trees.

The old farm area of Drakies which was once arable land is now built over. The group of trees was once much larger and screened the house. The house is probably over 200 years old (Drakies House). In one of the steading sheds the County Council kept an old steam road roller, black painted and an ST registration number.

In one of the Cottages in Back Street there lived an old lady who was a wonderful lace maker, and did macramé and glove making. The cottages have retained the original character . The right-of-way-lane for villagers going across the golf course to town was charged a fee of one penny a year. It went across the first fairway and the Club House, and the villagers' right-of-way took priority over golfers. The little gate which is in the wall beside the Curling Club premises was part of the right-of-way and known as the 'Steppie' – and led down to the main road – beside the burn – the County Boundary.

The villagers used to get their water from the village pump, but were not allowed to use it on a Sunday – so they had to go across the road and get the water from 'King Duncan's Well'. This was spring water. The legend goes that the burial place of King Duncan is where the filling station now stands. Spring Cottage stands beside the well and is probably called after the spring.

Castle Street

A street where I left my heart – happy childhood – wonderful parents– not very much of the world's goods, but my three brothers and I were brought up in a real family atmosphere, wonderful memories.

A street of houses and closes as they were called, small shops where one could almost buy anything – a street where most people knew each other – a place to 'play' in the grounds of the Castle where the Keeper of the Castle – Mr McBeth – kept the grounds immaculate – no modern machinery in those days – just an ordinary push lawnmower – how on earth did he manage, and have the patience to endure so many children playing around the grass which looked as smooth as a billiard table – not always patient I may say – many a time we were chased home depending on what mischief we were up to, but no vandalism in those days.

The entrance to the grounds had two beautiful ornamental sandstone pillars plus the iron gate of course and on the left of the entrance, the home of a Sgt Ross and his family of Inverness Constabulary. It looked like a miniature Castle and it was such a shame that the pillars and the miniature Castle were eventually demolished, it would have made an excellent small Museum – such is progress!

At least the statue of Flora MacDonald is still there, although maybe not looking so fresh these days – in years gone by the local Fire Brigade came and hosed down the Lady which made her all shiny and black – these days she has acquired a shade of green – Flora does not deserve that treatment!

The Street, cobble stones of course, where cars were very much in the minority – most vehicles were horse drawn – it was a thrill for my brothers and I as we had turn about to go down to the station to meet whoever and to be allowed to sit up beside the cabby as he drove the horse-drawn cab through the town – most cabs and their drivers were stationed down by the river awaiting their fares.

A funeral was a wonderful procession – two beautiful black horses adorned with feathered plumes on their heads – stately drawing the hearse – the mourners all walking behind and as the procession went down the street all the passers-by going about their business stopped – ladies bowed their heads – men took off their hats and waited until the cortege passed – very respectful and dignified. Another procession which trod the cobblestones was when a serious case had to be held in the Castle Court room. A judge who was chosen to preside along with the other officials arrived at the Castle resplendent in their robes – complete with wig – arrived in an open cab, after having paraded around the town – much to the excitement of those who gathered to watch this procession – it was a most dignified affair - the street was greatly honoured.

Castle Street – a street of houses and shops – busy shops. The following is as correct as far as I can remember. MacIver the shoe makers at the top of the street and as I remember before the Baptist Church was built Murdoch the antique shop – Mr MacKenzie, a chimney sweep, whose business was conducted from his home – it was a wonderful but trying day to get the rooms back to order after the chimney was swept. Miller – a fancy good shop, but I believe that this place was occupied by Hetty McPherson as a sweetie shop plus other goods – I do remember the pussy cats occupying part of the window display – lovely to look at but no place for pussy cats! MacKay a paper shop later occupying a site further down the street – I understand that there was also a fish shop or was it a chip shop? This I do not recall. Shivas & Ross – a furniture shop – where Mrs Ross made a wonderful job in the making of loose covers etc. MacIntosh a very high class fruit shop – how I drooled over the sight of the luscious black grapes (enter not within) but I did go in to buy the potatoes, which were all loosely scattered in a corner of the shop on the floor. Shaw or was it Horne, the umbrella shop – one could have their umbrellas repaired at very little cost. The meal store where one purchased the meal for the breakfast porridge – I liked to go in, such a lovely smell, but everything looked powdery, even the assistants, a dusty place indeed. Melvin the baker, one of two in the street. Galloway the chemist, it was said that the elderly gentleman in the shop was every bit as good as a doctor and most people took his advice. Symington the chemist, later I think known as Connan the chemist. MacIver, a first class butcher. MacIntosh, a music shop, Walton a draper where one could buy all the little useful things required – tape, elastic, pins and purns – I wonder how many now use that word for sewing reels. There was I was told a pub at the corner of the Raining Stairs – I cannot remember this, maybe because it was not the done thing for any female to go into a pub.

On the opposite side of the street, to name a few, a small grocer shop, the name I have completely forgotten, although I remember it was a very tiny place – Myrtle the baker – oh those lovely pies!! Willie Forbes an excellent grocer, Stewart the rag store, how we loved to go there if we had a rabbit skin, as we got a sixpence for that which was a huge amount of money, or we found a jam jar somewhere and then we got a windmill from Mrs Stewart. How we loved to run quickly and see the windmill on a stick blowing in the wind. Simple toys then which brought a great deal of pleasure. Miss Mathieson's shop – the lady was a stout loveable person who mainly sold corn beef and paraffin. No trouble to go for paraffin as we could scrape the crumbs from off the board on which a huge slab of corn beef lay on the counter. Miss Tulloch – later married and known as Mrs Shaw. She sold milk and grocery items and wonderful home made scones made by Mrs McBeth, the wife of the Keeper of the Castle, another lovely lady. Further down, the Castle Street Post Office in which Mr Finlayson was in charge. McTavish the ironmonger, owned by two brothers, a large well stocked business, who also sold paraffin, but alas no corn beef!!

At the corner of the street there was a small Gents' Outfitter – Munro – good quality clothing and then, the Clan Tartan – a very well known place for tartans and all kinds of wares, especially popular with tourists. At the top of this building up on the roof were the famous figures Faith, Hope and Charity – what more could one wish for in CASTLE STREET.

On looking back it must have been a happy street – the boys around had their own football team – The

Castle United – I do not recall any fame and glory but I do remember one or two mothers held a Fete – quite posh – in the grounds of the Miniature Castle. They succeeded in raising sufficient money to buy a strip for the football boys. They repeated the Fete raising the magnificent sum of £20 for the RNI, a fair amount in those days.

The 1914-18 War altered many things in the street. We had shortages of course and I remember as one example the milk we had. Our milkman on his horse drawn cart had two very large urns, which on turning a tap produced very blue milk – probably half water – we came out with our jugs to buy a penny worth, but all is forgiven, we did like our Frank the milkman, a nice man.

For adults it was a sad and worrying time. The cannons at the Castle disappeared, no doubt melted down to help the war effort, these were replaced later by more modern cannons, but not nearly so good for playing around. After the War it was so sad to see ex-servicemen, some without an arm or a leg, singing or playing instruments in the street, with cap in hand, trying to make a few coppers to help them live – not much thanks for war service. Gradually after the war shops changed hands or disappeared altogether, the cobbles were uprooted.

I just remember the landslide and my father up helping people with their belongings. That was in 1932. I was just a wee girl. I was very concerned because somebody lost their cat and that really upset me that the cat was gone.

My earliest memory of Castle Street, well I was very young at the time, but I woke up one morning to discover there was another two children in my bed. This was because there had been a landslide on Castle Street. Just at the back of the Castle the land had split and the people from the Council had very foolishly poured cement into the split. The whole banking came down on top of the houses. There was a lot of people lived there at that time but nobody lost their life. They lost their homes and the children that were in my bed in the morning were children my mother had taken in. Indeed she had taken in people who had lost their homes that night. You know the buildings just stood as shells for quite some time but the people were all re-housed in other parts of the Town. It was a great calamity at the time.

On the right hand side of Castle Street right down to High Street there was a fair number of wee shops. 'Dowsy' MacPherson had a second hand jewellery business and next to that Miss MacDonald the Hat Shop and further down was Hetty's. I can even remember a fish & chip shop where the West End Furnishers are now. Handford's had a furniture and carpet store, then Collie MacIntosh the fruiterers, MacDonald's the Meal Store and then Barney's. At the foot of the Raining Stairs was Melvin the Bakers, they had a beautiful tea-room upstairs above the shop. Then there was Galloway's and Connon's the two chemists shops, very well patronised by the locals. I remember the big coloured jars in the windows and the big weighing machine in the shop for people to weigh themselves.

On the opposite side of the street was MacTavish the ironmongers, George Davie the opticians and the Castle Street Post Office owned by Finlay the Stationers. These premises are now all occupied by the Council.

So many memories – the Street Party – held in the hall at the top of the Raining Stairs to celebrate the crowning of the Queen – the Castle land slide at a later date – another story which could have been a tragedy – houses being demolished for street widening including my own.

Domesdale Street or Castle Street? A street never to be forgotten.

My Blast from the Past
(Anon)

We rented a room in 11a Castle Street – 10/- (50p) per week. The building was very old and the rooms were large and cold, however with a coal fire it cheered the room and the smell of peat and logs it was lovely and warm - we did keep the sweeps busy. The coal merchants McGruther & Marshall or Riachs come to mind, we all had coal fires and the ranges they were polished so you could see your faces in them, mind you we didn't like windy days as the soot would come down by itself and what a mess.

It was a great comfort to know the Bobby on the beat would be coming in during the night (Dave MacLeod).

We took turns of cleaning the stairs, I shared a sink in the landing, we boiled our water, no running hot water as we have today. Some of the rooms had electric light others had gas and tilley lamps. We had pulleys outside the window for our washing.

It was always busy Castle Street, lots of shops, one was Hetty's – she had everything. There were lots of wee houses up beside the Castle itself and also by the Raining Stairs. We would go and sit up at the Castle most of the days when sunny, it was a good Street to live in.

Most young couples started in a room, mind you that was then – big changes now.

Opposite the Town House was Cameron's the Drapers, Faith, Hope & Charity statues stood on the roof. Woolies was always on the same place in High Street and not forgetting Castle Wynd and the Museum and Police Station. We also witnessed the awful destruction of Bridge Street and Queen Mary's house – it was a disgrace that lovely house was demolished, whoever was in charge of that should have been shot, the Town has no character left. Anyway we were happy enough the only thing I didn't like was the flat irons, so we didn't iron a lot, well I didn't!

No telly, I can't imagine being without it now and all my mod-cons. It's bliss, sheer bliss.

When we left Castle Street to go to Mary Ann Court, we felt sad, mind you we were up and down Castle Street weekly, going to town. It hasn't changed all that much.

The Haugh

Living in the Haugh we were never away from the River and the Castle grounds. We lived at No 21, the last house in the row and when they demolished Loch Ness Buildings the gable end of our house became unsafe and we had to move then. There was the jam factory at the Haugh and there was an opening up the side of Loch Ness Buildings which led up to the jam factory. Before you came to this opening there was the Tap Bar which is now the Haugh Bar. The mannies would go down on a Sunday to get their dram.

All the bobbies know my granny because she would be out at all hours delivering babies. She walked everywhere, no transport, even down to the Ferry for confinements. She brought a lot of babies into the world. She also made all the families' clothes on her old Singer sewing machine.

Beyond the jam factory was a bit we called 'the coalies'. It backed on to the hill beneath Godsman's Walk. It was sort of horseshoe shaped with wee white cottages all round it. There was a Mr MacKenzie who had a wee hut and he was a shoemaker and all the men would go into his hut for a blether. Where Haugh Court is now that was where 'the coalies' stood.

Then there was Mr MacDonald, a shepherd, who kept hens, and there was a shop there then, a Mr MacDonald had it. There was a tenement block just past the steps at the Ness Bank Church and a Mr Taylor lived in there, he was a cabby and next after that there was Melvin the Baker's stables. One of the men who lived above the archway drove the horses.

One of the local characters who lived in Loch Ness Buildings was 'Salome'. The Buildings had a bit of a reputation during the First World War. 'Salome' was slim and always well dressed with a hat on but she was known as quite a lady. When they were going to knock down Loch Ness Buildings about the mid-thirties people were being evicted. A local tailor who lived there protested by taking his bed outside and he put it against the wall of the stables and slept outside to show his protest. They were all being re-housed down the Ferry in the new houses. Then there was a row of little white cottages just past where the back of the Glenmhor Hotel is now.

I can remember a house with a thatched roof on MacDonald Street, it was the first house on the left hand side as you go up from Haugh Road and there was a yard opposite. The gentleman who lived next door to us was one of the last lamplighters in the Town. MacKenzie's had a wood and sawmill yard on Gordonville Road and I spent many a happy hour playing on a swing we'd made in the corner of the yard. I remember Hetty from Castle Street lived in one half of one of the houses on Gordonville Road and she had a parrot in the garden. At the other side was Paton Street and another yard where Johnnie Lawson had his vegetable cart and horse. He used to go round the streets selling fresh vegetables and ringing a large bell.

Towards the Town the jam factory was on the right hand side and up the side of the factory was Coalman's Lane, and there was also a shed where Mr MacKenzie repaired shoes. Across from the factory was a row of 'white housies' as we called them, they seemed very small to me. Next to the factory was a jeweller's shop with very little jewellery, perhaps this is because it was next to the Blacksmiths. Then there was 'The Tap', a pub which had sawdust and spittoons, today it's called the Haugh Bar.

The Town Centre

As far as I remember then High Street only had three of the national multiple shops. These were Wm Low, the Dundee Equitable (DE) boot shop, then there was Stewart the tailors, where you got a suit for two pounds ten shillings, that's where the name the Fifty Shilling Tailors came from. On High Street starting from the Post Office Steps (Market Brae Steps) between Eastgate and High Street there was MacDonald & MacKintosh the old firm of Inverness grocers. When you passed it you always got the aroma of steam coffee. Then there was the Income Tax Office, the Customs and Excise place and next to that was Howdens who were on High Street in those days. When you went in, there was a whole lot of drawers and if you asked for cabbage seed or whatever they opened a drawer and filled a little bag and you got it for a penny.

Then there was my father's shop which stretched up the back of High Street. He had a tailor's shop and there was an entrance in from the top of the Raining Stairs. Next was Liptons, one of the multiples which had just opened up and further along was C & D MacRae, then F A Camerons and at the foot of Castle Street the Clan Tartan Warehouse with the YMCA above it. Most of the shops on the other side were practically all local. Then Woolworths came to Inverness. At that time they had nothing dearer than sixpence. They were known as the 'threepenny and sixpenny' stores. You could get a tube of toothpaste for sixpence. They caused quite a sensation in Inverness.

There used to be so many good shops on High Street. There was Grants Clan Tartan Shop and the 'Glasgow' shop on the left hand side of the street. I liked that shop because it sold all sorts of things like jars of sweeties and boxes of biscuits. There was the Maypole grocers and the Buttercup Dairy where Marks are now. At the bottom of the Market Steps there was a shop (MacDonald & MacKintosh) where you could buy all sorts of coffee. There was a machine in the window (coffee grinder) and when you walked past there was always a lovely smell of coffee.

A great character in town was Victor Conn, he had sweet shops, one on Bridge Street and one on Inglis Street where H Samuels is now. It was a beautiful shop. He had a tearoom in the summer at the side of the Stand in the Islands. Then just before the war he opened a big restaurant on High Street, it was called the 'Conn d'Or', it would have been about opposite Woolies I think. Unfortunately when the war broke out it closed, it was one of the newer shops on High Street.

There was quite a few dress shops. Bethune & MacPherson, and Fraser & Campbell. Then there was the Maypole grocery, then Johnson the tailors, Timpsons were there for a long time. Then of course there was Grants the Clan Tartan shop on the corner of High Street and Castle Street. Benjy Grant was another character in Town. The YMCA was above the shop and the Faith Hope & Charity statues were on top.

I remember 'Woolies' especially. We used to spend Saturday afternoon in there, and getting sent down the Town on Saturday morning for the messages at Liptons, and then MacKay the Butchers in the Market, that's where you got the gigot for Sunday's dinner.

There was Liptons on one side of High Street and Lows on the other and the old Buttercup Dairy on Hamilton Street. Boots was on the corner of High Street and Inglis Street and of course John Forbes beside it. That was a great shop, then they split it and Boots took over part of it and there was a walk-through arcade between High Street and Inglis Street. MacMillans on Lombard Street was a great shop as well, just at the back of 'Woolies' and MacTavish the Ironmonger on Castle Street beside the Town Hall. They, were there for years, it was a big store.

Bridge Street

Going down towards the river, on the left hand side, there was a tobacconist. It was the first shop. Next to that there was a drapers, Camerons the drapers. That was a great place to go in there. There was gas lighting and I used to go in with my mother. She would say she wanted socks for instance – "Oh yes if you come to this other side Mrs Urquhart – this is the gentlemen's side" – we'd go to the other side for the socks and down would come a parcel, beautifully tied up with string and you'd open up the parcel and there would be all the socks. So then she'd say, "Well now I want stockings" – "Oh well you want the other side" because that was the ladies' side, and again down would come the parcel and out would come everything; everything was tied up in parcels because it kept it clean. It was just a wooden floor and the two big counters, one on either side and he had coats and dresses; and the fitting room at the back was just a curtain with a mirror when you went there to try things on. But what I remember about it most was the fact that there were chairs for people to sit on if they were waiting.

Och the Town Centre didn't change for many years, it stayed the same. The streets were narrow, that was the main thing and the traffic was very little. A few horse drawn cabs and lorries, no buses or anything like that, it was a quiet little town.

Eastgate

My father took over the business in 1920, it had formerly belonged to a Mr Ettles. There was a bakery there and as far as I know it was Mr Ettles who had built the whole building, the date above it is 1918. The bakehouse was at the back and five men worked there. When my father took over there were horse-drawn vans. I remember the horses were stabled in Falcon Square. Then we moved on to motor vans, one did the country rounds and the other one delivered in Town. In my time I drove the country van and sometimes helped out in the shop. I went down some mornings before the girls (shop assistants) were in to sell the morning rolls. The school children came in at the interval in droves to get hot pies.

Next door to us was Aeneas Lawler the fruiterer and he took over several of the shops next door to him. On the other side of the road there was Hugh Fraser the plumber and there was a Chapman's garage and the Plough Inn which was on the corner of Stephen's Brae and Eastgate and there was also a Saddlers. On Eastgate itself was Taylor's the Coal Merchants, Rigg's the Butchers and Davidson's the butchers further along. The Buttercup Dairy was at the corner of Hamilton Street and on the other side of Eastgate, Fraser & MacColl's the ironmonger, MacRae the jewellers, Noble the grocers and Ross the Grocers. Also was there was a hairdressers and lots of pubs, there was the Crown and the Clachan, the Lochgorm and after that Ferries' Garage.

On Saturday night in those days there would be lots of people around most of them shopping. The young ones of my age, we used to do what we called walking around the 'square', that was the highlight of our evening. We walked along High Street, down Church Street along Queensgate and up Academy Street and Inglis Street to the Market Steps. We'd meet all our pals somewhere on the square, and all the lassies walked the square as well. That's where you'd meet a lassie and maybe see her home. Oh it was a great parade, everybody dressed in their best clothes. Saturday night and Sunday night was the same but on the Sunday we were very, very quiet.

Well Fraser & MacColl was founded in 1891 by my uncle Charles Fraser and his partner Angus MacColl.

They'd both worked at MacTavish the ironmongers on Castle Street as apprentices. I joined the firm from school in 1931 and stayed until I retired, except for service during the War. There were a number of ironmongers in Inverness then, MacTavish on Castle Street, Campbells on Queensgate, MacDonalds on Bridge Street and Andersons on Eastgate.

My great grandfather established the shop in 1826 that was before we became a gents' outfitters. When the business started we were actually on High Street and eleven men were employed making umbrellas, top hats and portmanteaux for the stage coach passengers then we were on the corner of Queensgate and Academy Street before we moved to Union Street. We'd eventually moved into the men's outfitting business and I was in partnership with my father and brother. We had several Royal customers, they bought mainly kilts and sporrans and pullovers for the younger members of the family. We had a lot of overseas customers and as the business grew the trade with foreigners became more and more important. Cashmere and things like that sold well. When things were coming off the coupons after the war anything you could get was easy to sell because supplies were so scarce.

We were starting the hiring business in the 50's – mainly morning coats and black jackets for funerals and weddings. There was one fly dodge we had to tackle. We'd get a letter from the West Coast, it was usually the West Coast, and it would say

"Please send me a dark coat size 42 – urgent – funeral". So you'd send it with the bill enclosed and it would come back with a wee note "I'm sorry it did not fit". You'd put your hand in the pocket and there's the funeral card.

In the forties beside us in Union Street there was Tolmie's, a well known sweet shop, then Melvin's the book shop. There was a china shop opposite us and two chemists shops. The big store was Young & Chapman's in those days (was Arnotts) and also a bakers shop.

My sister had to do my Granny's shopping and I had to do my mother's on a Saturday morning. This was at the time of rationing during the war. There was two grocers on High Street, Liptons and Lows but you didn't get all your shopping in the one shop – maybe one would be better for the bacon and the other for something else. You would stand at the counter and watch the paper bags being filled with whatever you were getting. I remember my Granny had to get her bacon sliced at a certain thickness, and I took it home and it wasn't right so she went straight back with it and handed it back to get cut properly.

We were in the Academy and when we were on the way there we often turned left and had a look at the Eastgate Smithy where they would be shoeing the horses. Round the corner was Wordies and after that a pub – it was one of the key places. Wordies was at the entrance to the back of the Station where the horse drawn delivery wagons were. Then on Eastgate there was the Albert on the other side of the road and there was a pub with a gaelic name – I can't remember it now. Further on was Urquhart the Plumber and then Chapman's Garage. They sold cars and some of the earliest cars in the Town came from there. Then there was Rigg's the Butchers and a whole lot of wee shops including Mario's which at that time was owned by two Italian ladies before Mario Bernardi took it over. Next door there was another butchers shop and it became a Post Office and down at the corner of Hamilton Street there was Clubbs, the Buttercup Dairy and Mario Celli.

There was an occasion when a bull escaped from the Mart and went up the stairs in the Maypole and got stuck. The cattle took right of way then, everyone just stood back and waited for them to go past. Mind you, at one time people used to collect the droppings, you went and picked it up for manure for the garden.

Yes I was born in Inverness almost 86 years ago in No 10 Hamilton Street. It is not there now. I was born where Marks and Spencers are. Hamilton Street in those days was just ordinary. Nothing but warehouses, Castle Rait, Grigor's had Castle Rait, Fraser & MacColls, Danny Mann the blacksmith and three tenants. Mann had the blacksmith shop and the works at the back. My father was a machine-man in the foundry. (The foundry was a big employer in those days!) Yes it was. But he went to the War first – the first World War – he came back and was idle for a while, then he was on the railway for a while, but his main job was machine-man in the welders, the Rose Street Foundry. He was there for many years in fact until he died. There was four of us. I was the oldest, with two sisters and my young brother. He was the baby.

We played in Hamilton Street and all the back yards. We used to go round Falcon Square into Gallons, the fruit shop and the men would give us fruit, which they might be throwing away sometimes but was still quite good, and there was a cycle agent. There was a whole lot of warehouses behind Falcon Square. Now we used to go from Hamilton Street up through the back of Falcon Square and up to the High School and when we came home at night, at four o'clock, we would make our way down to – oh I forget the name – they used to give us locust beans – the place was just before you turned into the station – anyway it was a grain store, and they used to give us locust beans – long black beans and they were lovely. The men would throw them down, they were up with the chain things (hoist) and all the bags. And then we would go home, do our lessons – we always had to do our lessons – and we'd get out to play then after our tea. No matter where we were as soon as the eight o'clock bell rang, we all ran for home. The eight o'clock bell rang in the Old High Church there. I think it still rings! No matter where we were, you had to be home by eight o'clock at night. You got a telling off if you were late! We were all quite good. We got up to mischief probably. Well at the top of Hamilton Street, where Washington Court was, there was MacKenzie the auctioneer, the Courier office, and another fruit shop, Campbells, and wee MacGregor – you know, the man with the soft hat – and we always got fruit from them you see. Two or three of us – not a crowd. And there was a whole lot of places down there at the back of Rigg's the Butchers, the Templar's hall. We used to go to the Templars hall when we were young. The Templars, I don't know what is the equivalent now. A holy kind of thing – teetotallers! "The Templars are gathering from near and from far" – we used to have this song with Brother Taylor. And then they had competitions. Then the boys and the girls would all come out and have a fight and go right round the block. We used to go right round the block, Inglis Street, Hamilton Street, Washington Court. I don't know what else. We played reliever, you ran to dens and you would call 'reliever' and you would have to get to this den. There's a thing yet - a whirlie we called it - you know the Carlton? – well the back was opposite Mann the blacksmiths and with MacPherson's the sports store underneath – and there was this little whirlie thing that they used to take up ropes with – and we always used to touch the whirlie, one, two, three, and we were in the den and you weren't caught, but if you weren't there, if you didn't touch the whirlie, you were out. The whole gang of us, boys and girls together. And then we used to go round to Wordie's – in the lane – you went through Washington Court and there was Wordie's – horse people – delivery people – and at the side of that place there were all little flowers, and all the girls would have broken glass, and make little graves, all vying to see who would have the best grave. That is what you did in those days.

Academy Street

The best chips I ever tasted were made in a chip shop on the Academy Street end of the Post Office Lane and this was always a calling place on the way home from Scouts on a Friday night. You got them in a 'poke' (paper bag) and chips have never tasted the same to me since. And Burnett's pies. No-one could make them like that. At 11 am there were queues at Burnett's on Academy Street, office boys, message boys, all waiting to get the pies for their work mates.

You could also get a big bag of 'stalacks' (stale buns) if you were there early in the morning. Chipped (damaged) fruit and broken biscuits could also be bought at other shops in the Town and that was the schoolboys' feast.

Church Street

Well, Church Street was an interesting place in those days. My father's shop was next to what was the Cummings Hotel and beyond it was a close that ran right up to where the back of the BT building is now. Behind his shop he had workshops with corrugated iron roofs and beyond that was I think three little cottages and these cottages were used at the time of Culloden. Some of the men who escaped were sheltered in these cottages but they were caught and taken out and shot in the Old High Church Yard. The cottages were eventually pulled down because the Empire Theatre was building the high tower for the machinery to work their equipment.

On the other side of the little close was a bakers shop and they had the bakehouse in at the back of it, and at the next close was a hairdressers where I used to sit to get my hair cut for four pence. Next to that was Bow Court, which wasn't as posh as it is today. It was a pretty ropey place altogether – very, very poor. Then School Lane and the Dunbar Hospital. It had little rooms upstairs with very, very low windows. Past that was Stratton's and there were houses there at that time and another little close called Deacon's Court. There were three little cottages there, which was at the back of my father's house and they were very poor places. The back of them was into the next property and you couldn't get through to them so they became very run-down. They were closed and the people eventually re-housed out of them. Nearly all the properties were houses in those days, it was only latterly they were converted into shops.

On the other side of Church Street, coming down from Fraser Street was the bank, then the Hydro Electric shop and then Abertarff House. It was unoccupied for a long, long time and is about the oldest building in the Town. The next close down was Tullochs the painters and in there was one of the oldest Town houses. There were lots of little lanes going into the houses down the back, very old and very poor, backing on to the riverside. The next building was 'Clarkie's' Bar, it was one of the old places with sawdust on the floor and then there was 'Tackets' who had bought the property and had it done up, it was a shop selling furniture. The back of the Free North Church, the Ben Wyvis Hotel and

Church Lane and at the top of that where Coutts was latterly, there once was an old house. A bit down past An Commun was the entrance to the Old High Church and a Mrs MacGregor's house. It has steps going up to it and she used to take in boarders, the people who used to be performing in the Empire used to board with her.

On the other side of Church Street there was Edgar the Bakers, Fraser's Auction Rooms and on the corner of Union Street, Fraser Ferguson and MacBean the jewellers. Further up was the 'Crit' bar and the Northern Meeting Rooms.

The Riverside

Davis Square was a great area because it was just beside the river and my house. During the war years I ate well before I went to school because Dad used to go fishing at Friars Shott which is the area in front of the old Baths (Glebe Street) and I would have breakfast of a couple of small finnocks. Salmon also used to appear on the menu but not too often because the salmon used to go to the 'back of the Caley Hotel' to pay for next year's fishing tackle. We used to spend all our summers there in the river. The river was where the boys from both sides congregated, building castles, knocking each other's castles down, then we used to get a bit of fence wire sharpened and go down just in front of the Black Bull where there was a sloping area into the water where the boats used to go down, and the 'flatties' used to come in with the tide and we used to spear them and take them home and they also provided a light meal because some of them were quite small.

Another occupation we had was going down towards the Black Bridge where there was some deep holes on the Huntly Street side of the river and there we used to catch conger eels. We took them up to Wells Street to the Pieraccini's and old Ma Pieraccini would give us bags of chips for the conger eels. They were quite big conger eels in those days, they were quite fearsome to catch. They say she ate them!!

The river really played a major part in the kids' lives in those days. We spent much time in it. We would run around barefoot in the summer and get our feet all clarted in tar. Mother would have to put on, very sparingly, butter or marg to remove the stains. Also, of course we had flash floods in those days as well, in Duff Street, which no longer exists (behind the Black Bull – now the Waterfront) and Davis Square. Duff Street was very frequently flooded to a depth of about two feet and we used to sail boats there because the water used to come through the drains when the river was very high.

The flooding seemed to be part of life – they just got on with it. I can't recall any tremendous hassle. It was just recognised that every two or three years the river flooded and Duff Street got these floods. And also, of course, the top end of Queen

Street which was higher but the lower end of Queen Street sometimes used to be flooded. All the older boys used to go swimming in the river. I can remember once, well this was told to me, I was sitting on the banks watching the boys and I slid down the bank. My granny was looking down and here was me sitting at the bottom looking up until one of the boys pulled me out. It didn't stop us going back to the river. In summer that was our main attraction, the water in the river used to be very low in summer and you could cross quite easily. There was rivalry between the 'Castle builders' (the boys) on the one side and the 'Castle builders' of Greig Street side, these were kind of gangs. The Greig Street gang and the Queen Street gang –some of the older boys had skirmishes. I remember Queen Street especially, where my Granny and all the family came from (Nos 12/14 Queen Street) – it no longer exists, it's flats now. The boys used to congregate under the gas lamp at Alexander Buildings – that was the meeting point. The younger ones used to use that for playing 'kick the cannie' and 'reliever' and in the dark nights we would play round the area, ranging far and wide.

The bridge at Greig Street had a blue light over the steps leading up to the bridge and sometimes where there was a tree at the West Church – just opposite the bridge – and we used to hide in the branches of the tree with a pea-shooter and 'pop' at people coming down the steps when they were illuminated by the blue light. This was during the war years.

In those days there were a few good shops. In Muirtown Street we had the Fotheringhams. One of the daughters was one of the first lady footballers in Inverness. She played for the old Caley team. Then next door was Ross's Dairy and along from that the shoe repairer (Dougally?). Then on the corner was 'Clarkie' the butcher (at Celt Street) and further on was Benny's, at the junction just beyond the Thistle Bar. It was great to go into Benny's, there was a smell of paraffin, the bacon, the cat sitting on the counter, broken biscuits, a penny's worth were always available. These shops were all part of the scene.

Across Davis Square, down at the riverside, there was a lane going through, we had Dan the Butcher. I well remember going across there for the small pieces of mince because Mum had gone to school with the Butcher (Bell) so I think we were well provided there. Round from him was one of the first cars we saw in Inverness with the motor protruding through the front like an aero engine. That was a grocer's – it was right at the corner of Wells Street and that car was fascinating. It used to sit there and all the kids from the neighbourhood used to come and look at it. We used to go round through Swan Lane – there was a small church there, and we used to go to Sunday School there and they were very good to us and gave us little parcels of sweeties and things. We could get through from Swan Lane, where Polombo's the fish merchant was – piles of fish boxes which we used to stack up as castles – I can remember going home and my mother giving me hell because I smelt so strongly of fish after crawling around through these castles. Next, in Muirtown Street was Morrison's, they used to be show people. They used to have show grounds around Inverness. He was a great Punch & Judy man.

From an interview with Mrs Flora Jenner formerly of 43 Falcon Court recorded on 1ˢᵗ December 1992 who opened the Friar's Bridge on 23ʳᵈ December 1986.

The Town (Council) was hurrying the workmen and they were having such bad weather the engineers were getting fed up and harassed, they just couldn't go any quicker. One day out of the blue they came to the house and asked if Mrs Gow (Mrs Jenner's neighbour) and I would open the Bridge along with Mr Young. I said I didn't know. "What's Mrs Gow saying?" I asked "Well Mrs Gow is saying the same as you. Whatever you're doing she'll do the same". So I said, "Very well, we'll do it".

The man said "You'll be harassed with the newspapers but it doesn't matter. The reason we're asking you to do it is you're the only ones who never complained and accepted everything and were friendly with the engineers and interested in the Bridge. We had such a lot of complaints but not from you and Mrs Gow and you lived nearest to the bridge and had good reason to complain".

So we get our photos taken and then they had a meeting with the Council. The Council asked them "Who is opening the Bridge?" and they said Mrs Gow and Mrs Jenner. The Council accepted it but I don't think they were very happy but the town folk were happy because we were one of them. One of the Councillors had a letter in the paper saying we should have Royalty to open the Bridge but nobody wanted that and we had a marvellous day.

They took us over in a white Rolls Royce to be introduced and we had coffee and lunch in the Station Hotel and we got to keep the scissors we cut the tape with and a carriage clock each. Mine is inscribed:

Presented to Mrs Flora Jenner
by Edmund Nuttall Ltd on the occasion
of the opening of the Friar's Bridge
Tuesday 23rd December 1986

I learned to swim in the River Ness. Greig Street was a great place, there were lots of kids and lots of fun. We paddled in the River and the big day came when I was a wee lad and paddled right across. That was a gold star day. We used to play at the pillars of the Greig Street Bridge and the Church Street boys did the same, on the other side as we did on our side. We used to wade over and knock down each other's castles which were built up from the stones in the River.

When we were young the Salmon fishers used to be at the Riverside just down at Wells Street, Friar's Shott. The boat would go up as far as the Greig Street

Bridge and then one of the fishermen used to take the rope and that would be the net going down. The boat used to go right across the River, up and down. If we were lucky we got a scud on the boat right down till it came to the Shott again.

Down the Shore

You see the Merkinch and the other side of the river – if anyone from the Shore came over the Black Bridge – it was 'sudden death', and if the Merkinchers went into the Shore area that was 'sudden death'. They'd get thrown into the Harbour.

When I started work in the Gas Works it was 4/10d per week. My brother Jock, when he was serving his time, he was serving his apprenticeship as a shoemaker, a seven-year apprenticeship, and he was on half a crown a week. Home made jerseys, home made trousers. You'd no fancy flies or fancy zips then, just a wee 'shop door' – it would be quicker doing it down the leg of your 'troosers'. A home made tie, I don't know how we managed. Yet we never starved you know. It was tripe and onions we ate.

We lived at No 8 Shore Street which is no longer there. The upper half of the street had about twenty flats and houses and No 8 was the last house to be demolished. There was a huge yard between the house and the graveyard where the Co-op stabled their horses. That part had actually been a smithy. No 8 had four flats and the blacksmith lived in a downstairs one, Mr MacRae. Across from there was where the A I Welders started off and latterly it was used for stabling. We all spent a lot of our time down at the Harbour and round the Longman which was a great walk, very popular.

The Harbour always seemed very busy to us. A lot of wood used to come in on 'Batten Ships' they used to call them, and the tankers and all the coal and bricks. It was all delivered by sea. The railway line came round at the back of what was then the railway bridge and went right down to the Harbour, so the wagons could pick up the coal.

Well down the Glebe then there was MacMurray & Archibald the panel beaters and there was the pawnshop, it was a dirty little place and nobody ever seemed to be in it. Then there was Dick the bakers, this was a small baker's shop and his ovens were up the lane. Then there was a row of three cottages where the Undertakers is now and further along from that there was a little shop. Two old ladies had it and they made sweets and jam. We were never allowed to go into that shop because a cat sat in the window among the goodies. Well, I must have been about seven at the time and I came home and was violently sick and I had to admit that I'd bought a packet of sweets there on the way to school. So I was told, "Let you take it". Maybe it wasn't that at all but there wasn't much hygiene in those days. Then there was another shop next to that, a Miss Reid and it was a sort of haberdashers. She sold needles and thread and cotton reels. There were also the closes with iron gates that went back in off Chapel Street.

Friar's Street was nice before the Telephone Exchange was built. There were nice houses in there and one or two had little porches. They were on either side of the graveyard. Then there were houses where the green bank is at the Old High Church. They must have had a very small bit at the back for their washing. The children in the area then, well we played reliever and we went swimming every day at the Baths. The girls had dolls and dolls' prams, and we wore ankle socks till we were about fifteen. We used to paddle in the River and build cairns in the water – some traces of them are still there. We crossed the Greig Street Bridge to go to the Queen Street Church – you know the old Inverness expression "I stay across the water". Well we kept to our own boundaries.

Friar's Street changed a lot, there were some nice houses there. There were three big blocks with four tenants in each one and we lived in the end one. There was the graveyard there and a carpenter's shop, and then there was a woman who the actors and actresses lodged with when they were in the Theatre. Then there was a Mrs Campbell whose husband used to drive old Dr Kerr's car. I went for her messages every night after school and on a Friday night she gave me three half pennies – 1½d.

There was an old lady called Mattie Munro who lived in an old cottage in the street and when we were little and running around playing and making a noise she would get on to us. Down a bit further there were seven more houses and stables for horses and round the corner where the Baths are now there were more houses. All the streets were cobbled then and it was nearly all horses that were used for pulling carts like the bakers and butchers. In the middle of the street at Waterloo there was a big trough where the horses stopped to drink.

The 'Ramparts' was the old Cromwell's Fort and you could see it over by the old hospital. The 'scaffies' had their stables there and the 'Hoofies' family lived above. The football pitch that was there (Citadel Football Club) is now covered with petrol tanks but many a needle match was played there. Some of the boys would get staved fingers or knee caps knocked out of joint but Morrison the bone-setter had his caravan over by the riding school and we got free treatment. The riding school was used by the Horse Artillery who had their stables where the entrance to the Bus Station is now on Strothers Lane. Strothers Lane was only a lane then and there was a gate where it joined Railway Terrace, which they used to close sometimes, but we climbed over it.

I was born in Victoria Square, it was off Rose Street down past Milne's Buildings or you could come up past the La Scala and up to Railway Terrace and on the left there was a high wall with a gate in it which took you into the Square. We used to go to Innes Street when it was frosty and slide down the pavements from the top down to the bottom. But then the wifies would come out and put their ashes on our slide and spoil them.

Victoria Square was where the Rose Street multi-storey car park is now. My granny lived at No 8 and we were in No 9 and my other grandparents lived at No 50 Rose Street. All the family, aunts and uncles stayed round about. I went to the Bell School for about a year or so and then we all went up to the Crown School because the Territorials were taking over Farraline Park (1936/37). Farraline Park was a big enclosed square with the Bell School at the top, then the back entrance to the Rose Street hall on the left and the Lodge where Charlie's Café is now. There were big metal gates into the park and a lot of the TA was based there. On the way to school I would come out of Victoria Square on to Strothers Lane and cross over through the back station at Platform 7 past the old railway laundry, then through Falcon Square and we'd come out on Eastgate where the Northern Ignition and the blacksmiths were. On the way home from school we came down Stephen's Brae and down the little steps at the bottom of Crown Road and crossed over to stand at the Blacksmiths watching the horses.

I remember on Rose Street there was the Foundry and on the left was the Gas Works. Mrs Aitken's shop was on the corner of Rose Street and Innes Street, there were little shops on all the corners then. Our little shop was on the corner of Rose Street and Milne's Buildings, that was Duncan Urquhart's and Betty MacRae was the assistant there for years. On the other corner there was a little wooden shed we called 'Bronyan's'. This was a Mr MacDonald and he used to sit on an upturned wooden box. His family stayed in a flat at the top of Rose Street but old 'Bronyan' he would sit on top of his box and fall asleep and there was all those little cardboard boxes in front of him full of sweeties and he also sold paraffin. There used to be an overpowering smell of paraffin in the shop. If anyone was to drop a match the whole place would have exploded. In 1948 we moved to Dalneigh and not long after that Victoria Square came down.

Aye, well at the Glebe then was two four-storey tenements with a stone stair going up inside. They were becoming run-down because they weren't being maintained; it was private landlords that owned them. There were also a few cottages there. Before they were knocked down the Destructor was built for getting rid of the rubbish by burning it. The heat the Destructor generated burning the rubbish was used to heat the Baths and it was also used in the Electric Works on the other side. It was used to run the generators.

The Electric Works was where the homeless centre is now on Chapel Street and along from that going towards the Black Bridge behind that was the Destructor which was reached by going along the path behind the Eddie MacGillivray Hall. Then next to that was the Lord Roberts Memorial Workshop and then the Baths. The Destructor was bad for bits of soot and dirt coming out of the chimney. You could get it in your eye very easily and the washing out on the Maggot Green wasn't as white as it used to be.

The swimming baths were opened and we thought this was a wonderful place, and to stand in the showers this was even more wonderful. To put a penny in the hair dryer was the height of luxury, and to see this lovely bath when we didn't have a bath at home. We would go in at 9 in the morning and come out at one o'clock – four hours – we came out bleached white and having enjoyed jumping off the top board. We learned to swim – Roddy Dyce and one or two others kept a watchful eye on us.

It was rather a pleasant street in those days (Rose Street) apart from the foundry and the gas works which were very industrial. The houses on the right hand side all had beautiful gardens, lovely flowers and they all vied with one another. Quite a lot of the houses were divided, there were very large families, some of them had four or five children in one room. There was Milne's Buildings numbers 1 – 5 and they all housed six families in each doorway. A lot of children for the local school. I remember things like the chimney fires. They never sent for the sweep, the man who could clean their chimneys properly. They put a large chunk of paper alight up the chimney and up it went on fire. So we had the fire brigade almost weekly which was very frightening for all the other people, but they all did it so they couldn't criticise one another.

Some of the houses were divided. On one of the sides of Rose Street, near the Gas Works, there were six families with a couple of toilets out in the back yard. They had a kitchen sink for their washing, washing of clothes and dishes, and everything was shared, one per floor of the building. But in Milne's Buildings they had self-contained flats and they did have an inside toilet. You just washed at the kitchen sink or bathed by the fire on Friday night.

Oh I remember Victoria Square. The Square had lovely gardens, lovely little gardens, we thought they came from the war years (1914-18) when everybody produced their own food, it was a way of survival. The wages were something like £2 for a family of six, and there was no family allowances, and I think this was their method of doing it. They also had a little beauty in their lives, by having their gardens and their flowers. There was a little red gate from Victoria Square and you'll know the lady who used to tell us off if you left it open. It was not to be left open under any circumstances. (This lady was Mrs Ellen Grant, Grandmother of the interviewer). Granny Grant that was – we were in terrible trouble "Come back girl and shut the gate" – because it was kept nice and neat and very private. A little private oasis and they did enjoy their gardens. And there was what we called the 'Shepherds Hall' – The Loyal Order of Ancient Shepherds. With the mothers having all those illnesses and things, they paid in one penny per week and this was called death benefit. And also we paid into policies which we had in later life. It was a bit sexist because when they came to a certain age the ladies couldn't continue, but the men were allowed to become fully paid up members.

There was three shops in Rose Street, no four. I can't possibly count one of them – an elderly gentleman, and I think he just played a bit of shop keeping. Another lady shopkeeper at the top, but I can't remember her doing a lot. There was a grating outside her shop and I lost lots of half pennies there. I often wonder what became of them. Because it was clutched in your hand and you were making decisions on what you could buy, and occasionally it went down the grating and ended in the basement. The two main shops were Mrs Aitken who was very busy, at the top of George Street and Mr Urquhart, John Urquhart, he had everything from paraffin to Pease meal. They remained open till about nine at night and it was a sort of oasis in a dark world. We would be sent along to Johnny's as we called him, and I loved going there. I used to sit and listen to the conversations and I would say, "No it's all right, I can wait" and it was a most interesting place. I think I was an observer then. There was an interesting corner shop in Innes Street, it was run by two unmarried ladies and their brother, and they worked there till 9.30 pm every night by the gas light. As my mother was a friend of theirs, I was allowed to make up the sugar. Sugar came in great big bags then and it was made up into brown paper bags with a special way of folding it. There was also another very interesting shop in Innes Street for quite a long time, about number 16, and it was a lean-to place. The lady I think had been in private service and she supplemented her income by baking scones and pancakes and you got them hot off the girdle. They were absolutely beautiful. There was another shop down Chapel Street and two ladies, one very severely physically handicapped, and she stood there hours in the day making scones and selling them to the folks passing. I can still conjure up the smell of that shop, it was lovely.

At the old wall down at the Chapel Yard beside that cemetery wall, there was Eddie MacGillivray the butcher who was a character, well known in the Boys Brigade circles. And Mr Matti who did invisible mending – an Italian. He did some really beautiful work, my father and he were great friends. He also had some poultry. He told my father a story about a man who said, "Oh dear, Mr Matti this is very expensive for such a small hole" and Mr Matti said, "Oh well it's the expertise". He was reminded of a friend of his who was a surgeon and he was doing a private operation, and the man had said to the surgeon "It's very expensive for only 10 minutes' work" and the surgeon had replied "Oh well I'll let one of my underlings do it and they'll take two hours and you'll get your money's worth".

.

Friars Lane and Friars Street

Well, starting a the bottom end, looking on to the river and just below the Old High Church graveyard there was two beautiful white cottages. Then you went up Friars Lane and it was all houses up until you came to Peter MacDonald's which was a carpenter's shop – it was as you went up Friars Street and it was slightly to the left – and he was a great man for the Thistle. To get players he would give the carpenters a job on condition they would play for Thistle and that's how he got his players. Then there was a postman, Mr Young, and next was Cameron's, then the Ross's. Then there was a newly built wee house put in just opposite Friars Street and there was a man from Aberdeen called David Digance and we used to call him 'Half Pint' because he was always going to the pub on a Saturday night at five to nine so he would only have time for a half pint. Next to him was the carpenter's shop. Then MacLennans, then Patience, then there was the Old Technical School which catered for cooking, carpentry, drawing, laundry, sewing: all these things, all the technical aspects were done at this school. There was a man there that used to give us carpentry, a Mr Beaton, who stayed in Park Road. So that was Friars Lane on the right hand side. The Technical School was sited on the grass bank next to Leakey's Bookshop.

Going up from the river on the left hand side of Friars Lane there was only one house, which is still there, and then there was a high wall and a garage and that was the garage which belonged to Doctor Kerr. The entrance was on Friars Street but the retaining wall was on Friars Lane. Continuing up Friars Lane there was a very small shop which sold toffee apples and paraffin – all the shops sold paraffin then because it was all paraffin lamps, there was no gas or electricity. So I would go up to get paraffin for my mother and get my toffee apple.

Next to that there was a big white close and that led into a courtyard, and in that courtyard there was a row of houses on the left hand side – small gardens at the front – they were really superior houses at that time. That went right up to the graveyard wall – there was about six or eight houses there – that's where the Telephone Exchange was built.

The Model Lodging House

The ladies in Friars Street, they were very good to these men in the Model. I remember one in particular, a Mrs Rollo, she used to give them soup when they were passing. They would take the soup at the door.

Yes, that was what we called 'the Hawkers'. They would be stopping there. It was a big place, there were beds on each side. There were beds on the left side and on the right side probably twenty on each side. There was probably in the region of forty people and they did their cooking there and dried their clothes at the fire. It was a roof over their heads and a wee bit of comfort I suppose.

Well the Salvation Army was very prominent. They used to have a hall at the bottom of Fraser Street. I don't know if the women stayed there or not.

I remember when you went up Margaret Street, there was the Drill Hall on the left – that's where Spectrum is now – and that's where the Royal Artillery did their training and all their guns were in there. And along the side of that wall there was big doors and their guns would be wheeled in and wheeled out – big 20 or 30 pounders. I don't know much about artillery but that's where they were housed. We used to go up in the evening when the men would be training in the summer and they would have all the guns out and they'd be all in uniform. Then there was the Rose Street Drill Hall and that was used as well – the army was in there, I think it was the Camerons and they did their training too. Then to the right hand side of Margaret Street there was a lot of places and they were used as stores, for instance, I remember Peter MacPhee, he had a sweetie shop and he stored sweets there. There was about a dozen places just purely for stores.

Then there was the school – the infant school was on the right, then on the left hand side I think that was the intermediate class. I remember on some occasions the poor of the town, if they wanted a hair cut, there were people (I think came from Finlayson the Hairdresser) and they were learning the trade, so you got a free haircut. But, believe me, I went in and got one and another boy looked at me and he started laughing and I was laughing at him because it was atrocious haircuts. We were scalped, like David Beckham nowadays. Another thing that went on there – they used to practise dentistry but they weren't getting much trade. There was some apprentices doing their training – so we were told, "If you need any teeth to be extracted you will get a half day off." So I said to myself "Oh a half day off school is worth something so I'll go down". I got my tooth out and I got my half day. It wasn't a proper dentist, a trainee, and we were the guinea pigs. There was no painkiller – just out!

Where Academy Street and Church Street meet at the top of Chapel Street, oh yes I remember them well. When you went up Friars Lane and across Church Street there was a lane running through known as Nicols Alley and there was only one house, quite a high house on the left hand side. As you went through the lane you were looking at Anderson the Bakers and the old 'Catch my Pal' Institute. And if you went down on the left there was Fraser's Economic Stores. Then there was a barber known as 'Fray' Sutherland, a well-known barber in the town. He was a great singer. At the very bottom was Reid, the Newsagent, and that was a very busy newsagent and there were sweeties and newspapers and everything else. When you went up the other side on Chapel Street there was another wee shoppie, Mrs Cameron was in that shop.

Just about there an old horse trough stood because businesses used horses and carts in those days. That was the taxis really (horse cabs). Then you got your vegetables, the milk carts, and Wordies at the station – that was all horse and cart deliveries – so there was a lot of horses about. You could run across the street and not get knocked over then. Very peaceful days. There was another horse trough as you go down Chapel Street and it's almost looking up Shore Street, and a trough just where Martin & Frost used to be. There was another one on the riverside because all the horse cabs were on the riverside – at the back of where the Caley Hotel is now.

I remember before the Baths were built in 1936 (and they're knocking them down now – a damn shame) I used to swim there regularly. I remember what was known as the 'greasy bond'. There was a wall round beside the river, I don't know what was stored in it but we called it the 'greasy bond'. Then there was a big high tenement, Albert Place. I don't know if you remember 'Hill 60' when you went over the Black Bridge, well it was three or four storeys high with iron bars on the balcony, and a clear area in front of it. There must have been a lot of people lived there, mostly they went to the Bell School. Opposite where the Baths used to be, on the other side of Friars Street, there was a blacksmiths, Cruickshanks – he was a busy man. Then there was another blacksmith on the Shore, quite a few blacksmiths about the place with all the horses. Then there was a big store there beyond Albert Place – a meal store and opposite that there were a lot of houses, small houses. There was a sort of alleyway which went behind these houses and there was another crowd of people living in there. It was high density housing area really.

There were no mod cons at all until the Baths came. We had no means of having a bath. I had an uncle who moved into Denny Street about 1930 and they had a bath in the house so I used to get sent up every Saturday night to my uncle's for a bath. Then the Baths came and you could get a private bath for 6d.

I remember what the Glebe Street Baths looked like. Oh yes I remember it well. There was a row of cubicles on either side of the pool. When you went in there was the shallow end and the deep end and it was 16 ft deep – there was a lot of good divers in the club. On the cubicles was a half door and you drew a curtain and that's where you undressed, then you put your clothes in a big bundle. The private baths were beside the vestibule as you went in. I remember a story about when they were building the Baths, and there wasn't even tiles fitted in the pool and they filled it with water. There was a local man, he was in the Navy, he was a boxer, 'Stoker' Gunn we called him, he decided he was going to be the first man to have a swim in the Baths and he dived in, cold and all as it was and swam a length. The Baths was a great magnet for the children in the area. I was never much of a swimmer. I remember going up to the deep end, but somebody had to dive in and take me out. I never went back. I learned to swim when I was sixty-eight – so now I'm a swimmer.

We used to go in and play in the graveyard. We played hide and seek and ran all over the graves. We never gave it a thought. They used to have an iron gate, and over the gate was a semi-circular iron bar which was about 3" in diameter. There was two high walls and it used to be a dare in those days that you climbed up a wall and inched your way over the 10ft high wall – that was the Friars Street graveyard. We played there quite a bit. Nobody ever said anything.

The shoemaker was Mr MacLaren. He had a little shop – total chaos – but he seemed to understand the chaos. He didn't have lighting, he had candles. He seemed to work late and early. His shop was at the bottom of Church Street near Miss Ena Reid's shop, the newsagent, which was right on the point of

Church Street and Academy Street. He was a couple of doors up, looking on to a piece of waste ground. He used to tell me about the church yard, and where it was, and now the Telephone Exchange stands there. He was more or less opposite the old Technical School at the corner of the lane. It was a great place, the shoes were lying everywhere, but it was for Sunday shoes only. My father repaired the school shoes and the school boots for my brothers, but Sunday shoes had to be done properly for sitting in the Sunday School and my parents would have been black affronted if my shoes weren't quite right.

Once you got on to Chapel Street there was Cameron's the grocers and next to that a newsagent and across the road Howie had a shop and next to that Bergamini's had ice cream, Sunday papers and chocolate. Next was a Wine & Whisky shop and old George MacDonald and his son Lachie ran that shop. A lot of the locals used to go in and get a quiet nip in there because you could get a nip of whisky out of hours and George was always very compliant. Next to that was MacLean the Grocers and next to that was a wee sweetie shop with toffee apples and down a wee bittie was Dick the Bakers. So there was a tremendous amount of shops. Across the road was the Butchers. Then up on to Academy Street was Anderson the Bakers, Anderson the Grocers and a milk shop, Sweeney's Dairy we called it. Across the road from there was Mair the Chemist and next to that there was a furniture shop, Andrews (George Andrews from Telford Road). Next to that was Ernie the Fish Shop and Ernies was a very popular place. I remember the highlight of the week for my friend Alex Fraser and myself. We went in and for tuppence you had a bottle of Vimto and that was our Saturday treat, then you came outside and there was a machine there and for one penny you got two Woodbines in a small round packet and you got two matches. That was your weekly smoke.

Next to that was Johnny MacKenzie the Butchers. Och the whole place was a mass of wee shops. How they all survived and thrived I don't know. This was in the late 1920's. The reason they survived I think was because they gave 'tick' (credit) and once they got a customer on tick they could go in and buy something and pay for it on the Saturday and get messages for nothing during the week. The shopkeeper would make a note of what was owed and of course they couldn't get rid of these customers because they owed them money, and if they stopped serving them they wouldn't come back and they lost money.

I was born at what then was No 14 George Street but is now No 30 George Street. We all lived in 30 George Street although at the time it was No 14. There were three tenants, room only, the other side there was one room and a little bedroom. The couple who lived there kept a lodger, the Sewards. They had a woman lodger. The upstairs tenants had no water, they had to go outside to carry water up in pails, so you had a couple on one side and three on the other side having to carry everything – drinking water and washing water – for everything, upstairs and downstairs. There was an outside toilet shared by the three tenants. My earliest memory as a three-year-old was I went to a neighbour's house to play and the girl in the house – a little older than me – was a pupil at Farraline Park School so with my wheelbarrow I followed her up to school. I put my wheelbarrow into Glennie's lemonade store and went into the class with her. My mother thought I was in the neighbour's house all the time. Reaching the age of five, my sister was told to take me to school and enrol me, give all my particulars. She came home in a real rage saying that the school already had my particulars two years ago. My first day at school was very frightening. At the 11 am interval my sister found me standing in the shelter – that's the Farraline Park School – all alone when all the other children were playing. That condition only lasted for one day. I soon made friends and played along with the rest. I was only in the first class from Easter until the summer holidays.

The Longman

The Railway workers were on shift work so sometimes they were able to do other work during the day. They had little huts as you go down Longman Road. First there was the railway bridge, then the timber yard then you came to their allotments. On each plot they grew potatoes, carrots and turnips and some even had fruit bushes and nobody ever touched them, my father never even lost a lettuce. The allotments were a help in bringing up large families, they all wanted to produce some food. Burnetts moved there from their bake-house in Strothers Lane in 1934 I think it was, and they gave my father compensation to move further down the allotments. I think it was £2 he got to move and he had it for many years right through the war. I used to take the barrow and push it over the old Longman Bridge and I would sit and watch the trains and wonder where they were going.

Longman Road at that time, well the Post Office maintenance people were on the left hand side and then there was a row of very attractive little cottages all with beautiful gardens. Then you came to what we called the 'Powder Magazine', it had grass on top of it and was a gunpowder store from earlier times. On the right hand side was Alexander's buses, they had a garage there for washing the buses and maintenance. Right next door was the Highland buses. Eventually the Railway Hostel was built so the drivers and guards from the Perth train and other long journeys could have food and accommodation. Further down you could see Seafield Farm, a beautiful farmhouse. It was there till after the war and then squatters moved in and it was demolished. Further on, on the right was a cinder track we called 'the private roadie' and we'd go up to Millburn Farm. Then there was the Aerodrome. We got into trouble at times for going into places that said private but we disregarded the word 'Private'.

The Longman was our favourite picnic area and on a fine day most of the mothers in the street took the children there to swim and collect shellfish to be cooked on a crackling twig fire. In those days there was only the golf course on the Longman and some shooting butts for the Territorial Army and the Aerodrome. There were no industrial buildings. We could walk from the bottom of Innes Street and walk all round the Longman and come out at the top of the street without meeting a car. At night the Longman became an eerie, frightening place especially near the haunted house. This was a ruined house near Seafield Farm, it probably got its name because it was derelict and moonlight threw weird shadows from the nearby trees on to it.

The Longman in these days had a nine-hole golf course and the Territorial Army had their shooting range. If the 'Red Flag' was up on the 'hillock' you couldn't pass because the range was in use. There was also clay pigeon shoots held down the Longman and there was a haunted house about Seafield Farm.

Kessock and Merkinch

My earliest memory of Madras Street was a little shop directly opposite our house. It was a little tin shed or shop owned by a Mrs Walker. What sticks in my mind was that she used to sell bars of toffee, McCowan's toffee, and that was my favourite, a slab of that toffee. I think it cost a penny and even at that age when I was about four or five I had to do chores about the house to earn it. She also sold groceries and sweets and cigarettes. There was another shop on Madras Street as well – Goodalls. It was at the corner of Madras Street and Nelson Street. It was one of the first shops in the Town to get a liquor licence. That was away back in the days when liquor licences were hard to get. My great friends were the Spiers family, they were just on the other side of the street from us. I like to go down Madras Street even to this day. I was christened in the church at the bottom of the street. In those days it was called the Church of Nazareth and the minister, the Rev William Wilkie, was known for his parish work in and around Inverness.

When I was six we moved to South Drive. At nights we used to play 'reliever' and 'kick the can' on the streets. I don't know of anyone who had a car then, they would have been thought of as upper class if they did.

In the days when I lived in South Drive, Coronation Park was one long road from Thornbush Road down to South Drive. The road was about 4 ft wide and was lined on either side by trees and that's all there was on it. There were fields on both sides. The war was on at the time and we were surprised one day when we saw workmen with ploughs arriving. They ploughed up the left hand side as you go down and planted cornfields. That's where the School and the Community Centre are now. On the other side where the flats are, the Town Council in their wisdom, decided to give us a play area and that was one of the first football pitches there. It backed on to the old Thornbush Pub.

I was born in India Street practically under the Railway Bridge in February 1919. The whole corner has completely changed now, but they were a very friendly lot of people who were down there at that time. After you passed the Railway Bridge there were very few houses until you came to the Ferry. I can remember when I was a young fellow my mother used to send me down to the Thornbush where my father was working. I took down his flask, a blue enamel flask, for his tea. I used to see all the men who worked at the Thornbush, rough diamonds but they had hearts of gold.

I can remember when MacDonald had the Ferry bus service. It was an old Vulcan bus he had with a canvas roof and individual doors on the bus for people to get in and out. The railway line came practically over the top of our house at 31 India Street. I was just about brought up with the railway. I learnt a lot about it. I would lie in bed at night and I would hear the different trains coming in and I recognised which ones they were by their sound.

You used to have fun on the Kessock buses then. Remember Willie Michie, the Auctioneer. Well Willie Michie's father ran a market at the back station in Falcon Square. The wifies came from across the Ferry with tatties, butter, eggs, fruit and vegetables and they took all that to the sale and Willie Michie auctioned the stuff for them. The town folk would go there and buy whatever they wanted and then the wifies would buy their groceries with the money they got from the auction. They would come back to get the bus, fair loaded down with parcels to go back to the Ferry.

I sold the Football Times when I was a kid. You'd go up to the Courier office where they were printed on a Saturday night and buy three dozen. They cost tuppence but we got them for 1½d. We'd go round the pubs and sell them and by the end of the night you might have sold them all, maybe made 3/-. You took that home to your mother because in these days there wasn't much money in the Merkinch.

Grant Street had a gown shop called Bessie Johnston's just beside Rodgers and this was where you went to look for a dress for a dance in the Town or out of town. It cost sixpence on the bus for a dance in the country. You would be able to buy a dress for 2/- or 2/6. The last dress I bought there was green and sleeveless and had a cape trimmed with swansdown round the edge. The pair of shoes cost sixpence.

In Ross's Close there was a rag store run by Mr Jamieson and a bone yard. At the top of Grant Street there was a paper shop and next to it was a lodging house for men only run by Stewarts from Anderson Street. It was called Ness Square not Anderson Street and was known as 'Hill 60'.

At the Welfare Hall the dances were held on Friday nights, they cost 6d and folk came from all over. The band was local, Benjy Calder on the accordion and his brother on the piano.

The coal boats came in at the Shore across the Black Bridge at the Harbour and horses and carts took the coal to MacDonald's yard in Lower Kessock Street. When the youngsters knew a boat was coming in they would run down the lane and jump on the wagon and throw coal down and they would have bags ready to pick it up. The dockers gathered at the Black Bridge and Ness Square at the top of Grant Street and the kids would ask them when the coal boat was coming in. They would run home from school down Tap Lane or Shoe Lane and take turns in jumping on to the wagons and throwing the coal off.

We would sell scrap to Mr Jamieson and maybe get 2/- and we also sold stone jam jars and lemonade bottles to get money to go to the pictures. There was also a 'wine shop', which was open from nine in the morning and if you were there when the men were coming out they would maybe give you a shilling.

Be' West the Water

I was born in Mary Ann Court just off Ardross Street in 1927 and brought up there until I was about eighteen. It was a very compact area. It was really a great place to be brought up in. There were about eight or ten houses in a kind of enclosure facing inwards and some were flats, and in others some people had the whole house. They were all rented houses with a landlord and landlady, a Mr & Mrs Kemp, and he was a well-known music teacher. They lived there as well, their house was on Ardross Place, backing on to Mary Ann Court.

In the court there was also a large stable where an old carter named Ned used to keep his horse and cart and he came back every night and shoved his cart in there. There was also a wee garage at the end of Mary Ann Court, a chap Urquhart had it. It was just big enough to take one car and he used to do repairs. You could go into the garage and work if his mood was right and you behaved yourself. The people in the Court all knew each other. They didn't live in each other's pocket but there was a good feeling about it. We always used to go round to the car park next to the Cathedral, it was an open field at that time and we used to play cricket a lot in the evenings.

It was a dead rough field so you were always at an advantage over anyone who came in new because they didn't know about all the bumps and twists there. We used to do a bit of fishing in the river as well, at the steps just down from the Cathedral, now they're all overgrown, you wouldn't know they were there, but it was a dead easy place to go down with a rod and worm and chuck it in the river. I used to get 'flukies' coming up the river as far as that.

Ardross Street in those days was largely residential. Mr MacBeth the Minister lived there and Dr MacFadyen on the corner. There were little streets on Alexander Place which runs from Ardross Street to Young Street, there's a stone slab with the name Tanners Lane on it which was the old name before it became Alexander Place. There was big excitement in the area when the Palace Cinema opened, it was luscious, the height of luxury. It even had twin seats for people who felt 'close'. Going to the pictures on a Saturday night was always one of the great treats.

Around the area there were a lot of shops. There was Canessa's the ice cream shop and round the corner on Young Street the paper shop and then King's the Bakers. The Chip Shop is still there and The Tarry Ile pub and Munro's the Greengrocers. Down at the very bottom there was a sweetie shop on the corner of Ardross Place and Ardross Street kept by two old ladies where we used to go and get a half penny black bootlace.

You know as you go into Bruce Gardens Cemetery gates, well on the right down to what is now Maxwell Drive, that was all grass, and on the canal side there was similar big stretches of grass and now it's all filled in with houses.

I've lived in Park Road for 57 years and the houses are now over eighty years old. The local builders wouldn't take on the job of building these houses because it was all stone work they did then so they had to go out of town to get a contractor for the Park Road house building. After a couple of years they started on Dochfour Drive and all the contractors got a share of that job because it was such a big, big road. From then on there were plenty of new houses built but the houses on Park Road were the very first Council houses built in Inverness.

I used to play in the park which was right here. It was the public park all the way down from here. A Mr Fraser who had Dalneigh Farm took over all the land and the farmhouse in Dalneigh became the Dalneigh Church Manse. It was all farmland round here. We walked up from the Merkinch when we went to the Cemetery on just a cart track with grass on both sides. I walked and my mother pushed my brother in the pram all the way to visit the old folks' graves. They needed enough of a road there to take the hearses in by the Cemetery gates, just the one gate in Bruce Gardens. There was only fields all around, you can't imagine it now, can you?

There was a big house on Planefield Road owned by people called MacDonald and they had this big green where the children used to play. On that green you could do your washing and hang it out, and the kids played there although when they played football the balls were always going over the wall into the MacDonald's and they used to get mad and then we used to be mad because we wouldn't get the ball back.

Eventually the powers-that-be got them to make what we called 'the greenie' and my mother always knew we were safe there. Now it's the Planefield Bowling Club and the other part is the Cameron Club. It was supposed to be for the boys that came home from the First World War. The playing field was given in memory of these boys. We all saved up and all the boys who'd been in the War got £10 given to them. So we lost our 'greenie'. The other place where the Maggot Green is was also a playing green and you could do your washing there. There was clotheslines and I often saw blankets hanging there when I was young.

My cousins Alastair and Willie had the garage in Tomnahurich Street beside Rossleighs and my other cousin Andrew had the cycle shop opposite them. There were three garages in that area then. Further up

Young Street there was a garage on the left before you came to the Bridge. Further up was the chip shop, which is still there, then Bowes the newsagent, the Rendezvous and round the corner the Ness Café. Opposite was the Glenalbyn garage where the Social Security place is now and the Glenalbyn Bar on the corner.

It was two Miss Menzies that had that shop. Spelt Menzies but known as Misses 'Mingies'. Two of them had the shop and we used to go there to spend our pennies because they sold sweeties and all sorts of knick-knacks for younger people, as well as having groceries and that. We used to go from one end of Ardross Place – because they were at the very corner where Telly on the Blink is now. And I think there was another shop next to them but I can't remember now exactly. I've a feeling there was another shop across from them where Tomnahurich Street post office is now. I remember the shop on Montague Row – immediately opposite the Tomnahurich Street post office – that sells carpets and all that now – well there used to be if I remember rightly a wee café in there. He sold sweeties and all that as well but I remember he had a café there.

    Lollipops, liquorice, liquorice strap – that was a half-penny for the strap but you got a thick liquorice stick for a penny, and you could get a half penny lollipop, and you could get a penny lollipop. But there were another two shops near at hand where the West End hotel is now on Kenneth Street, that was a wee shop and we used to go in and I remember we used to buy sherbet in there. You know, you used to open the bag and there was a liquorice stick – and was it Tobermory tatties? And then at the corner of the other end of Kenneth Street – where all the new flats are now – there was a shop there where Bobby Bolt had his house. Do you remember, right on the corner? Well when you went in there the woman had converted a room on the right hand side as you went in the door to a shop which used to sell sweeties.

Oh aye, there were a lot of wee shoppies round about and then at the corner where Victoria Wines are now at the corner of Tomnahurich Street and Kenneth Street – that was Stewart Walkers, a licensed grocer, and along on Tomnahurich Street on the opposite side from Foxes shop there was Fraser's the licensed grocers. I think that is an insurance place now.

Oh yes I remember Foxes being there, yes. There were a lot of shops further down on Tomnahurich Street between Tanners Lane as we knew it – Alexander Place and Kenneth Street there were a lot of shops there because you had Morrison's the butchers, then you had Allen the grocers and you had a chemist who latterly was MacLeary the chemist. And then there was Munro the bakers, and there was Munro's the greengrocer and at the corner there was a Mr Brown who had a plumbing business in the corner shop. The other half of the chemist's, you went in the same doorway but you went to right to MacLeary and to the left to the bike shop. I think there is an optician there now. Bowmakers was there for a while – oh yes and the DIY shop was there. I think the DIY was where the butchers used to be, but all the rest have changed. It has all changed. Across the road of course was Falconer's garage but before Falconer's garage there was a shop there that sold tweed, and the man used to weave tweed at the back of the shop. He sold tweed and tartan. And above it there was a hall and that was the original Ebenezer hall. They are now on Celt Street. That was their original hall because I used to go there to Sunday school, in the Ebenezer hall. The start of King's Street and on the corner of King's Street was the Tarry Ile. It is still there.

Yes my granny stayed in May Court which was just on the other side of the road and I used to go down to sit with granny, and we sat in the bedroom window and watched them come out of the Tarry Ile. They were staggering. There was a garage there which became the Glenalbyn Hotel. That garage backed on to Albion Square so when they built the Inland Revenue and that, they knocked down that whole building from the Glenalbyn Bar right back and Albion Square was knocked down and all these shops on that side of the street were knocked down to make way for the Young Street premises of the Inland Revenue and the Department of Employment.

Again there were more shops; a chip shop – and there still is – but the chips don't taste the same as they did. Oh no! No! They just do not taste the same. We used to stop for a penny or tuppenny bag and they were good! There was a shop next to that, I think it is where the laundrette is now. Then the Carles had that as a shop. They sold various goods. You could get clothes and furniture and all that from them but I think it was a grocer's shop too at one time. There were plenty of grocers' shops. There were no supermarkets. They had a catchment area. People in May Court and Albion Square and King Street and Tomnahurich Street. All these houses were occupied. There were a lot of people round about in Kenneth Street. And then there was another butcher, and a photo developing shop there for a while. There was a paper shop there as well. That was Bowes. That's where I used to go for my comics – the Dandy and the Beano. Never missed them. And next to that was Kings the bakers. They had a little place where you could sit down and have a cup of tea. And where the Britannic Assurance is now was what we called Canessa's – you got great ice cream there. There was the Rendezvous and again you could sit down there for ice cream and coffee. When you think of it there were so many little shops and they all seemed to survive but now we've got these supermarkets and all the little shops are gone. All the character – all these little shops had character. That was that side of the street. King's had a double frontage, that's where Babarouskis is now. And then it was the butchers – I can't remember the name of the butcher that was in it then.

Before the Ness Café, I can't remember what the name was but there was a café before that and I remember it had sort of cream tiles or linoleum – very classy looking but it was just a café. And again you went down there for a cup of tea. I think they sold ice cream as well. And next to that was the Misses Ferguson's, that was another shop that sold sweeties and lemonade, next to the Columba Hotel. And I think that has now been all taken over by Riva. It was actually taken over by the Ness Café after the war. The two Misses Ferguson were elderly and of course during the war there was not much sweets to be had. I think we used to be able to buy lemonade and that was where people would buy lemonade going up to visit at the Infirmary. And then you had the Columba Hotel and the Palace Hotel and various places round here. There were lots of hotels down that side. The tourism trade I think was very well catered for in those days with hotels and when you came round the corner, on the corner of Alexander Place and Ardross Street you had the doctor's surgery. On the side nearest the river you had Dr MacFadyen's house and on the opposite corner of Alexander Place, immediately opposite the Cathedral, you had Dr George MacKenzie and then biggish houses occupied by families. The house next to Dr MacFadyen was let into flats – three flats. But I can't remember who was in the place next to them. That is where the Eagle Star had their office. And then after that was the Strathness Hotel which is now the Tower Hotel.

Mr Hector Bisset's father had an engineering workshop in Balnain Street and Bissets was renowned for skill in maintenance of steam engines – they could make parts, if necessary, and repair them. A house at the King's yard was occupied by William Fraser, quarrymaster, at No 7 Mr MacLean, cashier at McGruther & Marshall, MacKintosh's at No 9, No 11 Mr John MacBean Blacksmith, Mrs Cathy Murchison, No 12A Mr Fair at No 15, a rep for BP and had the second car to appear on the street – a two-seater with dickey. Then at No 15 was Miss MacGillivray, a popular Sheriff Clerk. Beyond Kenneth Street was the bus depot of Mr Roderick MacLennan who first started running charabanc type buses to the Ferry. His business was taken over by Willie Greig in 1927 and much expanded. On the north side, at No 2 was a policeman, then a workshop, then twelve flats of three storeys. Then along the street, Mr Edwards stonemasons' yard – children would play there when no work was being done. The yard was subsequently bought by Mr Donald Allan who constructed and let out garages. No 16 was occupied by Mrs Campbell, whose family had sheep farm interests in Patagonia, No 18 Mr Hector Macdonald, insurance agent and at No 20 Mr Glass auctioneer with Fraser & Co – his wife gave all the roses for school closing days.

'Wee Green'

Alex Ross was the architect responsible for the development of 'Wee Green' area. All buildings are of hand-hewn stone, and slated – a very labour intensive process. Names of the streets, Kenneth, Duncraig, Ardross, point to connection with Sir Alexander Matheson MP of Ardross, who purchased Muirtown Estate in the latter part of the last century. His factor and architect was Alexander Ross who was responsible for development of the 'Wee Green' area – Muirtown to Cathedral – and the buildings were erected around 1900 and before. The Cathedral is Ross's greatest legacy to Inverness.

On the south side was a newsagent and Post Office run by John Cameron whose father had been headmaster of Central School. John was of small stature and stood on a platform behind his counter – he was a loyal member of East Church. At No 4 the chemist, also John Cameron, well a groomed little man with a white moustache. He was as good as a doctor with his knowledge of medicines and gave free first aid in emergencies. Mr A Grant, grocer, at No 14 was also a Lay Preacher attached to one of the fringe churches which abounded in Inverness. Then there was a fruit and sweet shop run by Mr Rizza succeeded by Mr Salvadori. No 16 was the Farmers' Dairy and Mirtles corner bakery shop – Mrs Mirtle sold bread, scones, buns, teacakes. Next door was Mrs Mary MacKenzie's paper shop which sold sweets and tobacco too – she was very lame. The bakery lay behind these two shops and beyond it was a yard used as a sawmill, which was later taken over by the Milk Marketing Board as their creamery – the milk churns were very noisy.

On the other side of Greig Street at the bridge end, was a licensed grocer owned by William Grigor. No 5 was a barber's shop – Mr Scott, he had all the patter to amuse customers. No 15 was a confectioner's shop, Miss Bella Chisholm who was succeeded at that shop for a time by the Misses Tocher. No 48 was a sweet shop run by old, disabled Mrs MacKay and her son James. He ran a wholesale business with pony and trap, serving other retailers and he sang in the church choir at Queen Street Church.

At Tomnahurich Street corner, on the east side was the 'Tarry Ile', some say it was originally named 'Tarry a While' for travellers from the west. Across the road, on the west corner was Thomas Falconer's garage, originally a stables. Mr Falconer kept horse cabs and horse hearses. His hearse was driven by immaculate top hatted Mr MacKenzie. Falconer's followed by Rossleighs is now Tescos who have swallowed up what was King's Yard in Duncraig Street.

The small shop at the corner of Duncraig Street and King Street was Katherine Roy's shop for sweets and groceries. She would sell goods on credit to nearby customers and Miss Roy was deaf.

On Young Street starting at the Suspension Bridge end, No 1 had been a second hand furniture store and showroom for John MacBean and then became the most modern jazzy confectioners and restaurant in town, owned by Mr Canessa. No 5 was King's the baker who also had a restaurant. No 9 was occupied by Mr Paterson printer, brother of Andrew Paterson, leading photographer in the North. He handset all his type for producing stationery. Then for several years, Mr Joseph Bowes sold newspapers there. At No 11 was MacKenzie the butcher, two generations, and No 19 the West End Bar, then converted to a chip shop.

Across Alexander Place, formerly Tanner's Lane, at No 1 Tomnahurich Street was Robert Brown, plumber. No 3 was occupied by Willie Whitton, Chelsea player, then by Archibald Munro who sold fruit and vegetables. No 5 was Mackintosh, bakers, and their bakery was a little further along the street, and through the entrance to May Court. Their produce was carried on a tray on the baker's head and he walked to the shop – lovely smell! At No 5 Robert Macdonald, chemist, was succeeded by Dan MacLeary, whose son reached the top of his profession as a ballet dancer after early tuition by Miss Ross, daughter of Provost Allan Ross. Alistair Bullock sold and mended bicycles at No 7. No 11 was Elliott the butcher, whose manager had the name 'Melancholy Morrison'. Tavish Smith, hairdresser at No 15. Further up at No 47 was 'Fox's' selling newspapers, tobacco, sweets and finally No 63 was the confectionery shop of Miss Annie Menzies, now 'Telly on the Blink'.

Muirtown

I was born near the Muirtown Bridge in the Muirtown PO in 1920. The Muirtown Bridge was there then and the two distilleries, the Glenmore and the Glenalbyn and the Caley Park was further down the road. On the Clachnaharry side of the Muirtown Bridge was the Lion's Gate beside where the Muirtown Motel is now. There were two stone lions, one on each side and up on the right was Muirtown House owned then by a Mr Tarn, an author. When you went to the left there was Muirtown Gardens where Willie MacKenzie was the head gardener, and then there was Whin Park (not the one at the Bught). The fields up there were leased to Riggs the butchers. The cattle and sheep were taken there where Leachkin Brae is now, that was all fields then.

Clachnaharry was a busy little place then, the lock-keepers were there and there were workshops with blacksmiths and joiners. Then when you came back over the Muirtown Bridge on to Telford Street there was Calindus Foods, the canning factory and the New Inverness Laundry.

When we came to Inverness first we stayed in what's now the Loch Ness Hotel, it was let out in flats. There was six of us and we had two attics at the top of the house. We weren't allowed to go in the front door. We had to go round the back to get into our part of the house. I think there was three lots of tenants there and if anyone came in late, like if my father came in late on a Saturday and he'd had a dram, he had to come in through the kitchen where the people down the stairs were sleeping. He had to step over them to get to our attics. How my mother managed I don't know. She had a bedroom fireplace and she cooked and washed and did everything on it.

There was just the two attics and the ceilings were sloping. I mind the doctor came to the house to see me because I was sick and he bent to examine me then knocked his head on the ceiling and nearly knocked himself out. It was pretty tough then. There was a man Craig who was retired and he stayed on the same landing as us – the top landing. My mother had an organ which was kept out on the landing because there was no room for it in the attic and old Mr Craig asked if it would all right if he played it because he used to play the organ in a Church. So old Mr Craig used to sit down and spend the whole afternoon playing the organ. He was a grand old man.

Then there was the Canal keeper, old Sandy Nicolson, he had a ginger beard. When we used to hear the boats whistling for the bridge to open, two of three of us boys used to dash up on to the bridge and we used to turn the handle for old Sandy to open the bridge and let the boats through and then close the bridge again. That was one of the highlights of our days, opening the bridge for Sandy.

Clachnaharry and Leachkin

We lived in Clachnaharry until just before the war (WWI). It was a very open village, very friendly. Everybody knew everybody and everybody's business! But you just saw the younger children, you never saw teenagers because the girls went away to work in service, there was no work for them in the village.

Well the boys, there was the Canal and there were several families employed there then. And there were joiners, saw-millers, masons, plumbers, blacksmiths and the ship builders. There was a lot of work then beside the canal. It was a very, very busy time. We spent our holidays running back and fore to the sea lock at Clachnaharry to see the boats. If we were good they would take us up and then we would look down the Firth to see if there was a boat coming. That's how we spent our days.

None of us could swim but we were never out of the water, there was no entertainment for children in those days. But there was the annual fete at

Muirtown House which belonged to the Darwins. Each year they gave us a little treat. We were all dressed up and marched up there and we had a tea party and a walk round the gardens, much to the gardeners' disgust. We would be warned not to touch anything. Then we had games and tea and teacakes with raisins. Then we marched back to the house and Mr & Mrs Darwin used to stand on the steps and hand out an apple and orange, a skipping rope for the girls and a ball for the boys and that was the end of it for another year.

We used to spend a lot of time going up to Clachnaharry. The Canal was always a great attraction although my parents didn't like me going there. We used to go beyond the Canal and play cowboys and Indians at 'the Rockies' which was at the Munro Memorial above the railway. Then we used to venture on to the mud flats where there was an old barge. It's disappeared now but there's a few remnants sticking out of the mud.

At Balnacraig there was a primrose wood which was a favourite spot for Leachkin people. There was a pond full of tadpoles in the Spring but now it's all overgrown. The Barclays had a croft at Balnacraig and there were other Barclays across the field.

At Craig Dunain was the piggery – a fascinating place for all the youngsters. Jake MacKinnon was the pig man in those days. They say his house was once the mortuary and that it was haunted but I think that was the Leachkin boys' tales.

The pillars at the entrance to Craig Dunain, was the meeting place for the Leachkin lads and there was always quite a few of them. Across from the pillars and over the burn was Eck Fraser's croft and then he moved to Upper Leachkin. Down the road to the dump was a house later demolished and Bob Cassie put up the cabin there. In the field adjacent to the old dump, the farm cattle were burnt and buried there after an outbreak of foot and mouth disease. Further down there were two cottar houses at Mile End. The tenants worked on Kinmylies Farm. When we were children we used to have rides on the horses on their way home from the fields.

Another croft was Willie's at the foot of Craig Phadraig. Willie was a shepherd and he had two big shaggy sheep dogs which he took with him on the bus when he was off to the Mart. He never bathed them and the whole bus stank. There were many old worthies then, and they all had their nick names. 'Red Ally', Dunkie Billicans, Hugh the Cabby, Dan the Croft and many more.

Dunain House was taken over during the war by the Army and after that it lay empty until the Health Board acquired it. The other local mansion house is Tarn House at Muirtown. It had gates with a lion on each pillar and the lions were said to change places at midnight. Behind the pond at Craig Dunain is a grave yard used in the olden times to bury patients. Then after that they were buried on the bank next to the canal. Now of course things are different.

There were two shops in the Leachkin. The Post Office and shop was where the 'Brackens' is situated, it was owned by Jess MacLeod who was a sister of 'Dan the Croft'. She was a bit cantankerous but had a heart of gold. The other shop was at the foot of the back brae. It was little more than a shack but it sold almost everything. Both shops sold paraffin and the smell of it mingled with all the other smells in a grocers. Old Sandy Chisholm also had a wee shop in his house but his moods were unpredictable so I don't think he got much custom. On pension days he got quite 'obstreperous'. We also used to have a Mrs Wilson who went round the houses every so often with a basket which had all sorts of things in it and she always had a baby wrapped in a big shawl with her. There was also a coloured man, 'Jock the Darkie' we called him, who came with his big case during the war with black market goods. I still have a tablecloth my mother bought from him.

There were no houses from the foot of the brae at Muirtown then. The first building you saw was the Balnafettack Farm on the right. Then further up at the foot of the hill where you turn left for Craig Dunain you could go right over the Leachkin and there was a little shop there owned by Hugh MacDonald who also had a shop on Grant Street. That was a wee branch shoppie at the Leachkin. From there, mostly on the right side going up towards Craig Dunain were the rows of houses belonging to the Hospital mainly for attendants and other staff. Eck Fraser had a wee croft on the left hand side. He was a well-known character – 'Eck the Larkin' he was called.

Domestic Life – The Family

Coming home from school on a Friday, you couldn't get into the house for flour. That was baking day and my mother made loaves, pancakes and scones that lasted all week. The women all did that. They bought or grew vegetables and made meals out of almost nothing. My father had been badly wounded in the 1914-18 war and mother's total pension was about £2 a week. She had to bring up the four of us and herself. If you wanted to go to the pictures you had to earn it, lemonade bottles, bones which could be sold to old Jamieson the scrap dealer. On a Saturday I used to get the messages for half a dozen women and got tuppence or threepence – that was your pictures money.

When the swimming pool in Glebe Street opened in 1936 we went every day because it didn't cost anything. We got a ticket from school and it got punched because there was no way the three of us could have gone every day to the baths. The people in the Glebe in those days didn't have bathrooms or hot water but we were all spotless. My mother and father used the private baths – they were very popular. It was a shilling and you had to take your own towels. A lot of the houses in the area only had an outside toilet.

My father was a very keen gardener and a third of the garden was flowers and the rest vegetables. There was soup every day because we were totally self-sufficient with vegetables. We had mince and stew, sausages and fish – we had a lot of fish. We used to have a very nice lady – she used to come from Nairn – Mrs Hastings. She had a big creel on her back and we used to get fish two or three times a week when she went round the doors. She used to come to Milne's Buildings, stop at the corner and take the creel off her back, and we would go out and get the fish. It was a very plain diet, loads of rice puddings, semolina, tapioca (frog's spawn) and roly-poly. During the war my mother used to make potted head, she did it in a jelly. I used to hate that. I liked broth made with beef, but that wasn't very often during the war.

The Longman was our playground, the farms were there and we used to go down and paddle and have picnics. It was quite sandy there. Our garden was about the breadth of the car park (Rose Street multi-storey) and we kept poultry and played on the washing greens. We would take out two or three table covers, throw them over the clothes poles for a backstage and have concerts, maybe charge a penny or a halfpenny.

Although we were near the town we had everything delivered. There were fish floats with the Kessock herring. The man had to cover up the herring boxes because the seagulls were cunning and they would take off with half his stock while he was serving a customer. We had the baker, he had a very high van and he was from Edgars on Church Street. We didn't go in for the fancy cakes a lot, we couldn't afford it in that area. The milk floats came up from Citadel Farm, just by the clock tower and where the Citadel football park was. They came up about 5 pm with warm milk in what we called tap cans. We all ran with a jug and for a few pennies you could have warm milk straight from the cow.

We had no electricity in our house and my mother had a paraffin lamp at the top of the stairs and I used to be sent to get a pennyworth of paraffin – I used to take a bottle, about the size of a whisky bottle, and it would hold a pennyworth.

Our house was in Victoria Square, we had a kitchen, like a small lobby with a sink in it, a large living room and two bedrooms. We had lamps to start off then we got the gas. We had gas lamps outside too. The Square was like a drying green and across from our bit was the washhouse. We had outside toilets, one at the bottom of the outside staircase and one in the far corner of the Square. We had coal cellars over there too. We each had a bit garden and when you came in from Rose Street, down Milne's Buildings into Victoria Square, there was a row of cottages at Railway Terrace.

If anything was wrong there was always a neighbour there to come and help you or your family and we were all friendly and looked after folk.

My earliest recollections are living very happily with my parents and two younger sisters. My mother was a born homemaker and my memory conjures up pictures of the lovely fire burning in the range and in the evenings when we were ready for bed she would sing songs from the war (WW1) to us. Dad's contribution to the entertainment was to reach up to the tea-caddy on the mantelpiece and take out a cutting from the 'People's Journal' and read 'Wee Willie Winkie' and 'Bairnies cuddle down', after that it was off to bed, prayers said and I cuddled my cloth doll called 'Snora' and admired my little red-riding hood cloak which hung on the back of the door.

Money was extremely tight then but we never knew what it was to go hungry. Mothers made great pans of soup and dumplings for birthdays. There was nothing to eat between breakfast and dinnertime so we were ravenous by the time we ran home from school at mid-day. All the cooking was done on an open fire range and on winter days it was heaven to be sure our mother would be waiting for us with a warm kitchen, a good meal and a welcome.

It was paraffin lamps we had then and we had globes for putting on them, they cost sixpence. They were always getting broken but they gave a good light. There was a wick and you turned a little screw to make it go up and down to adjust the light. We were in No 6 Duncraig Street, and the people in the block were very friendly and neighbourly. When anyone was ill there was always someone to go and look after them. It was coal fires we had and there were no bathrooms then. We used to have to go to the public baths. The houses were very comfortable with long lobbies.

Well you had your porridge in those days, with milk, and mince and tatties for dinner and anything that was going. What was the favourite? Oh, mince and tatties I think, we liked mince and tatties. And you see there was no cookers and that sort of thing. My mother used to have the little hob fire, with a little oven on it – by that time there would be four of us – and she would be making pancakes. They had problems but they managed. And then there were spells when your father was idle you see – made idle from the foundry – and times were difficult – but we never wanted. Then we started growing up of course – then we started courting. Oh, we went to dances – we did a lot of dancing – John was in the RFA and we used to go to the RFA (the Field Artillery) at the Grant Street hall. Before I really started going with him, a clique of us had a dancing club at the Queensgate Hotel – four girls – used to go to the Queensgate Hotel and met other boys of course – oh I don't know what else. It was all good fun.

Oh aye, the pictures were on – the pictures were maybe tuppence or something – tuppence halfpenny for the matinée on Saturday – but we didn't get to the pictures that often because the money was scarce. There were four of us, four of a family then. Then on Sunday we'd go to Sunday School, with a halfpenny or a penny for the plate – sometimes we lost it – sometimes you didn't put it in! Probably buying a stick of barley sugar or a liquorice strap. And then your school days were fun! We went to the High School – the Crown now. No, we used to come out from Hamilton Street, go through Washington Court and up the lane. The High School was at the Crown then. Yes it was at the Crown then. We used to come out of Hamilton Street, through the court, up through the lane, cross Crown Drive and there were steps going up to Stephen's Brae, and we would be up the steps.

All Mod Cons

At the corner of Young Street right next to the Tarry Ile was Penningtons shop and I used to go down there with the wet battery for the wireless to get it charged up. We had two wet batteries, one would be in getting charged and the other would be in use.

Oh yes we had a wireless. That was our main interest for all the things that were going on then. Saturday night it was the same routine. The wireless went on, you waited till it warmed up and the sound came on, then there was 'The MacFlannels', Scottish Dance Music, it stayed on all evening. On the Sunday it was the 'Family Favourites' programme for the Forces abroad, and on weekdays 'Music While You Work'. Years ago you turned the wireless on to listen to it. The set was battery operated, with a wet battery, and you went into Peter Ross's workshop on Castle Street to get it charged up. It was a wee shop up a close on Castle Street. The batteries were heavy but I've seen my mother take the battery home in a shopping bag. In those days the ladies carried heavy bags home, it didn't matter how heavy they were. But then eventually we got a radio that plugged in to the electricity and to us this was very, very modern, then eventually television came in and took over from the radio.

When I was about fourteen in the early days of radio, my cousin and I would buy parts to make up three or four valved radios. It was an expensive hobby in those days but it was thrilling to make it ands hear it work, voices out of the ether. If we were using an accumulator battery it had to be charged up at MacRae & Dicks or one of the other garages or ironmongers.

We had a wireless set in the 30's and I liked the music. My father made our first crystal set (early radio) with the earphones and an accumulator (battery) which you had to get charged up. We had a gramophone too. My favourite tune was 'Soor Milk Cairt' and Donald Dallas songs. It was the round records then, but we used to have the cylinder ones first.

Poverty

My father worked long hours in the farming day and he worked holidays to get extra money, digging up drains where you were paid a penny a yard. It was very little money for doing extra work. Farm workers were very poorly paid because they got milk, potatoes and some coal and that was counted as part of their weekly wage.

I remember Sir Alexander McEwan when I was an apprentice in Stewart, Rule & Co (Solicitors on Church Street). During the Depression of the 30's there was great consternation among the staff at having to accept reduced wages, but nobody left. Life was hard in many ways then.

We used to see a lot of strange men around because that is where the model lodging house was. Some were tramps who wore a lot of coats and trousers for warmth. I think it was the Carrol's who had the model lodging house just as you went into North Church Place – they ran it. There were few beds, but there were mattresses on the floors and the people had to do their own cooking. They maybe had a couple of bacon rashers and an egg but they had to stay out all day – they were just allowed bed and breakfast.

There wasn't a lot of work, in fact the painters only had work in the Spring. I don't know how they existed. You see, the people who had plenty of money and were doing spring-cleaning needed painters, but that was the only time the poor souls got work.

After the war (WWI) it was very, very sad. The saddest thing was the knock on the door. There would be a young lad nicely dressed in the suit they all wore when they were demobbed, and selling newspapers. They shouldn't have had to do that, I could have wept for them.

The solicitors took it in turn to act as what was called 'agents for the poor' and we were expected to do this work for literally nothing.

We had an awful lot of people who came begging at that time – it was sheer desperation. Men were singing in the back courts where we hung the washing and during the week they sang all the well known Scottish songs. Some of them were beautiful singers but some of them had an awful struggle to sing. On Sunday they sang psalms and the pennies came flying down from Milne's Buildings. I was always told to go out and ask this particular man to sing 'Bonny Strathyre' for my father and on Sunday it was the 23rd psalm. This was in the 30's up to the war years and then a lot of them disappeared. They weren't on the road so much and some of them went into homes.

We had the model lodging house in North Church Place. My grandfather was a Baillie in the town and my mother talked of being there at the opening. She was fascinated by the very long range and everybody with their frying pan cooking. It was mostly men in the model and sometimes I think they had women. Many of the old men finished their travelling or their working lives there. Some of them had been injured in the First World War and had taken to the road, unfit for work, and there was no help for them.

There was one old man lived there (in the model) and he said they weren't always nice people there but it was his home. During the war (WW2) once a week he managed to get an apple somewhere and he always brought half to me. I worked at a dairy and I used to skim the cream from the top of the cans and put it into his can.

There were children in Farraline Park School who were in great poverty. I remember once my mother going up to my class and she brought my shoes and slippers that I'd outgrown. Miss Sinclair, the teacher, said, "Hands up anybody who would like these slippers", and hands went up all over the class. One child went home with my shoes and one with the slippers. That was the level we were at.

Drinking was a big problem on a Saturday night, we used to go out just to see the fights. There were always fights and we went just for the fun of it. There was a lot of unemployment, so where the money came from I don't know. It was a time when a lot of women and children went without.

I remember most of the men in the street were unemployed apart from one or two engine drivers. The railway provided work but the other men were out of work. They didn't get much work at the harbour, it wasn't until the war (WW2) started that men started getting employment. Some of them did casual work. The chap next door, if you wanted a room papered, he would do it. Each one helped the other out with difficult jobs like if you wanted a bit of fencing done they would do that. It was something for them to do, and they got a few bob for a packet of fags or something, or it would be the drink first. It was a pretty bleak existence.

It must have been murder. You had to bring every drop of water in and every drop of water had to go out in bowls, the washing water. There was no drainage, not in the houses. There was a village pump. When that froze over in the winter, it was simply dreadful. All the newspapers under the sun were used for burning.

You had to go down to the canal and it wasn't very good. We didn't use that water for drinking. We went to the Priseag Well – a well further out the road. That was always running and we took the water for cooking and that. But it must have been dreadful. You had open fires. It was hard then.

Oh all our clothes were handed down to the younger children and I was the youngest of the girls so I was well used to hand-me-downs. My mother made quite a lot of our clothes because she was good with her hands. With the hand-knitted jumpers she used to 'scale' them down (pull the knitwear back) and then knit them up again in smaller sizes. I was the youngest of seven children so I inherited the jumpers in a different guise.

There was a lot of poverty in the Shore area then and the Cooks who owned the sawmill were very good as they encouraged the children to join the Band of Hope and luxuries like a bag of buns were handed out at the meetings. The other thing they did was try to develop the talents of the local children by holding concerts and whoever won was given half a crown, a lot of money in those days. My uncle who was the eldest of a family of nine worked in a butcher's shop, he'd left school because the family were poor, and the highlight of the week was my uncle delivering the meat across the Ramparts area on a Saturday night and on the way home bought them all a bun with his wages. The shops were open till 11.30 pm then, and this was their luxury, they all waited up for their bun. My mother talked a lot about the railway and how often they were lucky enough to get bits of coal that fell off the wagons near the tracks. Life was hard down there but there was a strong emotional tie and the neighbours were very supportive of each other.

High Days and Holidays

Our first holiday was in an old van. We couldn't afford a car, but my husband was a good mechanic and we had a tent. We went up the West Coast and took our food with us. We went to Nairn for the Nairn Games. We went by train – there was a special train packed to the gunwales. We sometimes went across the ferry on Sunday on the boat and had a picnic. The boat went back and fore all day there was so many people going. My mother and father sat on a rug and we walked to the lighthouse and paddled.

On the first Sunday in May we went to the 'Clootie Well' – walking from the Town, and thought nothing of it. For most Invernessians there was no fortnight's holiday away. The answer to the question, "What are you doing for your holidays?" would usually be, "Och, just a day here and there".

Pre-war there was a tendency for all the trades' apprentices in town to stick together – like the bakers and the slaters. They all camped up on the canal banks, up by the old 'Sandy Braes'. They all had their tents and after work they went up there and stayed overnight and back to work in the morning.

There would be swimming and diving competitions. There were one or two fatalities – people getting caught in the cold water or on the Sandy Braes because they were quite treacherous at that time as well.

There was always someone who had a tent, a bell tent, and at the start of the summer we found a place, got permission from the owner and set up camp. We camped all summer and cycled to work every morning and back at night when the campfire was built and we had a rare time. The girls were invited at the weekends for a visit. We usually had a butcher's boy and a baker's and a vegetable boy with us so food was no problem as each boy got a 'parcel' home with him at the weekend – this was a 'perk' of the job. If we got a grocer's boy to camp with us this was living in luxury. The woods around the 'Clootie' Well, the shore at Stratton, and Holm Mills were the favourite spots.

We used to visit Clachnaharry and the Fairy Glen near Bunchrew and where we gathered wild rasps and brambles and blueberries to bring home to our mothers for making jam. When we were going towards Bunchrew from Clachnaharry we always stopped at a small cairn, someone said it was a tinker's grave. It may have been a spot where the coffin rested on the way to burial.

We went over on the ferryboat and spent the summer holidays – about six weeks. The man on the ferryboat had one of the little cottages up from the pier and my grandmother, my brother and I stayed there. We paddled and the boys fished. They used to catch eels and they'd chase us with them. There would be quite a lot of folk over for the summer holidays – you'd get over for threepence I think it was. It was great fun going over the ferry.

I don't have very many memories of Christmas apart from the school party which used to be down in the hall (Culduthel Hall). Santa was a great thing until you were quite a big age to be truthful. You were called out and you got a present. I remember it was a Meccano one year. I looked at it for a long time and I thought, "Gosh – this is great" because you never ever got Meccano sets or cars or toys of any kind at home. Our parents weren't in a position to give them to us. Christmas at home was – well no Christmas lunch, no Christmas dinner – it was just an ordinary day. A household might have a chicken or cockerel for lunch but there was no family lunch with crackers or anything like that. Farm work still went on – your father still worked on Christmas day. There were no extras.

The only extra we got at New Year was getting to stay up late and take in Hogmanay and get raspberry or blackcurrant wine and something to eat which you looked forward to. Midnight seemed to take ages because you were always off to bed early in the country. Midnight was a late, late hour to be up.

For Christmas you got a sixpence in your stocking and an apple and orange. I mind one time I got a wax doll. I sat it beside the fire and the thing melted. I was left with a lump of wax in my hand.

On Hogmanay night we all met below the clock at the Exchange, the clock is down in Grant Street now – we used to meet there and the band would play. There was a service first in the Wesleyan Church and they would all come up and meet us at the Exchange. It was great times at Hogmanay taking in the New Year. Then they would all set off first footing with a lump of coal.

On Burn Road there's a bridge in the middle, in those days (the 20's) it was a wooden bridge and some of the locals used to have dances on it, a fellow with a melodeon or an accordion playing in the street at night and they would dance there.

At Hogmanay there was a man Sutherland lived on Drummond Road and he came out and on the dot of midnight he fired a shot – he had a shotgun – he didn't fire at anybody but this was an indicator that the New Year had started – he did this regularly every New Year.

This boy at work was getting married. He thought he was safe because he was out in the van. Well, we let him empty the van when he got back and then we pounced – we had to get them in their whites (painters) so you didn't dirty their clothes. We didn't use things that wouldn't come off but you could do them up with syrup and feathers and butter. So we put the boy in a crate beside MacTavish the ironmongers, we borrowed their hurley and put the crate in it. We were going to run him round the town and then take him to his girlfriend's house on the other side of town, almost out in the country. However, the boy liked a drink, so we stopped and one or two of us went into the pub and told the customers what we had outside. They all came out with a dram for him so we got the idea to go round all the pubs in the town. There were thirteen of them and we went round the lot. When we eventually arrived at his girlfriend's door we tipped the crate up in sight of the door. The future mother-in-law was shaking her fist and threatening to set the dogs on us.

Clootie Well Sunday was always a great outing. The old Clootie Well is on the way out to Culloden, and for generations people have been hanging bits of rags – 'cloots' onto the trees, and throwing money into the well, and it's supposed to bring you good luck. Clootie Well Sunday is the first Sunday in May, but that was always a trip and buses took you out. It used to be mobbed. The wee footpath leading from the road down to the well, if it was a wet Sunday, it was churned up and very muddy. If it was a nice Sunday you took a picnic. If we were going for a picnic the mothers spent most of Saturday preparing the sandwiches and cake and hardboiled eggs, and the flasks we took with us. I can still remember the taste clearly, the taste of egg sandwiches on either Nairn or Rosemarkie beach. They were always crunchy by the time you started to eat them because the sand would be blowing into them, but they tasted like nothing else I've ever tasted before – it was lovely. That was a major outing and that was people's holidays. People didn't go away for a holiday for a fortnight. We were maybe particularly lucky because my father had an old aunt who lived in Rosemarkie just almost on the beach – called the Cabin. All the way through the war years we spent a couple of weeks there with my mother in the summer. It was a great adventure. We got the bus down to the ferry, then we got the ferryboat and crossed over, and then another bus took us from the ferry to Rosemarkie, and the same on the way home. We just played on the beach. I can still remember every single rock and little inlet of Rosemarkie beach – and it's never changed. I had my granddaughter there in the summer and I knew exactly every part to go to. So that was their holidays. If you had a Sunday, or two or three Sundays away in Nairn or Rosemarkie, or if you were really adventurous you went to Lossiemouth. It was so exciting and we looked forward to it for days beforehand and hoped the sun would shine.

Christmas was, I suppose, like Christmases will always be to children, it was very exciting. Probably the build-up was more exciting than the actual day when it came. There simply wasn't money to buy a lot of presents. We always got the traditional orange and apple and threepenny bit, or maybe a sixpence. We always got a book, that was something that always came every year. My own particular favourite was the Rupert Book and there was always the Broons or Oor Willie, they were always firm favourites. I know through the war, and a few years after, you got one or the other. It was the Broons one year and Oor Willie the next year. I think later on they started doing them both. The folk at the shops, Ann and Peg, they were always very good to us and they always put a book along as well. There were never big presents. I remember the first year I got a big present and that was a doll's house. Where it had come from I don't know. Looking back on it, it obviously wasn't new, and where it had come from I don't know but it was a lovely doll's house, it was beautiful and I often wish I still had it. But my father was one of these folks who couldn't bear to see anybody with less than himself, so he gave away so much of our stuff. The lead up to Christmas was always exciting. Mind you we always seemed to have a lot of white Christmases as well. I remember the first time we ever got Christmas lights for our tree. There had been talk of a big surprise one day when we were coming home from school. I remember coming home and it was a very snowy time just before that Christmas. We came into the house and there were lights on the Christmas tree, and it was Eric MacFarlane, the youngest son of the MacFarlanes who had got them for us. He had just left school and had started work as an electrician and somehow or other he got these Christmas tree lights. We were absolutely enchanted with this lovely tree.

The happy times were the weddings. Everybody turned out, even as late on as my own wedding in 1956. They all turned out and stood round the door and wished you well. You had a little present from everybody because you were well known. We always had a penny scramble and went round the cobbles looking for pennies. Everything stopped till they were found.

Medical Matters

The Fever Hospital – it was down beside the Ramparts. You went down Shore Street, came to the Citadel Bar, turned left where the petrol tanks are and to the right of that was the Ramparts and Cromwell's Clock. The hospital was closed by my day (late 20's, early 30's) but it was a building with steps up to it and it was known as the Fever Hospital where people with contagious diseases went, before Culduthel Hospital. We used to go up the steps and try and look in the windows. It was still quite a good building but unused by then.

When I was just starting up after the war I discovered they were pulling down the old Fever Hospital at Cromwell's Fort – the Citadel. There was a very well built corrugated iron building just beside it so I thought I could use some of that. I found out it was being dealt with by the Burgh Surveyor so I approached him – but oh no, they were going to make use of it. But then I found lorries carting away stuff so I went back and I was told if I took down my hurly I could get as much corrugated iron as I could take home and I built my first workshop with that. I was assured by everybody at the Fever Hospital that the old iron would kill me, but I'm still here.

When I was about three my father and I both caught diphtheria from my sister who died. She was two years older than me and my father caught it from feeding her and then I took it and we were both sent up to Culduthel Hospital. During the time we were there, there was a fever hospital built at the RNI. In the middle of our isolation period we were taken from Culduthel to the RNI. My father used to tell me afterwards we were just allowed to speak through the windows at Culduthel, and my mother came up just to give us a wave because we were in isolation. Anyway, we were taken down, probably it was by horse and cart, to the RNI and that's the building that became the Nurses' Home.

I had diphtheria and I was in the isolation ward, a little annexe beside the RNI – it isn't there now. There was a horse pulled ambulance, one horse, and Fraser was the driver and he stayed at the Lodge at the Infirmary – the house with the clock on it just before the bridge. The service was run by the hospital and I was taken by horse ambulance to the Infirmary.

I remember at the Poor House (Hilton Hospital) was a Dr Murray – he dressed in a black robe and rode on a tricycle.

Muirfield Hospital was then the Poor House run by Mr Bewglass – a very conscientious strict tea-totaller – he had an AJS motorcycle and sidecar. My wife went to Edinburgh as a passenger in the sidecar. There used to be corncrakes in the field beside the Poor House.

I began work in Hilton Hospital when it was called Muirfield Hospital in 1940. Before that it was called the Poor House and most of the patients were old people who couldn't live on their own, but we got lots of emergencies as well. Old Dr MacFadyen was the doctor for the poor. If they had no money they went to him if they had anything wrong with them and he sent them up. It didn't matter if it was first thing in the morning or night time. We also had a lot of single girls who went there to have their babies. We had a small maternity unit in the hospital. We had people from all over. When I was there was the blackout during the war.

When I was there the biggest problem was the blackout during the war. All lights had to be blacked out and some of the old men used to get up to the toilet during the night, open the curtains and there would be a knock at the door and there would be an Air Raid Warden or big Henry the bobby (Henry Smith). But this became an excuse to get a cup of tea if he saw the lights. He was an old worthy. At that time when I was working in that area bungalows were built on the other side of the road. Another thing we did during the war, although I'm not sure if we were supposed to do it – if anyone died round about, undertakers didn't do things then, and we invariably had to perform the last rites. We knew all the people round about and it was also an ARP station and first aid post, so any time sirens went off everybody arrived at the downstairs area. They had a part where there were no patients in two or three rooms. They always had their tea if they were waiting for any length of time and boxes of biscuits. The nurses never saw biscuits during the war but we got fly to that and we used to go along and have the odd one. The sirens went off quite a lot, a lot of planes went over. As long as an enemy plane went over they all had to be at their posts. On the 12th of January each year there used to be a gathering of lots of doctors – they celebrated the old year there. I remember Pringle from the Wool Mills – the old man, they had a party and a dance – I never knew why. The band was Fraser Sutherland. His son was Bud Sutherland, he played church organs and worked for Fraser the Undertakers.

When I went there first the Governor was called Mr Bewglass. His wife was a retired Matron. The Governor was the boss and he lived in the house beside the hospital on the corner of Muirfield Lane. His wife interfered quite a lot. She used to phone over to the hospital if she saw the nurses going out dressed in a way she thought was unsuitable. Two of us were going out one night and we did our hair up on top to be different and we were sent back. She phoned and we got to the gates and were sent back. Then, when – you know when girls worked in factories during the war and were allowed to wear trousers, well on payday two of us bought these grey flannel trousers, went out, Mrs Bewglass saw us, so back we had to go. But we thought we'd do her, so we just rolled them up, or pinned them and went out again and rolled them down once we got out of sight – she was a holy terror, that woman.

We had very hard work. The wards had fireplaces and when the sweep came he made a dreadful mess and the nurses had to scrub the floors. We had to scrub them from end to end, as well as all our own work. We had from old people to babies. During the war a lot of families followed their men if they were posted up here. Families used to arrive with nowhere to go and we used to get, sometimes in the middle of the night, four or five children we had to put up. We got lots of cases – potential suicides. We were worked very hard. I was on night duty in that hospital all on my own, and you know the size of the hospital. The only help you got was from patients who perhaps were not mentally balanced, but were able to help. I got fed up once or twice and went down to join the services, but nobody would take you once you said you were a nurse – that was it. There were happy times too. We used to go to the dances in the Caley Hotel, but we always had to be home by a certain time because there was a big gate in the gatehouse and the gate was locked, and the back gate was locked too. So if we didn't get in before it was locked, that was it. The Porter locked the gate. He lived down by the front gate. There were two houses, the Porter's on one side of the arch and what we called the Gatehouse on the other side. In the Gatehouse it was mostly patients' clothing, but a couple of men used to live there – old men. There was an old Quarter Master Sergeant from the First World War who was in charge of provisions in this little larder and he ruled the roost of course, and of course he thought he was in charge of stores. Many a time we were sent for things and he would just refuse. He threw a knife at me once.

When we were living in the blocks (tenements) everybody was kind to one another and they had great cures when people were ill. There was one old lady who lived there, she was very ill and I remember my mother was awfully good, if there was anything wrong they always came to her. This old lady had a bad chest and it was red flannel they put on it – that relieved her.

Culduthel Hospital was a sanatorium then, it was for TB and fevers. It was always busy because TB was rife then.

Culduthel Hospital was basically a TB hospital and we got to know a lot of the nurses, especially when I got a bit older and was more 'interested'. I had scarlet fever and I was put into Culduthel Hospital for about three weeks or so. They were worried at that time about diphtheria which could be very serious then – but scarlet fever wasn't so bad.

The original building (Culduthel Hospital) had been the Sheriff's house, Sheriff Grant, and then it became a hospital and they added bits to it. The TB patients would be lying out on the balconies, even when there was snow, they reckoned this was a help to them – the fresh air was good for their lungs. You would see them with the snow on top of them and sometimes they went from there to Invergarry and that was the end, they never came back from there. But some of them did recover from Culduthel. They were taken down the Loch by boat to Invergarry, the place was a wooden structure and when they were finished with it they set fire to it – just burned it.

I was a joiner and they were making the foundations for Raigmore Hospital – the old brick Raigmore. We pushed the barrow of posts and sticks to set out the sites for the various buildings. I couldn't tell you who drew up the plans, but I think it was the Government, it was a Ministry of Defence hospital. The labourers dug out the trenches for the concrete foundations, it was all brick and concrete. There were no lorries then, we pushed the posts in a barrow all the way from Friars Street to Raigmore. I'm sure it took us near three quarters of an hour, up Academy Street, along Inglis Street, Eastgate and then Millburn and then up the Perth Road. There were wooden houses in there then. What was on the site? Well, just a few cows. There were fields you see, right over to Cradlehall.

There was a lot of illness then. The condition of the school toilets I still remember were appalling. They were nearly always choked. I was OK because I lived just over the wall and I could run home at lunchtime but there were a lot of infectious diseases. Diphtheria was rife. I remember in Innes Street where a child had just been buried and the father came home and found the other child had also died. It just went right through the neighbourhood and we often thought it was passing round in the milk bottles because it went from door to door.

It was quite an occasion when this brown ambulance with a smell of burning oil came. I had scarlet fever and had to go to Culduthel Hospital and I still remember the ambulance and the awful smell of oil. I was taken up there and it wasn't very warm. There was only one fire in the ward but all the children were taken there and we were in for six or seven weeks. Tuberculosis was rife, we lost families with tuberculosis and there was no cure in those days. The terrible conditions they had and they had no privacy to live, it was very hard times.

He was buried in 1924 by Chisholm's the Undertakers who were in George Street at that time. It cost £7 for the funeral. That was an ordinary coffin and the burial ground was £3.10/-. I'll tell you an interesting story. My father died of TB which was rife at the time. He'd been gassed in the war – at the Somme. His lungs were a big weak and in the 20's he developed TB and in 1923 they decided to send him to Invergarry, a Sanatorium near Fort Augustus. So he was sent up on the 'Gondolier' which sailed up the canal. He was sitting on the deck of the Gondolier feeling pretty miserable and there were two ladies near him who spoke in Gaelic, and one said to the other, "You don't need to ask where that chap's going". "No", she said, "and I'll tell you another thing, he'll no come out of it". So my father who understood Gaelic knew well what they meant, and that wasn't a very nice thing to hear about yourself. However, he died there. I was just three and a half at the time. So TB was very rife then. I remember as I used to walk down Grant Street and in other parts of the town there would be signs up on the lamp-posts – very simply stating 'Do not Spit'. Because TB came out in the spit and if you spat on the ground, the bacillus dried up and there was a waxy envelope it formed. To ingest the dust in the summer which contained this bacilli – that was another case of TB. So this was the Public Health Authority trying to cut down on the incidence of TB. Now I don't know when these signs disappeared.

The Laboratories for the Ministry of Health, this was in the RNI. We started very small. When you go in the RNI you go left to the actual entrance to the hospital, and if you carry on there's a small building to the right, and that's where we started. When I started there was Dr Kirkpatrick who was in charge and to show you a sign of the times when he was appointed, he was appointed on Christmas Day. Christmas Day in Scotland in the 1930's was a normal working day. You got New Year's Day off and the day after and that was it.

He started off everything. Blood transfusion, biochemistry and he did everything – post-mortems and all that sort of thing. I remember a famous post-mortem that was carried out there – John Cobb who was killed on Loch Ness. I remember I helped to carry the body of John Cobb into the mortuary. I wasn't present at the autopsy or the post-mortem but I was asked to help carry him in. Poor John, he was a very popular figure up here.

The samples came in from all over the north and the Islands. It took a couple of days – they all came by post. The thing was to try and keep them as fresh as possible and of course one of the jobs of the post was you went down to the Post Office every night at 10 pm and asked if there was any post for the Pathology. We all had a week on duty and we had to do that every night of the week and on a Saturday you went at 5.30 pm. At the General Post Office you said, "Anything for the Pathology?" and there might be some came in late and you took them up. You put the specimens up that night and the same even on a Sunday. On the Saturday I remember going after the match at 5.30 pm and asking for mail.

I remember when I used to work in the Lab (RNI) we used to get the spits from Stornoway and all these places. But just after the war they got very good drugs against TB and slowly over the next ten years into the 1950's they were beginning to eradicate it. There was an interesting case in about 1946/47 when I came back from the war. There was a Sister in Culduthel (Hospital) and she developed TB/Meningitis, which was a killer. If you developed that you were as good as dead. But they had just developed a new antibiotic against the tubercle and that was Streptomycin. So she was one of the first in Scotland to be treated with this antibiotic. She recovered, but unfortunately the side-effect was that she was left deaf. But she had her life, and lived a good life after that.

The old Fever Hospital at the Ramparts was built in 1860 and was still in use in the Great War (1914-18), for smallpox, cholera and that. I think it would have gone up during or after that war. There was very bad diphtheria in the town and very bad scarlet fever which you never see nowadays. I suppose the improved hygiene is responsible for that. We used to go up to Culduthel Hospital and our friends would be in with diphtheria or scarlet fever and we weren't allowed in to see them, but we could look at them through the glass windows. You would see the TB patients and they were all on verandas, because at that time they thought the only way to cure TB was fresh air, so they slept outside. If you've ever been up to Culduthel, there's a lot of verandas outside all the wards and the TB patients were out there in all weathers.

So the first TB/Fever Hospital was in the Longman area. When it came down, Culduthel Hospital was built up in the woods. There was many servicemen used Culduthel Hospital during the Second World War? Then they started building Raigmore Hospital to accommodate the war wounded and a lot of them, including Inverness boys, were shipped to Raigmore Hospital.

That was the previous Raigmore Hospital, the red brick Units. That building was started in 1940 and put up fairly quick because they didn't know what casualties were coming. When the second front started there was a lot of casualties and the wards would be full up. I remember speaking to Mr Hamilton – Ronnie Hamilton, the surgeon, he was saying he would go in some mornings and wards would be full and you just worked for twenty-four hours.

They were from all over and they included local servicemen. I remember a chap Bob Wheeler, who's still living, and he's living in the Legion Homes on the riverside. He was brought there. He was badly wounded, he got a head wound which left him paralysed down one side.

Wartime Memories

A fortnight before war broke out the young Territorials, later called the 297 Inverness Battery, were called up. I had been friendly with quite a few of the boys from schooldays so my sister and I went to see them going away. They had got their papers when they came home from work and left Inverness about midnight. All the girls saw them off thinking how great it was that there was a war on. It shows how immature we were at the time. The boys went to Invergordon, then to Shetland.

The war broke out on Sunday September the 3rd. I remember my mother was bathing my baby sister when Mr Churchill announced on the radio that we were now at war and she burst into tears because she had lost her father and her brother in the First World War. As the war was going on Mrs Donald, whose husband was the Director of MacRae & Dick, asked me if I would help her knit some hose tops for the 51st Division. I knitted more than two dozen. I failed to get into the services because I was asthmatic. Then I tried to get into nursing at Raigmore but failed again for the same reason. I walked home from Raigmore hardly able to see for the tears in my eyes.

A boy MacPherson who was in school with me was the first of the troops from the town to lose his life, I think it was at St Valery. Somewhere between 1940 and 1942 the Italian prisoners came to Inverness and were stationed up at Drumdevan House. I used to visit an aunt at Drumdevan on a Sunday and would see the prisoners though I never actually spoke to them because my aunt was watching.

There was a regiment at Ness Castle, I can't recall who they were. When the Canadians came over they were stationed at Kirkhill and Beauly. They used to come in to the dances in the Caley on Saturday nights.

Half an hour after war was declared, the sirens went off in Inverness. We thought it was a practice but it wasn't. It was a German plane. We got used to the sound. We didn't have any bombing but they were trying to get the railway going north and the Caledonian Canal to put these out of action.

We had no shelter where we lived but we used to crawl under the table. Quite a lot of Anderson shelters were built beside the railway. My mother-in-law lived in Innes Street and they had a shelter in the back garden. The railway ran along the bottom of their garden.

Quite a number of churches were unable to have blackout conditions during the war because of the big windows. Our church, the West Parish, didn't have it, so we had services in the morning and afternoon. We used to go to the Methodist at night because they had blackout. The services were always packed, in fact it was standing room only with all the soldiers. After the service they served tea and cakes to the visiting soldiers and other servicemen.

During the war a lot of girls were called up for munitions training. They worked in the Rose Street Foundry and a lot of girls also worked in the Stage Door Canteen on High Street.

I was asked if I would like to come into the Post Office (now BT) at night to work at the telephones. I asked my parents who agreed provided I got home at night because we were staying on Drummond Road then and during the black out there were no lights and the area wasn't as populated then. So that was my War work. I worked all day from 9 am to 5.30 pm at MacRae & Dicks, went home and had my tea, then worked on the telephones from 7 pm till midnight when I was taken home in a Post Office van.

When the war got going in 1939 this was a closed area from Inverness north, you couldn't get in or out. You had to have a permit from here to further north or you couldn't get out. If you went out you met the roadblocks. There was one at Hilton, one at Culcabock and one at Clachnaharry. That's as far as you could go if you didn't have a permit. Coming back was a bit dodgy because you were usually challenged at night.

I remember the American sailors, I've still got the little invitation that was sent to all the little kiddies of Inverness from the American sailors. They were billeted in the Merkinch School Hall and before they left they erected swings and a merry-go-round and a Maypole in the playground and it's not that many years since they were removed. I used to play on them and many a time I went flying.

The war in 1939 – oh it was terrible. We stayed in George Street at that time, Jack worked in the Foundry. I didn't think so much about the war, I had the family and I was thinking more about them and

Jack. They were only bairns then. We used to hear the sirens go off and if the bairns were up the stairs I would take them down and we used to have a table and I put it in the corner of the room because there was a big tree in the next garden that sheltered half our house and thought we were safer there.

There was a pass issued to people who found it necessary to cross the canal and to enter the restricted area west of the canal. There were roadblocks at various points round the town – one at Island Bank Road at the Islands, and another at Drummond Road. It was the custom, if challenged by the troops, to stop the car, open the doors and get out. The foundation blocks for a bridge over the canal (in the case of an emergency) are still in place at the top of Fairfield Road.

About 1918 at the beginning of the First World War there was a sentry box and a sentry beside Old Edinburgh Road. My wife helped at the Northern Meeting Rooms to entertain American sailors from the fleet stationed in the Cromarty Firth. There was a Filipino from the S.S. Blackhawk who used to visit. He brought little canvas bags full of goodies that were otherwise unobtainable here.

During the war it was mainly concert parties and dances – there was dancing everywhere. It was mainly for the troops stationed here. They had troops everywhere – every church hall was commandeered with troops living in them, and all the hotels. So they had to get something to keep them occupied, keep them from getting too depressed. They trained during the day and had entertainment at night.

Because of the war there were certain places, restricted areas that were difficult to get to. You weren't allowed to go just where you liked – you had to get permission, but after the war the restrictions were lifted and you were able to go out to all the village halls to entertain.

One of my father's memories of 1900 or thereabouts was this story. A lot of the 20-30 year olds were members of the Old Volunteers – the forerunners of the Territorial Army. Every Saturday they would parade at 5.30 am in Farraline Park in full uniform. They would march to the Longman, fire nine rounds at 200 yards and 500 yards – fall in again and march back to Farraline Park, fall out and go home for a quick breakfast, into their civilian clothes and off to work at 8 am.

Everybody was looking forward to the end of the war. Some of the boys when they were coming home on leave, they used to land at Brackla and they used to stop there after they'd done so many raids over Germany. A lot of the boys used to come to our house in Ballifeary and they'd be there for the night.

I can remember making the big hoardings for 'Weapons Week'. There were big campaigns to save money and we used to make these big advertising hoardings – there was Spitfire Weeks and Battleship Weeks when all the savings were put towards that particular purpose. We used to put them up at the Memorial and at the great big rose windows at the Stewart's Restaurant on Inglis Street.

I believe just before I was born in 1918 the field at the side of our house on Culduthel Road was the site of a military post because it was outside of a special security area and they had soldiers there during the war (1914-18) and you had to have passes to get through.

There was a wee chicken farm down on Drummond Road next door to Miss MacBain. The owner was known as 'Willie the Hen'. Aye, he had a tragedy, he'd been shell-shocked – you would be walking past and he would have a 'turn' and he would pick up a hen and throw it up in the air. He'd be swearing away at the hens. It was all from shell shock in the First World War.

There was a canteen above A Cameron's on the corner of High Street and Castle Street. We served there during the war, we went there in 1939, it was a soldiers' canteen and there was one at the Station. It was immediately stopped after the war. (The Stage Door canteen.)

When war was declared in 1939 on a Sunday we were all in church. I remember Mr Edgar had gone out and heard it on the radio in his car and came in and passed a note to Mr Elliott (the minister) and he announced it. I was only eight and I couldn't understand why people were crying. But the church went on (St Columba) but shortly after that it was burnt and we were transferred to the La Scala and I remember the tremendous work the church did during the war. The La Scala on a Sunday night was packed with troops because films were shown after the service, so the troops made sure they had seats by coming to the church service. They were given tea and sandwiches the women had made – I don't know how they managed with rationing.

I remember one winter night my brother who was in Bomber Command came home and we met three Polish airmen outside. It was a bitterly cold night and we went up to them and said, "Come down to our house, my mother has something for you". What they didn't know was my mother gave them the lentil soup she had managed to make for Monday using a bit of ham joint the butcher had given her. So on Sunday night we all sat down to our soup which we didn't get on Monday.

These Polish men didn't know where their families were. They had left Poland and one was a Squadron Leader and the other two were also flying. They wrote to us regularly and then the letters stopped and we concluded they'd been killed in action. It was a very sad time.

One thing I remember, my father came home one day and he had a banana. I couldn't remember what a banana looked like. If there was apples or oranges you queued for them for hours and because we were all good neighbours someone would shout, "There's oranges at the Co-op" and we would all run round. Well this banana came and my father said, "Think of all the boys and girls in the Merkinch School who haven't seen a banana". At that time in the Merkinch School there was about 500 children or more so we raffled the banana and made £28 – a lot of money from poor children, and it was given for wool for knitting for the troops. By the time the girl who won it got the banana home it was black, but nobody younger than me had ever seen a banana – it was a very hard time.

Winter was especially hard when we were only allowed half a pint of milk. My mother and father went on to black tea and coffee with no sugar and kept the milk for me – but we never went hungry. The women learnt to bake with that terrible dried egg. After the war of course bread and potatoes were still rationed.

During the war the diet was very plain, but healthy. There was no sweets. I remember in the Merkinch School we had a hygiene teacher who came in and said, "Well I'm glad to hear that" (no sweets). We cut up carrots and took them to the pictures.

I had a budgie and I told the Co-op manager who was a friend of my mother that the budgie knew the difference between margarine and butter. We were only getting 2 oz of butter at that time. He came round one night for his tea and I let the budgie out and the budgie went to the margarine – wouldn't look at it and went straight to the butter. I went round to collect the messages the next day and as I was leaving the manager said, "Here's something for Jockie". Believe it or not, it was a ½ lb of butter.

My brother wasn't away, he was too young and as soon as the siren went he would run away up to the castle to do fire watching and my other brother's job was to get down into the shelter and light the stove and get the budgie under the table. Quite often we were up and there was a bad time in

1941 and we weren't in our beds all that week. We weren't bombed but they were bombing Foyers. I can remember the fear of coming out of our shelter and just getting to our front door and the siren would go again and running like mad.

I remember my mother coming home from town one day crying and saying she had watched these children coming out of the railway station with labels round their necks. We had evacuees at school but I don't think the teachers understood the needs these children had. I remember one evacuee being given a good strapping for not being able to spell.

During the war years 1941-45 my father had under his control large numbers of Canadians who were employed at the harbour loading timber, cut timber and pit props. Then there were all the regular shipments of ammunition, shells, mines etc to Invergordon and Scapa Flow.

At the time you had to have a special security permit to go north to the Tain area. It was one of the assembly points for heavy tanks training. My father had a permit because of the work he did. At one time the bridge used to have a man with a flag at one end allowing one car over at a time – that was the old suspension bridge – it had been surveyed and found to be faulty – the main Ness Bridge. So one car at a time was what was allowed over at the beginning of the war. But by the time the war was nearly over, all this equipment, heavy tanks, Bren guns and carriers and goodness knows what were going nose to tail over the bridge to head south for the invasion. The bridge didn't seem to mind at all.

The war was on and Kings (the bakers) used to supply huge quantities or rolls to various canteens in town. There was quite a few of them. They used to take maybe ten dozen rolls a day for all the troops who were resident in the area. The Palace Hotel had been taken over for the RAF. There was a tremendous amount of troops in the area, a lot of Polish as well, and the canteens were for their welfare.

The ATC was formed in Inverness about January/February 1940 and the first parades were held at the farm in of all places Culcabock, the barn and the farm. A few interested men, mostly ex-RAF from the First World War showed interest and quite a number of young men gathered in this barn, and that was the origin of the Air Training Corps in Inverness.

Being in the TA I was called up before the actual outbreak of war. I joined the local artillery unit, the 297 Battery. It wasn't my choice but I was sort of forced into it. I wanted to join the Camerons but my father had other ideas. Because of his experiences in the First World War he knew I stood a better chance with the gunners then I would as a 'Jock' which I wanted to be. He knew what I would do if I did join the Camerons. As soon as I got in I would do my damnedest to get a transfer to his old regiment, the K.O.S.B.'s.

I was stationed in Padgate in 1940 and my mother was up in court for overcharging for a pound of sugar. I had to come home from England. What a state she was in, she phoned me at Padgate and I got compassionate leave to come home and go to the court case. She was on a charge of overcharging for a pound of sugar – she charged fourpence when it should have been threepence three farthings, and she was fined £5 by Sheriff J P Grant. That was a lot of money then, he broke her heart.

There was an old zinc bath kept out in the shed and my mother used to fill every pan with water and boil it up in the kitchen and then the bath was filled. My sister and I used to pop into the bath on a Saturday night and it was nice and warm in front of the fire. I remember it was certainly through the war before my father came back, we were in the bath one Saturday night and a knock came to the door and I can remember she was in a terrific panic because this was the Minister. Our Minister was the Rev George Grant, a very well known local Minister from the West Church. But Och he came in and sat down and made himself at home, and I think my mother calmed down a bit after that. But it was certainly – compared to the lifestyle nowadays, and the housing conditions, I suppose it was primitive, but we were very happy and we never lacked for anything. During the war of course there was nothing like the range of foods available now. My mother had an old Aunt who lived on the Novar Estates up in Ross-shire. Her Uncle was one of the estate workers, and a hen used to be sent down before Christmas, by the bus. Just a hen complete with feathers and the lot with a label tied round its neck addressed to us. Then there was a plucking session, and the disembowelling of the hen prior to Christmas dinner. But that was really one of the few times we actually ate meat. We survived on tatties and onions and tatties and milk and porridge. I remember to this day the horrible smell and taste of powdered eggs. It wasn't pleasant.

I remember the excitement when the blackout blinds didn't have to be drawn every night, and this was the end of the war. I remember a party which was held, down where the Barclays lived at the market garden – now Delnies Road – there was a bonfire and the whole neighbourhood came along and there was a big celebration. I wasn't all that clear what it was all about. I couldn't remember my father because I was only nine months old when he went away. The men weren't home at that time but we did have a party and a bonfire. I think what I remember most was the atmosphere. All the wives and mothers – they were so overjoyed that it was all over and the men would be coming home. I remember my father coming home from the war, my mother looking out the window and saying, "Oh, here he is". He must have got a taxi up. There was certainly a great deal of excitement and I suppose it must have been difficult for people to learn to live together again. The wives had been so independent, bringing up families and struggling on their own for so many years and suddenly life had changed. The first euphoria lasted for a while and then people settled down again and the men got a job and tried to get to know their children.

I remember as well thinking about the snow. Again this must have been through the war or maybe just after. My father had sent clogs, wooden clogs, I think for both of us. Of course we had to walk to school then, there was no bus and I was in the Crown School. It had been snowing quite heavily throughout the day and I was walking from school and coming along Muirfield Road just where the Hospital wall is, the snow had started to pack up on these wooden clogs. I wasn't getting anywhere fast and it was getting dark by this time, it was quite dark. There was a squadron of soldiers marching along Muirfield Road, and I think I was standing howling at the side of the road, because my fingers were frozen and my feet were frozen. I just didn't think I could get home.

I was probably about eight at the time. A young soldier broke out of the ranks and he came over to me and showed me how to kick the snow off against the wall, and off he went. Again, during the war, there used to be an Italian Prisoner of War camp up Torbreck way and every night they were all taken home by lorry from wherever they were working through the day. We all used to stand at the top of the Brae and wave to them as they went past and shout "Eye tiddly Eye Tie" to them and they would wave and shout "Hello Blondie". I don't know if they understood what we were saying. I remember there was a German Prisoner of War, he worked as a gardener at the Scott-Swanston's house at 91 Culduthel Road, which was just across the road from us. He was a lovely man, he used to give us rides in his wheelbarrow. His English became quite good and I remember him telling us that he had two little girls himself in Germany. Obviously the poor man was missing his family and maybe we made up for a wee bit, but he used to play with us and take us around in his wheelbarrow. But it was happy despite not having much in material goods.

Births and Deaths

I was born on Bridge Street at No 31, it was a big flat above a shop and then it became the County Hotel. When I was being born it was to the sound of the Church bells on a Sunday evening. I've been told my mother was having a difficult birth and they put down what I think was called tan bark on Bridge Street to deaden the sound of the wheels. In those days all the traffic had iron wheels, horse drawn lorries and cabs and it made a fiendish noise on the cobbles. The streets weren't tarred, it was granite setts they used.

We were all born at home then with the nurse in and the grannies helped.

Behind us was the Central Park. It had a bandstand and there would be circuses and the fairs. There were several local families who had swings and roundabouts and my mother helped to deliver twins who were born in the caravan at the bottom of our garden to one of these families.

In Argyle Street we had a Miss F, a spinster on one side and another Miss F who was also a spinster on the other side. My brother was born on the 24th May and old Miss F said to my mother "It's an awful bad day for a birthday just before the term – whatever you do, see that the next one doesn't come near term day"! You see when people lived in rented housing that date mattered (possibly because the lease could be terminated at that time).

Death and Funerals

When I was a youngster living in Bruce Gardens, our road was en route to one of the gates of the cemetery and in those days, the cortege had horses, as many as maybe twenty horses. The Funeral Undertakers were Falconers, and MacRae & Dicks – they were the ones with the horses, black horses. In those days depending on the status of the deceased, you could have a two-horse carriage in front carrying wreaths, maybe two carriages, then the hearse with two horses. Then would be the minister in a two horse carriage and the nearest and dearest also in two horse vehicles. Then you would get about fifty or sixty people walking behind the hearse all the way to the cemetery. It was all men in those days, the women stayed at home. I'd a little business going following behind the horses with my little bogey and picking up the droppings and selling them to people for their roses (fertiliser).

There were nine in the family but only five survived, two sons and three daughters. One of the deaths was from meningitis, the belief at the time being it was because her father had taken her to the market and there had been a nasty rotten smell there and she had caught a germ and died three days later. Another Aunt at the age of 10 was burnt in an accident in the bonfire of a next door neighbour and she lived for three days with my granny nursing her. When this accident happened, it was about 1919, my mother told me her sister was left at home, she wasn't taken to hospital, my mother was left to nurse her. Maybe this was because my mother acted as midwife for the poor families around. If there was any births she went to help although she wasn't qualified but she had some nursing experience. When my aunt was burnt, after three days the doctor said "I don't think she'll go much longer" and we think her suffering was 'eased'.

When her granny who lived in Deveron Street was dying of cancer of the uterus she was left at home because there was no nursing available. She had great suffering.

It was a sad time and I think the saddest was the deaths that occurred. In Telford Road, we lost three boys – friends of my brother. His closest friend had gone right through action in El Alamein but he was killed the third day after D-Day. His mother received the telegram and she walked all the way up to the Crown School where his father worked to tell him. One of the boys was drowned, his body was never found but his mother believed to the end that he was still alive.

There was always good neighbours and people lived near their extended family in those days. If a daughter got married she tended not to live terribly far away from her mother. It was all rented property and you couldn't move around. Everybody helped out and there was always a collection for a wreath at a funeral.

The undertaker Mr Chisholm was struggling along with the terrible flu epidemic of 1922. One of my uncles went to help him there were so many deaths. The funeral parlour was a green kind of building on George Street, it seemed to be coated in tar. There was a disaster because it went on fire one night and we didn't even hear it. The whole thing went up and in the morning there was just rubble there. I remember the black horses and people just called it the 'Coffin-Van'. If the deceased lived in the area they waited until it was dark and the men walked with the coffin on their shoulders. They were very respectful. If the death was further afield they had a black van with the gentlemen on the top and two black horses. Then on funeral day they had that glass type of hearse, and we would all draw our curtains and stand very quietly behind the door. Children were taken in, they were never allowed to play and shout on a day like that.

One of the things I used to do when I was a boy, if I would see a funeral coming along the riverside, I would run home, get my cap and put it on and run back to the Greig Street Bridge as the funeral was passing, and take my cap off (as a mark of respect). These were the days when the hearse was horse driven and one of the drivers was a very forbidding man who lived in Balnain House. He had a pointed jaw and a big tile hat.

Churches, Religion and Mission Halls

There were a few well-known ministers in Inverness at that time. The Rev Donald MacLeod was in the Old High Church and his daughter married Dr George MacLeod who eventually became Lord MacLeod of Fuinary, and was well known because of his association with Iona. In the St Columba Church was Rev Cooper, in Ness Bank the Rev James Wright, in the East Church Rev Sutherland. In the West Church was the Rev MacLellan who had succeeded the Rev Gavin Lang (father of Matheson Lang the actor) and further down the river in the Queen Street Church was the Rev John Ross.

My grandmother was attached to the West Church but when she became too old to walk to church that far away she joined the Crown Church shortly after it was founded (1899). But my uncle continued in the West Church until he was in his eighties. The original minister there who baptised me was the Rev Donald Connell, that's on my birth certificate.

I attended the Crown Church Sunday School in 1919 and I remember some ministers, Mr Strang, Mr

Michie, Mr MacGilp and the Rev Charles Smith – he was there for twenty years before Mr Logan. My Sunday School teacher was Dorothy Campbell, daughter of a solicitor. The boys wore the kilt to Sunday School which was at 4 pm – they were teased about it. There were services morning and evening, and nothing else to do but go for walks on a Sunday afternoon.

On a Sunday we went to the Crown Church, so it was the same trek from the house up to the church and that was twice in a day, the morning and evening services, because my father was in the choir so I was dragged along.

No kids played out on the road on a Sunday and the majority of people went to church, and after church you had lunch and then you might go out with your parents for a walk. People walked through the cemetery and went up there with flowers on a Saturday or Sunday. The Islands were very popular as well.

I recall the Cathedral Provost was A.D. MacKenzie who retired to Conon Bridge. He used to preach at the Cathedral. The choirmaster there for many years was also the choirmaster of light opera – the Mikado and other D'Oyley Carte light operas. Before the 1920's the Cathedral did not have a screen before the choir stalls, the screen was erected as a memorial to those who died in the First World War.

We went to the Old High Church when we were young and the Sunday School. Dr MacLeod was the minister, Rev Donald MacLeod. Then we started going to the Methodist Church, it was in Inglis Street when I started, where the Stewart's Restaurant was. Then it moved to Union Street.

The first church I went to was the Cathedral and then I went to Ross's Church – the church that is now Chisholm's Funeral Parlour. John Ross was the minister – a marvellous man – and we used to have concerts. He came and visited a lot, ministers did a lot of visiting in those days. Mr Ross went away and I think he became a Moderator in Edinburgh and after that was Rev Tolmie.

We were getting older and we didn't like church then, but all the young people went to the Methodist Church. There was a beautiful round window (the Rose Window) in it but it became too small and they moved to what used to be the Music Hall on Union Street.

On Sunday they were not allowed to cook anything, so most of their meals were cold apart from the porridge which was reheated. They went to church for two and a half hours in the morning then had their cold lunch and the father opened the Book (the Bible) which we still have and read it to them for an hour and a half followed by prayers and then they got ready to go back to church again.

I remember my father saying how much he hated going across to his grandparents on the Black Isle, they would have been Free Church. My mother's family was involved with the St Columba Church and at the time of the burning (fire) we were all moved into the La Scala.

This was at 19A Church Street and there was three little cottages in the back which used to be where one of the men who was a bell ringer in the Old High Church lived. He used to ring the bells for the curfew at 8 pm and 10 pm and at 8 o'clock the kids used to go home or the bigger ones could stay out till 10 o'clock but after that – that was it. The police used to go round and say, "Move on boys" – they were chased.

On Lodge Road there was a little hall, it was donated by a Miss Fraser who lived in 'Redburn', Culduthel Road, she died in Switzerland in the 1880's and she donated it to the community in her memory and we had a Sunday School there. Eventually the Sunday School was taken over by one of the local churches but when I was a boy it was independent. It was run by a Mrs Fraser, a widow, who remarried a man called Jeremiah MacDonald, and we had one of these little organs. A lady used to come up and play and we sang hymns, Moodie & Sankey and so on.

A man came up in the 1930's to do up the paintings in the Town Hall and he squatted in this hall and he lived there for a long time. I'm curious to know where the authorisation came from because nobody knew – it belonged to the community and all of a sudden this man was in there.

There was a Mission Hall on Lodge Road where I used to go to Sunday School when I was young. I don't know how it was sold because it was built by public subscription. I queried this because I was looking for a house at the time and I went to a solicitor but I never got an answer. There was also a Mission Hall on Burn Road, but when I knew it, it was a laundry. Peggy MacIntosh and her sister Ann and their mother had the laundry. They used to do a lot of private work for Kilmartin and places like that.

A bus used to come there every Monday morning with a lot of washing. It was all hand done and ironed by hand.

The Mission in Balnacraig Wood was originally run by a Mr Fraser and a Mr Cameron, who were elders in the Old High Church. A Miss MacGregor played the organ and they all arrived on a Sunday morning in a taxi driven by Mr Proudfoot. Mr Fraser used a lot of his own money to pay for our prizes – bible knowledge, perfect attendance, good behaviour etc. We always had a lovely party at Christmas. This was the Sunday School and at night we returned for the Mission Service and they were always well attended. There was another Mission Hall at the top of the back brae up the Leachkin.

Sunday was the Sabbath, my mother went to church, and we went to church too and on a Sunday afternoon we went to Sunday School at Culduthel Hall from about 2-3 pm. Mr and Mrs Tom Fraser from Culduthel Road used to come on their bicycles to teach at Sunday School.

There wasn't many in the Sunday School. There was my brother and myself and Irene Campbell who lived beside us and Sheila Grant, and her sister Audrey – there was only about ten of us.

We looked on Mr Fraser as the Sunday School teacher, a big God to us. He would have his son Jock on the bar of his bike. You went every Sunday and thought nothing of it and you got dressed up in your suit.

There was always the Sunday School treats (parties) so you would join up to the Sunday School and you went to two or three different Sunday Schools as it got near Christmas and you would hope that the treats would be on different days so you could go to them all. You always got a bag of buns and maybe a fancy hat. I went to the St Columba, the Free North and the Gaelic Church Sunday Schools. I think they knew but they didn't mind because the families weren't well off.

Entertainment

The Theatre Royal – Bank Street

Donald Dallas was a great character in Town, he made some records. I remember they used to do 'Rob Roy' every year and it was great and Donald Dallas always played 'The Dugald Cratur'. It was an event every year and they also did the 'Mikado'. There was an old theatre on the riverside (Bank Street), it was lovely and we used to go there a lot. It went on fire about 1932 and we could see it from the windows in flames. Will Fyfe was there and that was the last performance. It was a real old-fashioned theatre, all red plush.

My introduction to opera was at the age of nine when a friend took my twin brother and me to the Theatre Royal to see 'Faust'. My brother was very keen on horses and he thought he was going to see horses when he saw the word 'stalls' above the front door of the Theatre. When the curtain went up we didn't have a clue what it was all about and he kept on asking, "When are we going to see the horses?" However, when Mephistopheles appeared he was so thrilled he soon got over his disappointment. On arriving home we were asked if we had really enjoyed the opera and in one voice we answered, "No it was just a lot of people bawling at each other".

The Theatre Royal presented operas performed by famous Glasgow Companies and those preferring drama were catered for with plays such as 'Mice and Men' and well known actors such as Frank Forbes Robertson. There was also Besrick Hammersley's Repertory Company presenting a different play each week. The maiden's heart-throb at that time was Garth Myers.

I remember the Theatre Royal on Bank Street. We were in it the night before it went on fire. It was Will Fyfe that was on and he lost the lot.

I was in the Theatre the last night before it burnt down. It was the old Theatre on the riverside and Will Fyfe was on. I was allowed to go because it was connected with schoolwork, at least that was my excuse for getting to go. We were sitting up in the Gods, my friends and I. When we were going over the bridge next morning to school the Theatre was no longer there, it was just a smoking ruin.

Empire Theatre

My memory of the Empire was drama festivals. They performed plays almost every night, three plays a night and the place was full, even what they called the old 'horsebox' at the back. It was such a wonderful atmosphere and they came from 'a' the airts'. It didn't matter what part you had, you were on stage and you were a star. But when the Empire closed we were all involved. I was in the Florians and also in the Opera Company on the last night – never to be forgotten – a tearful night. We were doing stuff from 'Oh what a lovely war' as well as 'Keep the home fires burning'. At the very end they raised everything, all the curtains and you could see the back wall with all the lighting and the baskets lying there. I well remember Jimmy Logan was there and I can remember his words to this day. He said, "That's the end of the Empire Theatre but remember, all of you city fathers, a Town without a Theatre is a Town without a heart".

There was some wonderful shows when the Empire came and at that time you could say to yourself after your tea 'Och I think I'll go to the Theatre' and just go. You didn't have to book weeks in advance to see Tommy Horne, Dave Willis, Tommy Morgan. All these people came with their shows and they were lovely.

We were unanimous that the Empire Theatre should have been retained as a Theatre. All it needed was new seating and new electric wiring. That was all it needed. It could seat twelve hundred. John (Worth) and I were very much against it. Why? Because it was in the middle of Town, it was about a 100 yards from the Bus Station and 150 yards from the Station. I put on a few shows in the Empire. David Hughes, the singer, and the Clyde Valley Stompers (jazz band). It was a shame when the Meeting Rooms and the Empire went to the wall, a sad day for Inverness.

At that time you had a lot of talent spotting competitions and Inverness had one. The Daily Express ran a talent competition and they had the finale in the Empire Theatre and I won that and went down to the finals in Glasgow, the Alhambra Theatre. I like to think I upheld the Inverness traditions.

Many of the people appearing at the Empire Theatre frequented the bar and stayed in the Hotel. People like Will Starr and many of the comedians of that time. Donald Peers did a two-week stint when he was at the peak of his career, Duncan MacRae who was a very quiet man, David Hughes, the singer. He died when he was still a young man but he stayed for a week when he was appearing at the Empire. He used to drive an American style car. Then there was Alistair Gillies, Calum Kennedy and his wife Anne. Russell Hunter, Sidney Devine, Joe Gordon and 'Chic' Murray and we had one memorable night when the 'Hollies' (60's pop group) were staying.

Cinemas

Aye, we had two cinemas, La Scala and Central Hall, both on Academy Street. The Central Hall later became the Empire Theatre. The Playhouse was built in 1928 and it was the first to have the 'Talkies' but mostly it was silent films. The film heroes were Charlie Chaplin, Jackie Coogan, Nick Carter, 'The Railroad Kid', Ronald Colman, Eddie Cantor, Jimmy Durante, Douglas Fairbanks Senior, but we never heard them speak until the 'talkies' came.

When we were wee, we used to go to the pictures on a Saturday morning, there were two picture houses, the La Scala and the other one was where the Empire Theatre used to be (Central Hall). It was a penny to get in. 'Pearl of the Army' and 'The Clutching Hand' would be on and when the excitement would be at its best the film would finish and we would have to wait until the next Saturday to know what happened. We would all be roaring and cheering and clapping, what a noise we made.

The cinema was the old Central Hall on Academy Street – there was matinées there and you got in for three pence. So if it was something special on we got three pence, but not every week, we couldn't afford it there was so many of us. Five three pences at that time was quite a lot. I mind seeing Pearl White lying on the railway line and the train coming towards her. The 'talkies' came then and it was the Playhouse had the talkies. It was 'The Singing Fool' with Al Jolson that was the first 'talkie' and I got to go to that and I got the following week but after that I was told I wasn't getting to the pictures every week. So that was that until I started work and paid my own ticket. I used to get 1/6 a week pocket money then and I used 1/- to get into the pictures and 6d for sweeties in 'Woolies'.

The La Scala was in the Town before the Playhouse but it was the silent pictures. The Playhouse was very nice and Mr Nairn the Manager, he used to do the cafeteria up at Christmas time, with all the Walt Disney characters – Fairyland – just like that.

I was in Urquhart the Seedsman working when they finished the Playhouse. When it opened Urquhart had the job of decorating the stage for the opening night and I was with him helping to set the flowers up on the stage. Because I was with him I got a complimentary ticket to go in and see the film. It was the first 'talkie' picture that came to Inverness. It was the 'Singing Fool' with Al Jolson and oh it was marvellous. Voices on the screen!

The matinée in the La Scala was always packed on a Saturday morning and the noise could be heard streets away. The queue to get in started first thing and stretched away up Strothers Lane long before it opened because if you got into the queue early you got a better seat. It was 3d to get in and if you got 6d for your pocket money you could buy a sweetie or a bag of Smith's crisps with a wee blue bag of salt. Once the picture started, usually a cowboy, the place erupted with some yelling for the cowboys and the rest for the Indians. And if you were sitting downstairs you would get all the crisp bags and sweetie papers raining down on your head.

There was always a serial, I mind one called 'Perils of Nyoka' and it always stopped just when the hero or heroine was about to meet their end and you had to wait a whole week to find out what happened next. A huge 'boo' used to go up when the action stopped. As soon as we erupted out of the La Scala the boys would be doing pretend cowboys all the way home or whoever the hero for that day had been. And all for sixpence!

Glebe St. Swimming Baths, showing changing cubicles and viewing gallery. (Mr A.M. Macdaonald)

Rose St. or Burnett Bridge showing the old Gasometer.

Huntly Place looking towards Upper Kessock St.
and Grant St. Circa 1930 (Courtesy, Olive Ross)

Inverness Area Life Boy Parade, Castle St. 1952-53.
(Courtesy, Mr P. Home)

The Islands

Well a few years later the Town Council decided to introduce summer concerts in the Islands and an orchestra was engaged to play in the old wooden bandstand daily for a period of, I think, six weeks. There were two performances daily, afternoon and evening except at the weekend. The musicians were all formally dressed. Mostly their repertoire consisted of light opera and classical pieces and in the beautiful tree-surrounded setting of the Islands with the river running by, it was absolute heaven.

The people stood around or strolled about but the enclosure in front of the bandstand was set out with rows of folding seats. The snag was that it cost fourpence, as far as I recall, to be seated and there were few amongst us who could afford such luxury and mostly we went on summer afternoons.

By the time we were teenagers (although that term was unknown then) we were allowed to go to Fêtes in the Islands. I think they were held on Friday nights and we always left home with the injunction "See that you're home by 10.30pm" ringing in our ears. In the darkening summer evenings we thought we had never seen anything as beautiful or sophisticated as the strings of coloured fairy lights which linked the trees along the major paths of the Islands together and were reflected in the River. There was a wooden floor laid in place of the seating sometimes, and if you were lucky enough to be asked you could have a dance.

We had so much to enjoy in those days. In the upper reaches of the River Ness at the Islands, which were linked by small foot bridges, on the centre island there was a pavilion and an outdoor dancing platform. The Islands were always lit up by fairy lights in the trees and under the sponsorship of Inverness Town Council, Herr Menny's German string orchestra played during the summer afternoon and evenings. It was so lovely to stroll through the Islands listening to the ripple of the water with the beautiful music of the orchestra wafting on the summer breeze.

My memories of the Ness Islands – well the British Legion Pipe band was always there and the stand was at the opposite end from where the last 'monstrosity' was. Victor Conn had a tearoom where you could have coffee. George MacBean, then the Registrar, used to produce shows and there were lots of local artistes. Once the concert was finished everybody went over to the other little island where there was a dancing floor, a little band and tuppence a dance. Then there was a firework display that took place in a garden in one of the big houses on Island Bank Road – it was very exciting. Sometimes there was a guest performer. I remember one time there was the band of the Scots Greys playing. There was fairy lights from where you went in at Ladies Walk and all the way through there was lights. You paid sixpence at the Bught to get into the Islands and then you could get a seat at the front of the stand that would cost tuppence.

The Islands were very popular, there was dancing there as well on the dance floor in the summer, and all the fairy lights were on. I remember the bands and the dancing, all the local worthies would be there. George Davie, the local optician, he was a great dancer. And 'Jockie Hen', aye there was a few worthies in those days. There was a quartet that played – and the woman who played the piano in the Caley for a long while – Hetty MacPherson. It was wooden floors they laid down for the dancing.

Herr Menny's orchestra used to be playing in the Islands and we used to go in the afternoons, Strauss and that kind of music would be playing. When it was raining they played in the Town Hall – marvellous. Bellfield Park used to be so busy, if you were playing tennis you had to wait to get on to the courts, we seemed to have longer summers then but maybe that's just looking back. I remember when Bellfield opened and there was golf, tennis, putting.

Another place at that time was Loch-na-Sanais, the little loch just over the Canal Bridge. When it was frosty or icy you had skating and they used to have a bit roped off for curling. The Caley Hotel on Church Street would have a sign outside saying 'Curling tonight'.

No, I didna like the loch, when you went in the boat it used to make me sick. We used to go walking round the Islands, and round the Ferry banks, that is all the distance we used to go. There were good concerts in the Islands, Pierrots and that. At the time of the Northern Meetings in September when they had the games and the ball was on at night we used to go over to see the ladies going into the Ball. Princess Margaret was there. The Caley Hotel isn't what it was then – it was lovely with grass in front of it.

The Music Hall (Union Street)

In the Music Hall concerts were held throughout the winter organised by Miss Sara Walker, a local music teacher and well-known violinist. She brought up many famous artistes from London. During the First World War two brothers from London Claude and Eric Baulbie used the Music Hall to present many shows such as 'Le Poupée' and a review of 'The Belle of New York'.

Well you see, in these days you made your own entertainment. Everywhere there was concerts, concerts and more concerts. Donald Dallas was the best man at my parents' wedding and he and my father were very friendly with Andrew Paterson the photographer and I have this photo where one of them was doing this bit with the apple on his head and a sword, I think my father would have been stupid enough to be the one with the apple on his head. Well my mother fainted and had to be carried out of the Music Hall. The poor soul probably thought the sword would have gone right through my father's head.

We gave concerts on the back green which was shared by the Innes Street neighbours. My father rigged up a stage, a square wooden platform for us and many a budding trouper showed his or her paces there. Our concerts would be packed full but the entrance fee was just minimal. I remember paying 2 pins as an entrance fee to view a Laurel and Hardy film on a cinematograph owned by one of my brother's friends.

At the time it never occurred to me to wonder what he did with the thirty or so pins he received.

Och there were concerts nearly every week in the Town Hall, there were lots of concerts in Town, I have a bit in my scrap book of 'The Wool Fair' concert. Lee Fraser was in a lot, he had A & S Fraser's, a ladies shop on Union Street, and Carrie Cruickshank and a Mr Gall who managed Hipps the gents tailors on High Street. 'Sergeant on Parade' was one of his favourites.

We used to go round all the homes and the hospitals and the Prison with the concert parties. I remember in the Prison one time and one of the songs I sang was 'In eleven more months and ten more days I'll be out of the Calaboose (prison)'. The concerts were held in the Prison Chapel and my mother was sitting there and I looked at her and she was in stitches and the prisoners were in stitches as well. There was one of the verses said:

"The prisoners in Porterfield were very very sad,
The warders couldn't stand it anymore
They said now dry your tears, you're here for three years
There's time to learn a chorus, and they all began to roar"

They enjoyed that. Then we were at the Isobel Fraser Home of Rest and the Poor House on Muirfield Road and the Highland Orphanage on Culduthel Road.

We did dancing, there were always Highland dancers, and singers. Some played an instrument, sometimes the piano and sang duets and we'd have sketches. It was quite a variety we had. At that time I was going out to concerts virtually every night of the week. I've seen me frequently going from one place to another to perform. There was always fund-raising, we used to do concerts all over the Town for cancer, the Imperial Cancer Fund and the Provost's Coal fund was one we did a lot for in the early days.

At the top of Strothers Lane was the Scout Hall and there used to be concerts there. I remember Mrs Swanson from Rose Street and she used to do monologues and Mr George Wiseman would play on the musical saw. There was accordions and fiddles and someone would dance.

When the Canadians were over during the War there was a Garrison Theatre put on on a Sunday in the Empire Theatre. We used to go to the Garrison Theatre very much against our parents' wishes, but once we met some Canadians and it turned out that the father of one of them had met my father in the First World War.

(Note: The Garrison Theatre was held in the Empire during the war on a Sunday night for soldiers stationed in the area, to provide them with some entertainment away from military surroundings)

We played over on the Capel Inch, there were no flats or houses then, just a grassy place and the circuses and shows came there to provide entertainment for the children.

That's where the shows were at the Capel Inch, and the Maggot Green. The Pierrots used to be there and I remember listening to them sing to a crowd and the song they sang :

"An old new fashioned cottage stood
Beside a blade of grass
The white washed walls were painted navy blue
The iron doors were made of wood
The windows made of brass
And on the roof sweet peas and water lilies grew"

One of the comedians sang that on a platform erected at the Maggot Green. The shows came to the Capel Inch, swings and roundabouts and wee cars and stalls and hoop-la. They used to come in the summer.

We opened the circus in the public park, it's not there anymore but there was Bruce Gardens on one side and Glenurquhart Road on the other, Victoria Park it was and there was railings on the outside and shrubs and trees and a band stand. I've seen boxing booths and a zoo and a circus in the tent. There was four circuses held in there and crowds used to come to see them.

After the war in 1919 when my uncle came home that was when they started the Circus up again, with my grandfather. They went around buying up horses and building caravans. I remember going down George Street, down Deveron Street and Innes Street, along the Shore up Academy Street and out that way. The reason was we had big engines as well, steam engines. We used to pull three or four loads and the corners weren't very handy for getting round the corner of Rose Street, so we used to go the long way round.

We had the Northern Meeting games in the Northern Meeting Park and that was a two day event. The first day was for the 'high and mighty' and the second day the people from Inverness were allowed in. As youngsters I recall, all the cars were parked in Bruce Gardens, nose into the kerb and all the way up. We used to go round and take the registration numbers of the cars, but if it wasn't a Rolls Royce or a Bentley you ignored them.

Then there was the Northern Meeting Ball which took place in September or October in the Meeting Rooms and that ended the social season. Half of Inverness turned up on Church Street to see who was going in and what they were dressed in.

It was a terrible loss to the Town when they pulled the Northern Meeting Rooms down. That was where the chandeliers in the Town House came from.

When the Northern Meeting Ball was held at the Meeting Rooms we used to go and watch the 'Toffs' arriving. The ladies would be beautifully dressed and the men would be in Highland dress.

Well the Americans took over the Northern Meeting Rooms during the First World War, they were requisitioned. Then when they went away we were allowed to have a little dance in the supper room downstairs, but not upstairs, that was separate. We did old- fashioned dances, the Lancers, Quadrilles and jig-time quadrilles – that would teach you something!

After the night classes finished at 9 pm we would team up and walk round 'The Mat'. That was Queensgate, Academy Street, High Street and down Church Street. And then start again to watch out for the 'talent' we would meet. We would all meet up and have a good laugh and then we would be escorted home. For entertainment there was dances held by the Boys Brigade in Burnett's Tearooms, upstairs on Academy Street. The Clach Football team held their dances in the Merkinch School Hall, and the West Parish BB's had their dances in the West Parish Church hall. Everyone knew everyone else and they all joined in and danced. But at the last waltz you would wonder "Will he ask me for the last dance?" because that would be the boy that would see you home and you were always hoping it would be the one you fancied.

We used to have our staff dances in the Queensgate hotel and sometimes in the Caley. Oh there was plenty of boyfriends then, those were the days eh!

I remember when the Caley Ballroom started and we were dared to go there. We just weren't allowed because there were so many stories told by people who came into the house. But my sister Peggy was dance crazy and my father found out she'd been to the Caley. She said to him, "We can't do anything in Inverness – everyone runs and tells on you".

I learned to play the melodeon with Varro Salvadori and I've played it ever since. We used to play a lot of Italian music during the war but the blackout would cause a bit of a hiccup. But we used to play jazz stuff as well, and play at concerts. There was a time I was in a quartet with other chaps and we played in St Mary's Hall in Huntly Street. We were thoroughly rehearsed and there was one part of the music which had to be repeated but one of the blokes forgot and it was just a complete shambles.

I was involved with the Northern Meeting Rooms for some years because I was a great lover of big band music. We had Ted Heath, Joe Loss, Johnny Dankworth, Jack Parnell, Doctor Crock, Freddy Randall, Ken MacKintosh and many others. All of them came up to play at the Meeting Rooms. Very big crowds came to hear them, up to a thousand no bother, they came from all over. One night I'll never forget, I got tipped off that buses were coming from Keith, Huntly and Elgin and the place was completely sold out. I'd asked for Police help but I got none so I told my bouncers to let them all in. We had 1553 people in that night to hear Chris Barber.

We had big bands up every week and for the likes of Joe Loss we charged five bob. There was one particular band, it was with me for years and that was The Clyde Valley Stompers. They used to pack the place out. Yes we had many funny incidents at the Meeting Rooms. We used to have one bouncer and though we never really had any trouble at the door unless a real drunk came along, this chap had a magic thing he always carried with him, a safety pin. If there was any trouble at the door with a drunk he poked him with the pin in the backside. No problems after that.

There was dances in the Town once I got to the teenage stage. One of the great places we all loved going to was the 50/50 Club which was at the top of the Raining Stairs. There was no alcohol of course, it was tea and buns at half time. That was a great place and all the teenagers used to go there. It was basically just an old Hall, formerly a school, but that's where the car park is now at the top of the Raining Stairs. Then we graduated once we got to about sixteen to going to the Caley Ballroom or the Northern Meeting Rooms and there was marvellous bands. All the big bands in the country used to come up and play there. Ted Heath and all the big bands of that time. So you could almost be at a dance every night of the week because the Caley was on a Wednesday, the Meeting Rooms on a Thursday, Country Dances with buses to take you on a Friday night and then back to the Caley on a Saturday. There was also open air dancing in the Islands on a Wednesday night in the summer. There was a big bandstand and it was a super place for open air dancing. The Islands was very much a focal point of the entertainment scene locally, because there would be concerts. In fact it was dancing there I met my husband. So hundreds of people would be in the Islands at night, walking through, stopping for a while watching if there was a concert on, or going to the open air dancing – it was really lovely. There was lots of things to do. We didn't drink, none of us drank because well, we didn't have money and in those days it was frowned upon. The boys would maybe have a pint, but at half time in the dances it was mainly orange juice or a cup of tea, but we still had a great time. We didn't go to pubs, or certainly the girls didn't. I think the girls would be looked on as a fallen woman if you went into a pub, and I doubt if any of us would have the courage to do so. Yes, the social life in many ways was better than it is now for youngsters. There was always plenty to do.

There was a lot of concerts. The Churches would have their concerts and also the Empire Theatre. A lot of the Empire Theatre chorus girls used to lodge in Church Street, because it was so handy, and a friend of mine, Robert King, his mother used to take in a lot of girls, four or five girls. The entertainment used to be quite cheap. You used to get into the pictures for about four pence. I remember going to the Empire Theatre when it was both a Theatre and a Picture House and you would get a seat for four pence. In the La Scala you would get a seat for four pence. That was before the Playhouse opened. We would go in and we always had a 'piece' with us. We'd go in at 2.30 on a Saturday and we were there until 10.30 pm and there was three rounds of the film. You just got a cheap seat down at the front and you stayed there for the whole three rounds, whether it was rubbish or anything else. You had your 'piece' and how you sat through that boring pictures I don't know. We had jeely jam pieces. In that days you used the fruits of the country. You'd be out for brambles, you'd be out for rasps, that was the traditional outing and you made your winter stocks from that. The whole family would be out gathering brambles on the Canal Banks and other places down the Carse. Everything was used, not much waste.

The Little Theatre and the 50/50 Club

We did a lot of our shows in the Little Theatre in Farraline Park. It seated about a hundred and the wing space was very small but it was a nice wee theatre. In the old days they used the old building at the top of the Raining Stairs, that used to be the 50/50 Club and I remember we played in there as well.

We used to go to the 50/50 Club, Doc Hay's club at the top of the Raining Stairs. It was a youth club for the age group between fourteen and eighteen and it was run by Doc Hay. It burnt down years ago. It was very popular and had a stage and dance floor. Of course it was all live music then, no disco's and the bands were all local. The 'Blue Union' came through from Beauly and the 'Wild Cats'. 'Size' MacKay played in one of the groups and he's now a barrister in Edinburgh.

There was a drama group, the Blue Triangle Players and they did lots of work with the youngsters in Inverness. They moved up to the Little Theatre at the top of the Raining Stairs. It was also at one time the Flora MacDonald centre/YMCA. My father would say to me "Mary, you should take your bed up there".

Halls

Oh the concert parties were all over the Town. There were all the Church halls, the West Parish, the Old High, the 'Catch-My-Pal' at the bottom of Church

Street, the Co-op hall in Fraser Street, the Parish Hall on the riverside next door to the Courier Office and the Registrar's office. The Merkinch Hall on Grant Street, the Crown Church and the Methodist Church halls. There was a hall on Celt Street and also St Mary's hall. The concerts were packed out all over the Town.

There was another hall down in Grant Street – the Welfare Hall. That was gifted to the people of the Merkinch for the use of weddings or parties and the like of that and every Sunday there used to be a Mr Shand of Shand and Lindsay's (they had a drapers on the corner of Queensgate) and he used to wear two or three pairs of glasses, and every Sunday he had this meeting and if it wasn't him it would be the Salvation Army and we used to have good meetings there and good nights – that was the Merkinch crowd you see.

There were other bigger stores like Gordon's and Young & Chapman's and they used to sell dresses for the Northern Meeting Ball. We used to go up and watch the ladies of the County going into the Northern Meeting Rooms.

The other great place was the Merkinch Welfare Hall in Grant Street and they used to hold concerts and whist drives and all these get-togethers.

The children from the Merkinch School used to do Scottish Country dancing there, the Cumberland Reel and they also sang the songs the teachers had taught us. That was part of the community.

Well there were dances there in Lochardil Hall and we used to play badminton. It was a very good badminton club because it had a low ceiling and when people came to play against us they were accustomed to high ceilings so they couldn't play with the low ceiling and we used to beat them all. It was a great club and the number of marriages that came from that Lochardil Hall was quite remarkable. It was run by trustees and some of the farmers in the neighbourhood.

I remember the Coronation, there was a big dance in the hall, everybody went to it, young and old and it was a really happy occasion. If there was anything memorable that I can remember it was always to do with Culduthel Hall because that was where everyone went for something special. Old Mrs Grant always used to sing at the doo's at Culduthel Hall and it was always the same song she sang 'Westering Home'. She used to clean the school at Culduthel and come and do the school meals as well.

(Note: The above hall has been known locally as Culduthel Hall or Lochardil Hall over the years.)

Catch My Pal Hall

If it was a Friday night you'd find your pals watching 'Punch & Judy' in the Shepherd's Hall in Milne's Buildings or in the Catch My Pal Hall beside Andersons the Bakers on Academy Street.

We used to do a lot in the Catch My Pal Hall. My brother and I used to do a duet and singing and dancing. We sang 'I'll be your sweetheart' in a duet and my brother used to do his music hall turn of bird and animal impressions.

Yes. Well to give you a brief outline it was known as 'The Catch My Pal Union'. We had an organisation founded sometime in the 1920's by a William Anderson who was a great leading figure in the Town. He was a great churchman and he was an Elder in the St Columba Church. He had a very strong character, strictly TT and absolutely hated the drink.

220

He started doing business in Inverness in Grant Street – in a Licensed Grocers funnily enough, Anderson & MacKay. But he broke away to form his own bakers and grocers in Academy Street. Next door to the shops was a very good hall. With £10 the organisation was formed. There was also a Mission Hall down beside the Shore near the Citadel Bar, which was sometimes used. But apparently him being an Elder with St Columba he ran a Sunday School in this Mission Hall down beside the Citadel Bar and there sometimes was an overflow from the Catch My Pal. So it was used for that purpose as well. On joining the Catch My Pal Union we had to take an Oath or a Pledge.

My first memory was of going to their annual concerts with my mother. This was one of their highlights of the Social Calendar. Remember there was no radio or TV in those days. The admission was sixpence and there was a fight to get tickets. They were very scarce, but being good customers of both Anderson the grocers and bakers we were always lucky.

Among the many entertainers I remember was the late Alan Cameron, Derek Henderson, a retired Minister, a Mr Wilson the 'Barber', and there was George Strachan. I think it was Mr Davies who was a ventriloquist and the Anderson's sons also played their part in it. Then there was a lot of sketches by members. I remember putting on sketches myself with my friends. So two friends and myself joined in 1936, principally to enjoy a game of Indoor Bowls, Darts, Dominoes etc. At the AGM we were at, I was appointed for some unknown reason Secretary/Treasurer and my friend Alex Fraser, Assistant. In 1938 after a year of this office we found the job a wee bit irksome and we decided the only way to get out of it was to 'Break the Pledge'. We chose to do this by going what we thought was really up the Town, but it was only the Haugh Bar.

Feeling very nervous as I was only 17 and my friends a year younger, I went up to the bar and ordered three half pints which I remember tasted horrible. We duly confessed our lapse and were re-admitted, but stripped of our office bearing. Shortly after this we were all away to war.

After the war the hall was taken over we think by the Military and after that the Gas Company used it as a store for gas cookers.

With Mr Anderson's death and the advent of war, we think it was probably disbanded in 1939 or 1940.

(Note on Catch My Pal: It was a Protestant Total Abstinence Union for young men founded in 1909. It began in Inverness on Celt Street and then moved to Academy Street where it eventually closed during the Second World War.)

Childhood Games

We played skipping, ball games, skeetchie and 'Tap the Finger' – we used to be blindfolded with our hands behind our back and you had to guess who tapped your finger. There was 'Reliever', we all hid and one was left in the 'den', and then they had to go and look for us and whoever was caught first had to stay in the den. 'Kick the Can' was great. You had to kick a can as far as you could then you would run and hide.

In those days we all played games in the streets because it was quite safe. There was a cycle of games – there was the time for rounders and reliever and various ball games, then marbles 'derbs' we called them.

Oh yes, we had lots of games. Reliever, the 'Hedgies' was a great place for that up around the Castle Hill. Then there was 'skeetchie' and we played conkers and marbles – we had a great collection of marbles. We would take a picnic of a bottle of lemonade and a packet of biscuits and we'd go off to the Islands and have lots of fun there, paddling and watching the fishermen, climbing trees and playing hide and seek.

The Castle Hill was our play area. We weren't really supposed to play there and there was a keeper of the Castle – a Mr MacBeth – and he used to chase us every time he found us playing there. We would shout out "Cherry-beak" because he had a red nose, and then run for our lives. We used to play at the 'Hedgies', that's the banking that faces the riverside and the Castle Street children had a gang and the Haugh children had a gang as well. We would meet at the top of the brae and have a real 'ding-dong'. It was just the top of a dust-bin lid or a wooden sword we had.

As a group of youngsters on Greig Street we would wrap old newspaper into a round ball and tie it with string, that was our first football. Then we would go swimming in the river between the bridge and the Greig Street Bridge. We would dive off the temporary bridge (1939-1961) but if we were caught by the Police we were in trouble.

There was a lot of children growing up in Church Street but there wasn't much traffic on the street. We used to play rounders and we used to hide in behind places round all the corners. One of the other great things we had – och it's still there – on either side of the Greig Street Bridge there was the 'Castles'. The

'Castles' were piles of stones which the boys on either side of the river – our side and Huntly Street and Greig Street – would build on their side of the River. There were four castles which were raised and then raided by the ones who would go and pull them down and then build them up again.

We played 'Catty'. You made a stick and had numbers on it 1-4 and a point at each end. Then you took a big stick and hit the end of the 'Catty' stick and up it went in the air. If the other side caught it you were out but you'd try to get it past them and the further it went the better. Then the other game was, you made a circle of buttons and you'd to lift the buttons without dropping them and if you did that you got the buttons for yourself.

In Greig Street we played football in the street but the local policeman was quite harsh on us, he chased us so we used to go round to Balnain Street and play there. At the top end of Kenneth Street one wintertime we made this gigantic slide which must have been 15-20 yards long and 6 feet wide and it was a great thing. Along came the Bobby one day and into the grocers he went and got a packet of salt and ruined our slide.

We had different seasons for everything. Skipping, marbles, skeetchie, bowlers, kick the can, football, cricket – we were never bored. At the first fall of snow we were away to the playground to make a figure of eight. Then we'd get the sledges out and make a run down the fields. We only went home for meals.

Oh a great attraction, the river, a great attraction. We used to fish in the river. I remember we went fishing from the banks especially for flookies or flounders. We used to go home very proud and give our mother a flookie for our tea. That's the flounder, you know.

Then we built a castle which is still there. You go down Friars Lane and then just about 50 yards out you'll see a castle with just stones, a mound of stones. That was the Friars Street Castle. On the other side of the bridge, just immediately over the bridge, was another castle. That was the Church Street boys' castle. There used to be great fights on the river knocking each other's castle down, and stones would be thrown. When I go down to the river I always look to see if my castle is still there.

Schooldays

I went to the Bell's School in Farraline Park, where the Library is now. It was a big school and some of the teachers were very hard on us. There were three Dallas brothers in Inverness and one of these was a teacher in the school and Miss Taylor was the head mistress then.

The Bell's School was a very big school with a lot of children at that time. There was a very good standard of education. We started in the 'baby-room' and Miss MacLeod was the assistant to Miss Susan Fraser. Miss Fraser became crippled with arthritis but she didn't take early retirement. She came to school in a taxi and was carried in. But she was still able to thump with a very long pointer and prod you when it was necessary – she had a far-reaching pointer.

I went to the Bell's School when I was very young. Because of my mother working I was shoved off as soon as I was four years old so I was always a year behind the other boys. I was there till I was eleven years old then up to the High School (now the Crown). I remember one character who used to take us for PT, his name was Donald Dallas. He was quite hard on the boys, you know. A colleague was telling me a story about Donald Dallas – although it was a bit before my time, when they had the baths in Montague Row. He would make all the boys line up at the deep end and then he would say, "Jump in", whether they could swim or not. If you didn't jump in he took the cane across your buttocks.

This was Colonel MacKintosh, he was the Colonel of the 'Battery' and they used the Bell School playground (Farraline Park) as it was partly military ground then. They had the guns out in the playground and that sort of thing. The school was started by a Doctor Bell, an Englishman. We all went to the Bell School, my brother, myself and my sister. Probably the earliest memory I have is Mr Horne, the janitor. He would come along with his long pole to the classroom about 3 pm to light the gas lights. I was taught by Miss Kate Martin, she was a delightful old lady, then Miss Alexander and the final step was Matthew Dallas. He was the last of the old bowler hat and big tie pin generation. I still remember how he walked down the playground in the morning with his little case in his left hand. He raised his bowler hat to every little girl who said good morning to him.

"The Bell School is the best school
It's made of stone and plaster
The only thing that's wrong is
Its red-headed master."

The Ragged School

I only know a little about the Ragged School as it was gone before I was born but I do know my grandfather was involved with it. He was a Town Councillor and a Baillie called Thomas Snowie and he had a gun-shop and taxidermist on Church Street (now Ashers). My mother told me he was involved with the Ragged School through the Council.

When you look at the building of the Bell School, at the frontage, the front section is different and there are two distinct sections possibly built at different times. One part has central heating and the back sections are all just fireplaces. It was for the very poor children to give them some education and meals.

My very first school was a little prep (preparatory) school in Inverness, which had been run for quite some years by a German, Herr Vack. Herr Vack went on his holidays to Germany in 1914 and of course he didn't come back. His school was then taken on by a Mr Simpson, who eventually took over the old Inverness College (this building is now part of the Highland Council HQ).

The prep school was a semi-detached house on Muirfield Road run by a Herr Vack. He had an assistant master, Mr Simpson, who after Herr Vack died had a little building beside the tennis courts (on Bishop's Road) where he ran a school for boys. I think it was called 'College House School for Boys'. It had its own uniform and purple cap with initials on it and had about ten pupils. The boys from the Bishop Eden Boys' School used to harass the College House boys when they went past the Bishop Eden building.

There was the Bishop's boys' school and the Bishop's girls' school where I went to school. In those days it was really sort of 'High English'. The Provost of the Cathedral used to come and visit the school a lot and they were very, very fussy in those days. When we went to school we had to wear white pinafores and our hair in two pleats, that's what we all had to have. In the mornings we had prayers, being an English church school it was pretty religious. We got ten marks if you had a nice clean pinafore on and your hair was in pleats. We all had long hair in those days. Then we had prayers, grace before we had our lunch, grace after it and prayers at night.

There would be three classes and one teacher in that room. The teacher would be doing three classes at once – they had to work much harder in those days. Then we would have a medal for the pupils who were first and a little present from the teacher. We also had a blue banner which was hung on the wall and the class that had the best attendance and was the cleverest always got the banner on their side of the room, and a little treat as well of course.

We used to have to go to the Sunday School, St Michaels, it was run from the English Church. Then the Bishop's boys' school was closed and the Bishop's girls' school was used as an ordinary (non-denominational) school. All the other schools used to get out for lunch in the morning, but we were always locked in – we weren't allowed out. The other school children, as they were running past, used to yell 'Crabby School' and we would yell back at them.

I was seven years old when the First World War started and we were staying in Abban Street so I went to the Merkinch School. Mr Ross was the Master – 'Bumber' Ross he was called – that's how Carse Road was called 'Bumber's Roadie'. When he retired we had Coutts Morrison as the schoolmaster. My sister went to the Bishop Eden girls' school in King Street but I went to Merkinch. After we were twelve we went up to the High School – that's the Crown School now and were there till we finished. I left school at fourteen. I remember some of them, oh aye, fine that. There was Miss Chapman – 'Necta', Miss Urquhart, she was the one who had all the bells in her room, she was the English teacher. There was a maths teacher we called 'Snoosh' – MacLean I think his name was and Mr Bray was the headmaster. Then we had Mr Dallas, he used to come and give us our drill on a Friday.

The Central School was divided into two schools, there was the little school (Infants) which was on Planefield Road and the big school on Kenneth Street. After the third year you went from the little school to the big school. I had Miss Dobbie, then Miss MacDougall and then I had Gracie MacDonald – she was a great teacher. She was the one that took the qualifying class (before going on to secondary school) and she could get the best out of her pupils. She was strict but fair, but I remember one time she was doing the seven times table and she asked somebody what seven times seven was and they said 51, and she asked someone else and they said 50. So she went round the class and only two people said 49 so all the rest of us got the strap. No one ever forgot what seven times seven was after that.

Then there was Miss MacLeod who used to do the banking every Tuesday, the day we took in our sixpence or shilling. It was entered into a book and when it came to a pound it was put into the TSB (Trustee Savings Bank). It taught us early on that if you put a certain amount away every week that it builds up.

My father went to the Central School when it was on Queen Street and he finished his education at the age of eleven and he paid a penny a day for his education. I went to the Central School aged four and a half and the headmistress was Miss Adam who taught the first class (P1). A Miss Milne taught the second class (P2) and the third infants' class teacher was Miss Anna MacKenzie – a well-built disciplinarian and in this class pupils first met 'the belt' on the hand if they didn't meet her standards.

The 'big school' headmaster was Mr J Shaw, he'd been a Captain in the Camerons in WW1. He was a good disciplinarian and only used the strap rarely. Sometimes he would bring war relics to the class – shell cases, .303 bullets and a German revolver.

There was a tragic accident on the road at Kenneth Street, a little girl was killed and thereafter the trees which had been at that part of the road were felled and railings put up. The shrubbery there was converted into a rose garden and Mr Shaw tended it, sometimes helped by the pupils. There were also football and shinty teams.

Miss MacDougall taught the first two classes in the 'big school' and she used the strap almost every day for poor performance in spelling and sums. At Christmas each class held its own concert. The school closing (summer holidays) was a big event with the prize giving in front of parents. The pupils rehearsed songs for weeks beforehand with the music selected by Mr Shaw. The pupils were all in their Sunday best and each wore a flower presented by Miss Glass of Duncraig Street.

Then at the bottom of Brown Street there was what they called the 'tinkers' school'. They were segregated, I forget the teacher's name, she was there for years. The hall's still there, a wee gospel hall or something, that used to be the 'tinkers' school'.

Then we had a Miss Campbell in the Merkinch School, she was a real lady, but she only had one bad habit. If she caught you swearing she used to put carbolic soap on your tongue. Aye she did!

I went to Clachnaharry School when I was five (1907). I was only tiny then. Going to school all dressed up and a clean handkerchief pinned to my lavender woollen drawers. You couldn't go anywhere without a clean handkerchief. We had a two-teacher school and I was awful happy at school. There was about sixty children there at one time because you had families used to come from Bunchrew and other places, but then it dwindled down. The children all walked to school. They had to walk in all weathers. I think they would take a 'piece' with them. There were big families of about six or so children. We went into infant school and then moved into primary in what we called the big room. You were there till sixth year and then you went into town to the High School (Crown). I loved school but unfortunately Granny died in 1915 and I had to go and stay in Harrowden Road with my Aunty and Uncle. It was war time (1914-18) and my uncle was stationed in Aberdeen so we went there for a few weeks and when I came back I was behind everybody in the class and everything was new to me from the village. There was a class of 35 girls which was frightening for me and I was in class 1F. I was 35th in the class, not surprisingly, but the next time I came up to first. It was quite a leap so they decided to put me into an A class and I had to take French and Latin. I had a great headmaster, Mr Braine, he was a wonderful man and I loved school, but some of the girls were very badly behaved. I was fourteen when I left much against the headmaster's wishes, he did his best to make me stay, but I had to earn my living even then.

One thing I remember was the Coronation of 1911. I remember the girls in each school had to dress in white pinafores with a sash of their school colours. Our colour, Clachnaharry, was purple, and we all got dressed up and went by train from Clachnaharry Station into Station Square and from there we marched up to the Academy (IRA). They joined us and their colour was royal blue, then the High (Crown) School, the Merkinch colour was green and the Central School yellow. We all marched down View Place, along by Ness Bank Church to the bridge, crossed over to the Northern Meeting Park and went in there. We got a bag of buns, a coronation mug and milk. I don't remember what else we got, I was only eight then and very much lost in the crowds of youngsters. But it was quite an event.

I went to the Crown School in 1930, although it was called the High School then, and the infant school was on Midmills Road. When the new Technical School was built we shifted out of the Crown and they must have saved an awful lot of money because we had to hump all the seats and benches over to the 'Techie' ourselves. Two journeys in the day, with big long benches and seats and half of that was carted over by the pupils. But it was a very good school (the Technical) for its day. Roller blackboards, big windows and a beautiful gymnasium, all modern stuff.

The headmaster of the Crown School was Colonel MacKintosh and another Mr MacKintosh (Charles MacKintosh) took over during the war when he was away. One of the teachers was a Mr Dallas – not Donald Dallas who used the microphone – "Come out boy till I flog you", he used to say. I had the other Mr Dallas for my last two years in the Crown. He used to take the bank money, we used to put in a shilling a week. I had the job of going down to the bank with the money for a while but I took advantage of it so it stopped. Two of us used to go to the Savings Bank in Lombard Street, Peter Ferguson and myself and he had a granny who lived in Bridge Street so we used to go for a cup of tea. We were supposed to be down and back to the bank in ten minutes but we took about an hour.

There was a lot of children in this area so crowds went to the Crown School. There was Friar's Street, Academy Street, Church Street and the Shore and if you were on that side of the water you went to the Crown. We came home at lunchtime, then run back again and up Stephen's Brae all in an hour.

I loved the Crown School, they were very good to me. I remember Colonel MacKintosh the headmaster although he was away during the war, and we had Mr Charles MacKintosh. I remember once Colonel MacKintosh came in, he must have been on leave and he went round all the classes. He was in his full military uniform with a brown belt and he was very smart, we were all impressed. We had some wonderful teachers like Miss Connie Smith, but there were one or two who were hated and feared. However we had an excellent education.

I started at the 'Wee School' in the Crown aged four and a half to try and keep my older brother in school as he kept running home. After that I went up to the 'Big School'. There was a corrugated iron building beside the Crown School and this was the science and sewing rooms. This day we were all sitting in a sewing room doing silent reading because the teacher was out. We were sitting at high tables when all of a sudden the door behind me flew open and in came Mr 'B' the maths teacher. He caught me by the scruff of the neck, pulled me into his room and insisted I hold my hand out. I said, "No", and he belted me round the wrist. Well out came my right hand and it landed right on the point of his chin and he sat down on his backside on the floor. Then he hauled me into my brother's class and his mates thought all this was marvellous but I walked out and went home and explained it all to my parents. They said I must have been doing something wrong, but there were plenty people to say I was not and my mother knew their families and they would vouch for me as this man was a brute. My father wrote to Mr 'K' but he wouldn't entertain listening to my story. So I walked out and went to the Labour Exchange on Church Street and got a job as a message boy with Maypole Dairy and went home and said I'd left school. A letter came saying as I was only fourteen, I couldn't leave school till Christmas but I ignored that. However much later I was told by Mr 'K' that the teacher concerned had been dismissed during the war for 'brutalising youngsters'. He had walked with a stick, and the fact was I'd hit a man who had a walking stick and I never forgave myself for that.

I have four younger sisters and all of us attended the Crown School, then called the High School. The leaving age then was fourteen. There was no indiscipline, we sat in regimented rows, arms folded and feet together. Children knew their place in the scheme of things – even the wildest 'playground performer'.

Not all pupils were brilliant but I can't recall anyone who left school unable to read, write and do mental arithmetic. Unless parents could pay, no one was taught a musical instrument and parents had to supply jotters, pencils, sewing materials and knitting wool and this was a considerable burden in a household of five daughters. Textbooks were supplied but had to have a brown paper cover put on immediately (and the corner grocer was usually very cooperative with this.)

Later on I finished up in the Crown School (then the High School). That was where you sat your qualifying exam. The headmaster was a man Braine and by gosh he could give you the strap. I was on the receiving end a few times. Nobody minded the strap from any other teacher except Braine, he was tough. He put out your two hands and you held then above the desk. So you got double when the belt came down and you hit your knuckles on the desk.

1950's

Culduthel School was a couple of hundred yards down the road from us, on the main road and the headmaster was James Steele who came from Skye. The school had three classrooms. Primary one had a room to themselves and P2, 3 & 4 had a middle room and P5, 6 & 7 were taught by the headmaster himself. Mr Steele used to get us to go out and work in the garden every Friday afternoon. Culduthel School closed in 1968 when Cauldeen opened and the children transferred. It was a great school to be in, there was only about ten or twelve children in each class, nearly all the children from the farms.

1920's

We've been in this house since 1922, the five of us grew up here. The school was down there, Culduthel School. It was a very nice school and our teacher was Miss Moyse, and her father was headmaster. There were two teachers and the headmaster and around 80 or 90 children in the school at that time. There were big farms then with the workers and big families of them. There were farms all over, Oldtown, Balmore, Leys Castle, Slackbuie.

1940's

Culduthel School was a country school, the headmaster was Mr Steele. We had three classrooms and when I was there you left school at fourteen or so, but then it all changed and when you were twelve or thirteen you went to the Techie, the High School. At Culduthel School we had the 'Teacher's Garden' and in the afternoon sometimes we were out in the garden weeding and things like that, but it was just part of being in a country school.

There was the MacDonald boys, their father was a sort of gamekeeper at Leys Castle, and there was the Cummings from Essich Farm and they had to walk all the way from Essich. It was a long, long way. We had no distance to go compared to some of the children living on the farms. There was a boy Ewan from Balrobert Farm and the ones from Knocknagael. They were all nice school teachers. When we went to the Techie school we found it so different. The children from the town schools, their upbringing and their lives were completely different to kids from the country.

There was a boy Petrie, he came from way up Balvonie of Leys which must have been about four or five miles to walk to school. Just before I left they got organised with cars taking children from a certain distance to school. You had to be a certain distance away to get this transport. There were school meals because I remember a van coming with them all in steel containers to keep it hot. It was just dished up at the table in the classroom so you got your lunch at your desk. The dishes were washed in a sink with kettles boiled to heat the water and there was a lady came in and did the serving out.

In winter we always got to school with us not being so far away but the ones from the outlying districts, they wouldn't always be in school. They could be off school for maybe a week or two until the roads were cleared. Some of them came through the fields, they didn't come on the roads because through the fields was a short cut and going by road it would have taken long enough to get home.

In 1920 aged seven I went as a boarder to Heatherley School on Culduthel Road. My first dormitory was the Blue Room opposite the drawing room which had blue curtains at the windows hanging on brass rails. We drew these and modestly retired behind them to dress and undress in our own little bed space. Later on I went to a bigger dormitory higher up at the other end of the building. This had a trap door in the floor which was our fire escape route. Occasionally we had a fire practice when we climbed through the trap door, down a ladder into a bathroom, then down a stair and out at the side of the house.

One night after 'lights out' we lifted the trap door to reveal a terrified housemaid enjoying a hot bath. Great giggles. Only staff, prefects and visitors were allowed to use the carpeted front staircase, the rest of us clattered up and down the back stairs.

At the end of each spring term we performed a play. I have a photograph of when we enacted The Tempest on the side lawn. Charades and dumb crambo were enjoyed on winter evenings and we could amuse ourselves very simply with a piece of string playing cat's cradle. We played noughts and crosses and performed tunes with a comb and lavatory paper (it was thin and shiny in those days). The mistresses joined us in the dining room for mid-day dinner and while they enjoyed their coffee, we were encouraged to talk politely to them and each other.

We went to the La Scala occasionally for special events such as a lecture about a Mount Everest climb with black and white slides by Mr

Mallory the year before his final fatal ascent. We were told never to say 'the La Scala' because 'the' and 'la' meant the same thing.

We wore navy blue gym tunics, navy Viyella blouses in winter, green girdles and black stockings. In winter we had black felt hats and in summer straw ones encircled by the Heatherley hat band. Our shoes were cleaned by Blaney the boots. I suppose he was an odd-job man, who did many odd jobs about the place. Girls who bit their nails were sent to Matron who smeared them with bitter aloes which deterred us. Once it was discovered that one of the day girls (with distinguished parents) had nits in her hair. Poor child, we all looked askance at her and all the boarders had their heads scraped by Matron with a small-tooth comb.

There were few teachers in the Leachkin School. There was Mr MacQueen who was headmaster and after him David MacKintosh, Miss MacFadyen and Miss MacFarlane. For many years it was a three classroom school and at one time Latin and science were also on the curriculum. I remember my first day at school. A Miss Robertson was then my teacher and her classroom had a 'Modern Mistress' stove which was used by the cookery class. It was one part of a big room divided by a partition which went across from wall to wall and Miss Fraser was the teacher for the older pupils. In my years in the Leachkin School until after the war there was no electricity. We had lovely coal fires and in the winter we went to school in the daylight from 10am till 2pm. Paraffin lamps were used for our Christmas parties. In the summer, before the war we had our sports at Dochfour House courtesy of Baroness Burton. We had a lovely tea with jelly and fruit. I remember at King George VI and Queen Elizabeth's coronation a huge crown was erected at the front of the very new nurses' home overlooking Charleston, and we had ankle socks with crowns on them. During the war we held concerts and whist drives for money for the Leachkin boys when they came home from the war and we had cookery demonstrations for the wives which were great fun. Everywhere was pitch dark (the blackout) and we all had a wee torch with a dimmer on it.

My oldest brother got Dux of the Merkinch School and at that time you were only allowed two years' free books when you went to the Academy (IRA). All the rest were paying to get in you see, and I remember my brother going up there to the Academy with the home-made jersey and the home-made 'troosers' because my mother was a widow. She had 10/- a week to bring the three of us up. So he went up there and came home crying. The snobbery was so great then, and he had no school blazer but he did his two years there. He was in the cricket team and he was the only bloke in the team that never had a clean white shirt on. Well my mother had no money to put him to college so he just had to struggle on his own and he did it on his own.

The first two years (post war) were very hard because Britain was a poor nation, little food and rationing went on for a long time. I was in the IRA by then. It was a great thing for Merkinchers to try and get the Bursary and get in. The year I sat it (the Bursary exam) we had a wonderful year because twenty-one sat the exam and twenty of us got the Bursary and of that fourteen went into the A class. That was a hard time because socially there was a lot of snobbery and we were made to feel very unwelcome although our parents had struggled to buy our uniforms. If anything happened it was always "We don't want that kind of Merkinch behaviour here". I don't remember any of our behaviour being worthy of statements like that. I'm afraid it amazed me the numbers of teachers who were not socially of high class but suddenly became very distinctive in their way of treating children. That tag of being a Merkincher – which I'm very proud of – stayed with me until the 3rd year when I won the Control (examination) and went into 4th year and suddenly I became integrated.

I started school in the Academy and that meant walking from Bruce Gardens as a youngster of five right up through the town to the Academy, back home for lunch, back again at 2 o'clock and then home at four – on my own. My route to school was down Bruce Gardens, along Tomnahurich Street, up past the Town Hall – we always had a bit of bread for the cabbies' horses there – and I always had a drink of water at the fountain outside the Town Hall – then along High Street and up Stephen's Brae. It was quite a trek.

Yes I was educated in the Academy and the Rector when I was there was Dr George Morrison who went to be Rector of Robert Gordon's College, Aberdeen. He was followed by Mr Crampton Smith, and it was he who was Rector during the greater time of my stay. Miss Rhoda MacLeod was in charge of the primary department and Miss Kate Kennedy had the senior class of the junior school. I remember when Mr George Morrison was still there he used to come out of his office and have a walk round. If anyone had been naughty or done something they ought not to have done, the punishment consisted of standing outside the classroom door. Then George Morrison would come round and usually take them by the ear into the classroom and find out what the trouble was.

In those days in the Academy, at 11am the luncheon hour, you either went down, if you were fortunate enough to have a penny halfpenny (1½d), to Skinner's the Bakers at the foot of Stephen's Brae and get a pie, or you went to Bowman's the Bakers where you got a nice fruit slice for a penny.

I went from the Crown School where I got the bursary to the Academy for the next three years. I liked the Academy very much because the education you got was second to none, but at that time there was still an element of snobbery. At the Academy, because there was still a fee-paying Junior School attached to it, there was a tendency to think you were a bit above everyone else if you'd come up from their Junior School into the Secondary. My parents were ordinary working people and they didn't have much money and there were times when I felt there was a division between the 'haves and the have-nots'. The deciding factor when I decided to leave was that I'd had my school blazer for three years, school uniform was compulsory then, and I would be going on to the 4th year and was going to need a new blazer I knew my parents couldn't afford at that time, I knew I couldn't compete financially. The Rector, Dr D J MacDonald, he was a great man, he took me into his study and tried to persuade me to stay on, but I couldn't tell him the reason and my mind was made up.

I was born in Thornbush Cottage in my grandparents' home in 1921, and went to the Merkinch School at the age of five right up until I went to the Academy. The top pupils went to the Academy and the rest went to the High School, now the Crown School. When the Technical School on Montague Row was almost ready for occupation, pupils who were in the Academy but wanted to take business courses like typing, shorthand and book-keeping could move there so I opted to go.

I started in the Merkinch School in 1920, there were a lot of children in the Merkinch at that time. We were not very well off, the families then, it was big families and not very much cash to spare but we made do and were actually very happy. I can remember things that I was taught in the infant school. In the first reading book it was "Pat is in a pit, a pot is in a hut, it is a hot pot". This was teaching us the vowels. The headmistress of the infant school was a Miss Campbell and we thought she looked wonderful. She had a beautiful midnight blue dress and white chiffon scarf with a brooch and white hair. We had a teacher called 'Jess Bun', she was a bit of a warrior of a teacher. She was from the West Coast and she spoke Gaelic. She used to teach us Gaelic songs for the Festival but we just mimicked her words because none of us were brought up with the Gaelic.

Rigfoot

I had intended to be a nurse but my father didn't think it was a very good idea so he said he would rather pay for me to go to Rigfoot, the Secretarial College, so I went and did a year there. It was on Southside Road and it was the Misses Urquhart who ran it. You were taught shorthand and typing and book-keeping.

After I left school I carried on at night school and went on to advanced work, book-keeping and shorthand typing for three years up at the High (Crown) School. I went to a gym class on another night, that was in the Academy, which I did not like at all. I didn't like the headmaster because we were at the High School we had to go to the Academy for science and art and the headmaster used to look down on us. We would all come in at once and he would think we were criminals. We wouldn't make a sound, but it was very evident he didn't like us at all. That was in the 20's.

When I was eleven we shifted to Lochalsh Road and I carried on in the Merkinch School and then later on went up to the Academy for a year or two. Then I went to Miss Fraser's, a shorthand/typing college on High Street. She was called Miss Elsie Fraser, a very elderly person and she lived in one of the closes beside Cameron's Stores which used to be on High Street. She ran a little college there and lived in the building. It was a commercial college, and I was there for a year. We were supposed to finish the course in a year. We were there all day and we took the three subjects, shorthand, typing and book-keeping.

Early 1900's

We went to the 'Pudding School' at the foot of Church Street. Next to the church (now Leakey's Book Shop) there was a great big building, a sort of Technical College. One week we went to cookery and the next week to laundry. There was a great big wringer roller. For ironing you brought a large white gent's hanky and what a palaver to iron a hanky. You had to stretch it and pull it. You started with a handkerchief you see and then you went on to a pillow case or something like that. You advanced very slowly – what a palaver. There was a stove with flat irons all round it and you picked up an iron and got on with it. It was part of our education going to the 'Pudding School'. The boys went to technical carpentry down below. At cookery we made bread there. One time we had to bring a piece of scrag-end to make broth or something. My Aunt said, "But I wouldn't send you for that myself". "Well that's what they want so I'll have to go and get it". I think it was a bit of neck or something I got. It was all so serious. It was all lady teachers we had and they were all so serious.

We went to cookery and laundry with the Orphanage children. They went with us to a big place down at the bottom of Church Street. We went in there and one week we got laundry and the other week cookery. It was great fun. We used to be allowed to take home whatever we made – if it was 'puddeen' or anything like that. It was learning us and it was a treat to take home with us.

The old Technical College used to be at the bottom of Church Street. We used to go there for laundry and cookery on schooldays. That's why I still iron dishtowels the correct way, the way I was taught in the school on Church Street and I still fold the towels as I was taught.

The MacKintosh Bursary

I went to the Merkinch School and my teacher was Annie MacKay and headmaster Mr Black. My granny was a MacKintosh so I received a MacKintosh Bursary and went to the IRA which was fee paying then – of course I had to get the necessary marks to get in.

When you were eleven you sat what was called 'The Bursary'. There was such a thing as the MacKintosh Bursary which had been endowed by the MacKintosh family. If your name was MacKintosh you went through without any bother. We wondered at the time – because the biggest dunces in the class went up to the Academy because their name was MacKintosh. Some years it was all MacKintoshs that passed.

The Blind School Ardconnel Street

I went there in August 1927 and the Matron then was Mrs Rettie, and there was a cook and a maid. As far as I can remember there was heating and gas lighting, but no electric. That came after Miss Asher came. There was no gas in the boys' dormitory. In the winter time when you went to bed and got up it was dark. The food reminded me of Dickens' days when you had the long tables and the forms you sat on and the bread was put on the table in front of you – no plates or forks and knives. Sometimes you got a mug for your tea – not a mug like you have nowadays but like a milk jug. We ate with spoons all the time.

When Miss Asher (Matron) came it all changed. She got tables where four could sit and we got knives, forks and spoons and cups and saucers.

Some of the people in the school must have been taken in to live just as a home because they were short-sighted. In those days poverty was so widespread across the country it was probably the best place for them.

The parties in the school were really good and the Christmas party was good although our normal food was plain but it was substantial. At Christmas you got your stocking filled. I got much better presents at the Blind School than I would at home. The Christmas dinners were done by the Board of Directors. That came out of the funds that were collected and donated by the public.

We used to be taken down town to the barbers for a haircut, to MacKenzie at the top of Bridge Street. We were never given any pocket money. The only money we had was when we left home at the beginning of term and our family would give us some money. Sometimes we climbed over the wall down the back way into Castle Street but we were never supposed to go out on our own.

Early 1900's

I have vivid memories of my first day at school. The procedure in those days was for the pupils to be lined up and for each child to hand the teacher a note which contained his or her name, address and date of birth. Then it was most unusual for a mother to take her child to school. Most children entered school under the supervision of an older brother or sister or a neighbour's child. This helped to make us independent from a very early age. The classroom was very sparse, there were no desks, only forms, but that's not to say it was a grim or dull place. Most of us found it very exciting and challenging.

As an example of the lighter side of our school day – I remember we were all asked to bring a penny to school in return for which we were entertained by a conjurer. We all sat enthralled while he pulled rabbits out of a hat. At a later stage of my school days, I recall the death of a much-loved teacher. The headmaster suggested that, as a token of our affection and respect some of the children should sing a hymn at the graveside on the day of the funeral and so six boys and six girls were chosen to perform this sad duty. The children were all asked to wear black armbands.

All mothers in those days had a black hat 'in case', so we six girls decided we would wear our mothers' hats as a mark of respect and we all arrived at school wearing the hats, either with a tuck taken in or stuffed with paper.

We were then marched to Tomnahurich Cemetery, the burial service was performed and the coffin lowered, followed by a volley fired by a detachment of the Royal Volunteers after which we sang 'Earth to Earth and Dust to Dust'. I must admit that I don't recall any of us being unduly disturbed by this our first experience at a graveside.

The Highland Orphanage School

I was appointed to the Highland Orphanage School after the bombing in Glasgow. The bombing was so severe and after that we had to leave our home in Cumnock. I was appointed to the Highland Orphanage Primary School after two years at Rothiemurchus Primary School. The roll at the Orphanage School was 20-25 but whenever it passed 25 an assistant was appointed. I had all classes aged from five to twelve.

There was a bell hanging outside the school with a big long chain and I had to ring that at 9 am for the children to come over to school. One morning the bell fell down with a thump and as I had a little girl by the hand, it was a blessing we weren't killed. The local blacksmith was contacted and he came and re-hung the bell, but I didn't ring it again.

A NARROW ESCAPE AT HIGH ... SECONDARY SCHOOL

There were two rooms in the school divided by a partition, plus a small store room, and a tiny cloakroom. The cleaner was an excellent lady, Mrs Grant. I shall always remember her because she always had the coal fire on in the morning and the school was exceptionally cleaned. The coal came in now and again, twenty bags at a time, and I always sent one of the big boys out to count the twenty bags so that I could sign that this was correct. The coal fire was in one corner of the room and it was surrounded by a big nursery guard. The heating in the wintertime was never more than $45°$ and sometimes it was only $40°$ so one had to be very well clad to teach there.

There were no visiting teachers, only the Dentist came and of course the Inspectors. But I insisted on the school nurse giving us a visit now and again and also the children getting their little bottle of milk. I put the bottles round the fire every morning so that the children had it hot if they wanted it or cold if they didn't.

Now as there was no gym teacher, and nobody else, I had to take all the subjects. I took the gym in the spare room when we couldn't get outside, and there we had gym such as it was. There were hoops of various colours. One day a gentleman appeared at the door and I thought he was selling books and I said, "Good morning" and he replied. I said, "I don't want any books, thank you". He said "I'm not selling books – I am the Inspector of Gym". So I took him in and I was very pleased to see him and I said, "we have the gym next door". I got the children ready and into the room we went. We did all kinds of things, bunny hops I did as well, and so did he, and just as he was doing a bunny hop everything fell out of his pockets. We managed to get him back in order again. Now I thought it was a good thing to take the children beyond the walls, and on a good day we went out to the lawn to do gym. There was a very nice old lady, Miss Sutherland, who lived just over the wall and she used to come and watch us. I took the children to Music Festivals and twice a year I had to have a Concert – one for the AGM of the Orphanage when the Governors and friends all arrived and once the Provost came, Provost Grigor and his man came as well (Town Officer). Now I had nowhere for him to dress properly, so his man had to help him just in the lobby. But he came in and to our great pleasure he had his regalia and he also wore his chain of office, and he let the children touch it and I think that was really wonderful. Now on Coronation day (June 1953) we had to combine with the Crown School. It was pouring rain but we managed there safely, and we gave little concerts and a little happiness and home we came.

But for the Coronation Celebration there was a great celebration in the Bught Park and all the schools in the town took part. Each was given something to do, a project. We were given the 'Queen's Mary's'. I was very fortunate because I had a friend who was very good at sewing and with ideas. I used my one and only evening dress which was made of blue velvet for the Queen. The other girls, the three Mary's, were beautifully dressed in pink and mauve and yellow and they were lovely. We went across to the Bught Park and we sang there and it was very well appreciated.

At Christmas time the children were asked to sing carols. First at Ness Bank Church, and at St Stephen's Church for the evening service, and at the Columba High Church evening service. But at the Ness Bank they sang at the morning service, and I was thrilled to find that what they sang was well received because Mr Lawson, the Assistant Director of Education, arrived in school the first day of the new term and said that he had never heard 'The Holly and the Ivy' sung so beautifully. The children of course went to church on Sundays on their own. Another day I took the children home here to have a little outing and walking down the road we met a herd of cows, probably coming from the Mart and going up to the fields at Hilton. The children were terrified and one girl rushed and said "Horses, horses, Miss Fairbairn". I said "No they're just cows and they won't touch us", and we got safely down the road. For another outing I took them down to Queen Street to see a horse being shod, and everything was lovely at the smithy. The fire was on, the blower (bellows) was on. The children were allowed to give it a little puff and there was the horse getting its new shoes on. There was one thing that disturbed some of the girls, at that particular time they were boiling a sheep's head. From there we went through the town to Woolworths and just as they were going in the door I gave the children 1/- each and told them they could buy what they wanted. So in we went and they did spend their 1/-.

Now, later it came to be, that the new houses at Hilton were ready before the school. (When old Hilton was built after the war and the new Hilton School.) So the school roll began to rise. It rose to ninety-six children and we had to have another teacher, and now it was a two-teacher school. A Miss Bethune was sent to take charge of the infant department and this infant class came up from the Crown School and joined us. This went on, and more children arrived, and children began to come from Hilton, and another way had to be opened for them. They couldn't come in round the front of the Orphanage so there was a fence and gate made, and that gate never had to be opened except when the school was opening. I had to open the gate every morning. Well the very first day that gate was opened my children ran away. They ran out into the field, hither and thither, and one of them was a wee while longer in coming back because he did a little more exploring, but back he came and all was well. Every night after the children went away, the children going up to Hilton and my children going across to the Orphanage building, the gate was locked. Instead of being called the Highland Orphanage School, it was now called The Hilton School Annexe. It finally closed and all the children went up to the Hilton School proper. I was appointed Senior Woman Assistant to Mr Fraser who was the new headmaster and who had come from Skye.

The Highland Orphanage building then became a house (it was sub-divided into flats). Some of the children were moved down to Rossal Home (on Island Bank Road) a new Orphanage. The children went on to other schools from there.

In my time as headmistress the school was run by the Governors and the Council Education Department as well. The Governors were nearly all lawyers, so don't talk to me about them! I got such a row from one of them. I was so angry. I asked for milk you see, for the children, and the Matron said "They're not going to get milk – they'll wet the bed". I said to Mr ….. "They don't just take the milk and wet the bed". He took me down and carpeted me and gave me an awful row.

Youth Organisations and Clubs

My uncle, Charles Fraser, spent his life devoted to the Boys' Brigade – he ran the 6th Company in the Free West Church, ultimately St Marks and now the Trinity Church. Prior to the war the Company had 80-90 boys. Mr Fraser was the Captain for many years. As a tribute to many years of work in the Brigade he was made a Freeman of the Burgh on the 14th December 1938.

Most boys were in the Boys' Brigade or Boy Scouts but these were not approved by the Free Church or the Free Presbyterian Church. Most United Free Churches and Church of Scotland had Boys' Brigade attached to them. The only Scout troop with such a link was with the Cathedral. There was much rivalry between them, despite the declared aims of both organisations, there were often fist fights between the boys, although no serious injuries, just black eyes and bleeding noses.

I was in the Boys' Fourth Brigade for many years. Well, my contemporaries in the Boys' Brigade were Willie Cattanach, who eventually became a minister, a chap Donald Kennedy, Raymond Meiklejohn and

Willie MacLeod was the Captain at that time. That was during the War – from 1939 onwards.

The Fourth used to have a clubroom round at the back of Falcon Square, on the very top floor of one of the tall buildings, and on a Saturday this used to be open to the youngsters, and there was a snooker table there and you could have a cup of tea. There was a big old standing-up stove and a pianola and we used to have some good evenings there. There were a lot of B.B. competitions at that time, PT and ambulance ones. Competition was fierce, there were quite a lot of Boys' Brigade units then.

There was usually a sort of general drill on meeting night when you were 'bashed' into shape. There would be another night for ambulance and first aid training and another night for PT They used to have a weekend camp at Balvonie of Inshes just above where there was a whole succession of little trout ponds, that's where we camped.

The Bell School in Farraline Park, it was quite imposing with the architecture and columns and the parade ground in front of it, and the gates leading on to Margaret Street. I was in the Scouts and we had a Scout hall on Margaret Street. We went through one of the warehouses containing coffins and other carpentry work in the semi-darkness to get up the stairs to our hall on the top.

We went up the side of the East Church, there was the East Church Hall then the warehouses. It was a dark sort of street because it was narrow and there were these high stone buildings. Latterly our Scoutmaster built the Scout hall above the garage which is now Farm & Household Stores on Millburn Road.

I was in the 21st Old High Scouts and one of our jobs was to provide 'casualties' for the Home Guard. There was an old house just round the corner from Queen Street where the present Methodist Church is, that used to be the building where the Home Guard used to have to 'retake' it from the 'invading troops'. I remember one of the chaps in the 'invading troops' used to appear at the window with a moustache and give the 'Heil Hitler' salute.

Well the Home Guard boys were crawling along the riverbank to be able to shoot blanks into the old house and we used to be the casualties. We used to get made up over in Farraline Park (Drill Hall). Sometimes we used to be put out to the old mill in Old Mill Road which was another area the Home Guard used to use. We used to be bandaged up and then taken back to Farraline Park for food, that was where the Home Guard got fed. The Guides were there as well and they would also provide casualties for the Red Cross.

I recall as a Boy Scout, being part of a guard of honour, along with the Boys' Brigade when the Duke and Duchess of York opened the York Ward in the RNI (King George V1 and Queen Elizabeth) in 1929.

The first Leachkin Guides and Scouts originated in the Leachkin School. I can't recall the Scoutmaster but our guide captain was Miss Ivy Tocher. At different times the bigger girls went out collecting for flag days. My friend and I always got Blackpark, Upper Leachkin and down by old Whinpark at the canal.

Heatherley School had its own Girl Guide company and Brownie Pack and in the school grounds we would enthusiastically build huts from dead branches and enjoy 'tracking' through the rough ground, tie knots in the grass to show where we'd been. We marched, changed step if necessary, halted, formed fours, stood at ease, saluted as a Brownie should and of course always stood to attention when the National Anthem was played. We did our best to keep our promise.

The Boys' Brigade camps were at Carrbridge every year, the second week of July, trades week. It meant a great deal in those days. It cost each boy 14/- and there were BB companies from all over the North, sometimes five hundred boys there, and they were well run. Boys even came from Stornoway and they always wanted a day to go and see Inverness. What they wanted to do was watch the Railway trains, most of them had never seen trains before.

I'd a wee bit of a row with my mum, something I'd done or should've done and didn't but I thought I'd better get out of the house and I went over to Charlie Fraser in Fraser McColl's. He was president of the Boys' Brigade Battalion at the time and I asked him if he could sell me or hire me a tent, a bell tent, you know, the bell tents that they used when the Boys' Brigade went to camp at Carrbridge or at Drumnadrochit. And he said, "Well, I could. How much have you got?" And I would be what ….I was in the Boy Reserves at the time as a matter of fact, I'd be ten or eleven. But I said to him "Thirty shillings". He says "Thirty shillings for a bell tent and the floorboards and that". I hadn't thought about the floorboards. But I said "Yes". He says "Oh well, have you got the thirty shillings on you?" "Oh no" I said, "I'm too young for that sort of money but I can pay you one shilling a week", that was sixpence from my pal that was going to camp with me, Malcolm Grant. And he said, "One shilling a week". I said "Yes, that's a lot of money from us". I was working at the time because I was getting twelve and six a week from the Blind Institute as a messenger boy. But he gave it to us and said, "Well I'll tell you, you give me a shilling a week and I'll get the tent out to where you're going. "Bunchrew. Up in the wood. You go underneath the railway right opposite the house at Bunchrew, Bunchrew House". And there used to be a faucet of water coming out of the wall and it ran all year. We knew that. Good water. We went and looked at it – so we got a camping place there and we pitched that and our floorboards round about the beginning of April, we always started camping the 2nd of April and packed up when we felt like it.

So in April we got our camp together and my father had made a bed for me with straps – four posts and straps across – and he put them in two boxes. And Malcolm had done the same thing. He'd got the same kind of bed, I think, if I remember rightly he had a spring bed. Anyway, we had the beds and we had a cupboard to hold the food. Of course the cupboard was nearly empty for all the food we had, but it was wonderful how we began to stock up and stock up, with our dishes and all the rest of it. And we got a collapsible primus stove. It cost me twelve and six but it was a honey of a primus stove. And then we'd to light a fire outside and that meant preparing the fire and putting sacking or something over it in case it rained. You prepared your fire outside the night before and then you had the primus stove inside, which gave you a kettle of boiling water in 10 minutes. And you could make your brose – two tablespoons of meal in the bowl, a little salt and a little water and you stirred it up until you got the thickness you wanted and you started eating it right away. And before that, while one was doing that, the other one had gone to the farm, Bunchrew Farm, for a pint of milk fresh from the cow, no pasteurisation or anything. Terrific, and thick cream on it by the time you got back at night. Usually we just had our porridge or our brose and a slice of bread, maybe two slices of bread and tea, a mug of tea. And then you cycled into work, straight into work. You went home for lunch, or dinner as we called it then. But at that time you went home for your dinner and then straight back to work and at night, in the evening, after you finished work, straight out to the camp and you made your tea.

We had got bagpipes, we had a fiddle, we had an accordion, well a melodeon rather. We'd a cupboard full, well stocked with various things and foods and two more primus stoves. We had cut steps down to the bank and dammed the river so we had a big well of water and it came through a filtered pipe and out at the end of the pipe. An ideal camp site.

There was the Working Man's Club on Bridge Street – we were neighbours but I was never in it. It was a Mr & Mrs MacGillivray who were the caretakers.

The Working Man's Club was a wonderful place. There were four tables, three for billiards and one snooker table and upstairs table tennis. We also played a lot of solo whist. If you were a keen card player believe you me that's where you were taught. It was 10/- a year membership. That's the kind of club I would have liked to have when I came back from the forces, but it must have gone when Bridge Street came down. There was no drink allowed and no undesirables. There were never any fights, it was good clean wholesome company and we had a marvellous man in charge.

We had the Strathspey and Reel Society. Mr Grant was the leader. He was a wonderful man, he was the farmer at Tomnahurich Farm and he made violins. There was David MacAskill, he was a beautiful violinist and of course Mr Riddle who started the Society, Mr Williams who was blind, Mary MacLean, the Camerons and myself. Also at that time George MacPherson and his sister, they had a shop on Castle Street, he was great with the button key melodeon.

Sport

I played hockey for Inverness Academicals, but I
didn't play shinty. The Academicals played hockey
at the Bught, we played against many teams
including the Artillery, Elgin, the Abbey School Fort
Augustus. We enjoyed playing against them, we had
a good meal at the Abbey with the Monks sitting
looking on.

My father used to take me to play golf when I was
little at the Longman Golf Course, but then it was
commandeered by the military and made into an
airfield.

Inverness had a good shinty team in these days, Tom
MacKenzie was involved and George who had the
Crown Bar. I used to go to the shinty quite a lot
myself. One of the strongest sides was Newtonmore.
I can remember Cameron Ormiston (one of the
players) getting the stick across his nose in the first
five minutes of the game. He just shook his head and
carried on and at the end of the game he was taken to
the Infirmary with a broken nose.

There used to be the swimming baths on Montague Row but when they closed, the swimming area was the Harbour or the Longman. Some of the better swimmers would swim to the Capel Inch, but not me, I hadn't the stamina. If there was wagons on the line (railway) next to the Harbour I could dive off the top of them. The Longman often saw us and it was quite usual to take a dip there mostly in the nude. The breakwater was our diving platform.

My uncle was a very keen water polo member of Inverness Swimming Club. He was the goalkeeper of the Inverness Water Polo team when I was a young boy and he used to take me up to the pool in Montague Row. The building was demolished a few years ago and outside it had 1892 on it, the swimming club originated from the turn of the century. It was privately owned by a group of Inverness businessmen and there was also a commercial laundry. It was a joint venture and for many years it was very successful. I remember the pool was very noisy and a terrible noise of all the men shouting and bawling especially during the water polo matches. They actually won the Scottish Water Polo Championship one year and they sent players not only to British Championships but also the Olympic Games. George Cornet actually played for Britain in the Olympic Games and another very good player was Gordon Myrtle of Myrtle the Bakers on Lombard Street.

The Montague Row Baths, it was very austere, there was very little luxury and the water was very cold. They didn't have chlorination then but it was functional. To clean the baths the water was just emptied every now and again as far as I know.

When they closed about 1926 the Inverness Club had to go to Nairn and the Nairn pool was just seawater pumped in, very cold and cloudy. Then in 1936 the Inverness Council built a swimming pool at Glebe Street. Some of the Councillors were sportsmen and businessmen and we used them to put pressure on the Council. They built the most beautiful and up-to-date pool. Certainly it was the best in Scotland and swimmers who came from all over Scotland up here to compete were amazed at the facilities we had.

One of the main feature of the year's swimming in Inverness at that time was the 'Ferry swim' and many, many swimmers participated in this and it was a great achievement for them to swim from South Kessock to North Kessock. Some of them used to do double crossings and one lady swimmer, Sandra Whyte, she crossed four times during the tide. It was very important that you caught the tide at either ebb or full and she was such a powerful swimmer she swam four times across during the ebb tide.

Sometimes we had to cover the swimmers in grease because the water was pretty cold, we used to buy a big bucket of Vaseline and all the swimmers were coated with the Vaseline. It was a big event for them to say they'd swam the Kessock Ferry. Sometimes the weather was a bit boisterous swimming in the Muirtown harbour but we enjoyed it and I think we encouraged others.

We had a football team called 'The Castle United' and we ran a sale of work in the grounds of the Castle Lodge and the money we raised bought strips for the football team.

We used to go skating on Loch-na-Sanais. The winters were such in those days we would have anything from a month to six weeks' skating. Prior to the War when cars were a bit more popular one or two of the more well off people in the town would come out in their cars. They would sit on the banks of Loch-na-Sanais and point the headlights down on the ice so we'd get skating at night. It was flood lit until the batteries gave out. In addition there was the curling as well and there was the curling hut where the Torvean Golf Course and offices are now.

There was an open space at the foot of George Street which backed on to Innes Street and we used to play there in what we called 'The Parkie'. This was our training ground for sledging until we graduated to the slopes of Culcabock Golf Course when we were older. The Cresta run had nothing on the run down the Golf Course brae, all the more thrilling when it ended with a 'dook' in the burn. It seemed as if the whole of Inverness resorted to the golf course with sledges in winter. Sometimes we would go to Loch-na-Sanais when it was frozen over. It was there I learned I could never balance on ice skates although I could roar up and down the street on roller skates.

There was a skating rink between the end of Queen Street which led on to King Street and Kenneth Street, it's now a block of flats. Queen Street led from the river right along to the skating rink and when I was young I remember my mother mentioning she was not allowed, as a young girl, to go near the skating rink because it was a place of 'ill repute'. It was an old church originally before it was knocked down to build a block of flats.

For our 14th birthday my twin brother and myself each received a shilling and at 4 o'clock we ran all the way from school to Gilbert Ross the ironmongers where we each bought a pair of skeleton skates for nine pence. To our dismay we discovered that we needed to buy a strap for fixing the skates to the front of our boots for the extra cost of three pence. Our heads dropped because we'd already spent three pence of our shilling on a pie. Our plight touched the kindly heart of Mr Ross who provided us with a thick piece of cord to keep the skates attached to our boots. Now that we had our skates we made our way to Loch-na-Sanais about a mile from the Town. There was a coffee house where you could buy a cup of coffee for a penny and for the same price leave your coat for safekeeping. Needless to say, if a choice had to be made we chose the cup of coffee and hid our coats under a bush.

Sometimes this led to difficulties because we were told to leave the skating pond when the 8 o'clock curfew bells rang and of course we were in a panic as we tried to find which bush we had left our coats under. When these were finally retrieved, we skated nearly all the way home but on reaching the town centre we thought it wiser to take the skates off in case the 'Bobby' caught us. As we grew older our skating time was extended till the 10 o'clock curfew. We enjoyed many happy times on Loch-na-Sanais as in those days the winters were long and hard.

In my early days I was involved in horse racing. We stayed in Grant Street above the dairy. At that time there were lots of stables in the area. They had very good horses so as a kid I wandered in and out the stables. The first of my riding career was the trotting horses. I rode those for 'Poker' Stewart the fish salesman on Anderson Street. The first horse I rode for him was when I was twelve.

They tried to reintroduce racing in Inverness. There had been racing before in Inverness on a track at Dunain, right opposite Dunain Mains Farm. I think the track would have been owned by Baroness Burton of Dochfour – it was a private track. It died out but then in 1936/37 they tried to start it again at the Bught. It was run under the auspices of the Scottish Pony Turf Club. The first year they came to Inverness was September 1936 and the races were run in conjunction with the Northern Meeting Ball. All the gentry had house parties, I suppose they were up for the shooting, but in September these balls were run for two nights in the Northern Meeting Rooms. The horse racing gave them something to do during the day.

You were paid £1 to ride the horse and if you won the race you got 2/6 (half a crown) commission. The races were about £50 prizes, they weren't big money, but it was still good money in those days.

At least I had the entrance fee to see our local football team 'The Citadel' or as we called them 'Sheep's Bags' because of the proximity of the slaughterhouse at the Citadel Park. The first Highland team to be in the Qualifying cup before it was played in areas like nowadays was the 'Citadel'. I mind some of the players' nicknames, 'Poacher' 'Pockets' 'Bachers' and 'Boophan'. Street football teams were common and matches were played at the

Bught but whoever got from the match to the 'Football Times' office on Hamilton Street first put in what score he wanted. I've seen some of us beaten 10-1 when the actual score was maybe three to one in our favour. I remember the dozens of kids selling the Football Times on Saturday nights. Some of them were in their bare feet shouting their wares and some weren't older than seven or eight years of age. That was a sight I'm glad has been terminated.

The whole area is changed now but the focal point in these days was the Clach Football Club. The crowds that used to go down there was tremendous in these days.

In our sojourns up towards the Caley park, we were all great Caley supporters, the horse trough at the end of Muirtown Street next to the toilets was the meeting place.

In 1921 when I was nine, Rangers came up to play Clach in the first round of the Scottish Cup. In the Caley Park on the same day Caley played Kilmarnock. That was the two first division teams in the Scottish Cup. The Rangers tried to bribe the Clach down to Ibrox but we weren't having any.

One day I got a knock on the door and here it was a chap from the 'Corinthians' Football Club so I went and played for them. I played for them for two years, it was an ex Boys' Brigade Team but then it folded. As the years went on there was less and less (members).

Although there were still a few ex BB's in the team, I retired from football for a couple of years and then got involved with Hugh Falconer of the British Legion and we decided to form a football team for the Royal British Legion. The team included Evan Lumsden, who was a Police Officer and who died in a diving accident in the canal at Fort William.

I was a great Inverness Thistle supporter. The first time I went to the Thistle Park was in 1936, the year they won the League. Sherlaw was in goal and there was Bain, MacKay, Munro, Ballantyne, Robertson, Gray, Clunas the coach and Jimmy Roy.

278

The Central School had a football and shinty team and the football team had a struggle to keep up with the Merkinch and Bell Schools. For a time the trainer was Willie Whitton – ex Chelsea, who ran a fruit shop in Young Street. In shinty the Leachkin School was the rival, always urged on by their head-teacher John MacQueen. A shinty pitch was formed at the Bught after having to leave Bellfield Park. The School sports were held at Victoria Park or the Caley Park and the inter-school sports were at the Northern Meeting Park. Donald Dallas presided at all sports meetings.

On sports day you would have a ribbon in your hair or sash and apron with a hankie pinned on and white sandshoes. Each class marched from the Merkinch School to the Clach Park for the sports.

I was dead keen on the Caley. I played for the Bell School and we played at the Citadel Park. It was all local lads in those days and run by the boys themselves and the parents. There was a bloke played for Citadel, Jock Paterson from Ardersier. The Citadel were the first team to win the qualifying cup. When they won the cup it was for the whole of Scotland. We went down to Edinburgh in the final and played Murrayfield Amateurs and came back to great celebrations. That would be about 1932/33, before the War.

There were four Inverness teams at that time, Caley, Clach, the Citadel and Inverness Thistle.

What happened to Citadel? I think it was administrative, and it was a terrible cold park, support dwindled, bad times came and they packed it in. There was a lot of BB's football teams, Scouts, School teams and Juvenile teams then. Third Caley, Third Clach, Third Crown, Third Thistle and Third Citadel, they all had their teams. Quite big crowds came, three or four hundred. I've seen three or four hundred in the Caley Park with teams like Third Citadel. A lot of the boys went south to play with the South teams.

If you strolled down Innes Street in my young days you would have seen a football match in progress between the lamp-posts. If you heard 'Copper' being shouted, all the kids disappeared but they were out again as soon as he was past. The area football team was composed of George Street, Rose Street, Innes Street and Railway Terrace, and our team manager was known as 'Fab-a-link' but he had a few nicknames. Although he was cripple he was about the best young goalkeeper in the Town and we all admired him. Our biggest rivals were the Shore Street boys and a challenge game on the Ramparts at the Citadel usually ended in a fight of some sort. Still we were all good friends and we all went to the Bell School.

Street football, that was a great thing. We didn't have teams, just picked sides and threw down a couple of jackets (for goal posts). Then there was always an argument – was it a goal or not? We used to play in the back greens which we called 'The Backies'. The clothes ropes were in there and we tried to play football through them. I remember a fellow, quite a good footballer, he was playing with us one night and he was chasing the ball and this clothes rope was a bit low and it caught him and nearly garrotted the boy. He couldn't get his breath and we had to get the doctor for him.

Inverness had a lot of good fun going on. The High School (now the Crown) on the Hill, their team was Thistle. They had the use of the Thistle Park for all their football matches and sports. That was their 'Home ground'. At the Bell School we had the Citadel football club and we played in their colours, a dark red. The Merkinch School had the use of the Clach Park and they played in black and white. The Central School had the use of the Caley Park and they played in the blue and white colours.

Swimming

I've been great for the swimming over the years. Oh aye I still am. I started off in the Montague Row baths, the first swimming pool in Inverness, which was opened in 1892. It was owned by the Montague Row Laundry Company, who built it next to the laundry, so the laundry boiler could supply the heating. Nairn laundry had already built one in Nairn, so they followed suit. The pool was 25 yards long and about eight yards wide, six feet deep one end and three feet at the other. It had a three foot spring board and a fixed diving board at about four feet and eight feet high. There was a chute with the water spraying down. At ten feet there was ropes with rings from the roof girders so that patrons could swing from the deep end to the shallow end, from ring to ring. There was a wire across the shallow end with a wire rope hanging and a belt for teaching non-swimmers. Along one side was dressing cubicles, with a gallery on top for spectators. And there was one warm water shower and two toilets. Along the other side was folding dressing cubicles, which folded flat to allow seating for swimming galas. On the pond side they had coconut matting to keep swimmers from slipping. The pond was filled every Sunday with water from the Caledonian Canal and heated by a narrow steam pipe from the laundry, covered with a wooden box so swimmers wouldn't get burnt. There was no filtration plant and if the water started to smell they would throw in a pail of chlorinated lime – to kill the smell. On Saturday afternoons the pond emptied and the coco matting thrown into the water and all the surrounding area hosed down, and the young boys would brush out the sides and the bottom of the pool until it was completely empty. The pool was filled on Sunday, opened on Monday and at four pm the water was clean but cold. The ladies' night was Monday and after the ladies night on Monday, and Tuesday the club night, the water was brown and you could write your name on the bottom. We did quite often. The swimming club had Tuesday and Thursday nights, seven to eight pm and they held their annual gala on the last night of the season in September, when the pool was closed for the winter. It re-opened in the April holiday. As the pool was leaking it became too expensive to heat so it had to be topped up with cold water.

The Town Council refused to take it (Montague Row Baths) over and ten years later they built the new pool at Glebe Street. The Burgh Surveyor went to Glasgow to see what kind of pool was required. The pool was built a hundred feet by forty feet, with a depth of nine feet to three feet. For diving it had a firm board at four feet and five metres, and spring boards at one metre and three metres. The bottom of the pool was laid with nine inch by four inch glazed white bricks, so it never had loose tiles on the bottom. The water polo goals were first suspended by ropes from the girders in the roof. This was changed after the ropes became worn, and they were then stored behind the diving platforms. Footbaths were situated at the shallow end and all swimmers were asked to use them, and the showers, before entering the water. Showers and toilets were built on the main building, a third of the way up the side.

Dressing boxes, which had teak stools and mats were situated along each side of the wall, with a balcony above for spectators. Teak woodwork was first finished with linseed oil but this had to be washed off as mildew was forming in the corners. The bath staff washed all the linseed oil off and varnished the teak with yacht varnish, this cured the mildew. All the surrounds were covered with red tiles and all walls in cream tiles. There were private baths for men and women, a laundry with washing machine and a hair dryer, and also a boiler for melting down half used soap which was then used in the washing machine. The front vestibule was cream tiled with terrazzo flooring, a notice board on the wall and a glass fronted office with a turnstile. The back office was used as a store for all cleaning materials etc.

There was a committee room with a large table and chairs so that the baths' committee or swimming clubs could hold meetings. A small back office was for the bath's manager. Men's pool staff had a small room at the back door above where the rubbish bins were kept. The filter plant was built on the north side of the pool. There were four filters, electric pump, steam chlorifier and ammonia cylinders and soda and alum feeds. Steam was supplied from the town destructor. The pond was brushed with a long pole and a gym brush and four inch square logs were floated from end to end to skim the pool every morning. Any dirt was lifted out with skim pans. The staff consisted of a bath superintendent, one office girl, an instructress who relieved in the office, two girls for the laundry and private baths, two swimming instructor/attendants, and one cleaner who relieved at the pool side.

The pond staff worked in shifts, eight to one and three to five or one to three and five to nine, working alternate Saturdays and Sundays – forty-seven hour week, for £2.18s. No increase for unsocial hours. At the opening gala the pond staff had to do six rescues of swimmers who swam half way up the pond and then went to put their feet on the bottom and found they were out of their depth, and panicked! For the first few weeks all males had to wear full costume, and no mixed bathing. All ladies had to wear caps and were warned not to wear pink or white costumes which could be transparent when wet. Everything was changed quickly, and males were allowed trunks and mixed bathing except Thursday mornings and Monday nights, when it was ladies only. Miss Margaret MacLeod was the only staff member with life-saving qualifications, but Dan Davis and myself were very quickly past the bronze medallion and silver medal and instructor qualifications. Then Mr Lumsden the pool manager followed suit. There were many staff changes during the first three years. Molly Brown the office girl was the first to go, then Helen Fraser left to be replaced by Margery Barnet. I left to go as baths manager at Elgin, replaced by Uisdean Fraser who later became a police inspector in Aberdeen, marrying Margery Barnet as it happened. The war broke out and I was away all during the war. During the war years there had to be lots of changes in staff as each attendant was called up and replaced by members of the swimming club – part-time some of them. After the war, on the return of the servicemen, the pool staff was settled down, with Ian MacBean, Rod Dyce and Alec Cowley MacGillivray. Dan Davison was manager.

Water Polo

The development of water polo in Inverness? Well the first record of water polo in Inverness was a game of aquatic football which took place in Nairn swimming pool in August 1892. Teams from Caley and Clach, Inverness took part. Clachnacuddin won. On SASA re-organising water polo Caley/Clach combined to enter as an Inverness amateur swimming club for the water polo cup. They also entered for the standard trophy in Aberdeen, winning it the first year it was put up for competition. First time I heard of the game was when my father pointed out George Cornet, as a man who played water polo for Scotland. To play water polo you must be able to swim which I did not learn until 1922 at eleven years old. Ian Mellis and Tommy Syme and I were at the Longman just where the Kessock Bridge now stands, and where the Caley football club is. I had a set of cotton wings which were watertight when wet, and Ian Mellis pulled them out from under me and I found I could swim without them. Before we left the water all three of us could swim. Farraline Park school boys had a swimming period after school on Friday evenings, from four until five. Donald Dallas was the schools instructor at the Montague swimming baths. This was a twenty five yard pool with diving board, spring board and chute. The school periods were voluntary and not well attended. I soon found that Donald Dallas was quite pleased if boys from other schools attended as there was room for them. Harry Maclean, a boy slightly older than me, then got me to join the swimming club. This had one hour on Tuesday and Thursday nights. He also taught me to swim side stroke, over arm stroke, trudgeon and eventually front crawl. We were at the baths every night except Monday – ladies' night. We were allowed in free as we cleaned out the pool on Saturday afternoons. At the swimming club a Mr Tom Allan who was an Insurance Inspector with only one arm, taught us boys to pick up a water polo ball by holding it between the hand and the wrist, and also to get our shoulders up to throw, both front, back and sling shots. At that time the Inverness water polo team was Jock Sutherland – the goalkeeper for Inverness Thistle – backs were Tom Fobister – who also played for Nairn, Lyle Finlay who only had one leg, but was a strong swimmer, Gordon Myrtle – easily the best player – who was a member of Burnetts the bakers, Bert Myrtle his brother, Jim Davison – bonny Jim who played football for Clach and Ally Rose a postman, who played for Caley. Here I heard stories of great players of the past. George Cornet, who played for Scotland from 1898 to 1911 and Henry Masdall who also played for Scotland against Ireland. Another player who made an impression on me was Tom Douglas, bank manager at Nairn who played for Inverness in Scottish cup games. He could swim six lengths of the crawl after playing his polo match. At that time crawl was used only by a handful of swimmers. Gordon Myrtle, Bobby Gordon, Dan Davison, Harry Maclean and myself were among the only people to swim crawl in Inverness. At this stage I got an Olympic training medal for swimming twenty five yards in under fourteen seconds. Gordon Myrtle tried but could not do it in ten seconds. Young players were encouraged and at one stage the Royal Academy played the other club members but although the Academy were older boys they could not beat the club boys.

I purchased my first copy of water polo rules in 1924 and I still have it. I also have the latest amendments mind! As a fourteen year old I was first picked to play for the senior team as a forward. This was when I learned to make space for myself by concentrating on the play even when not directly involved, also how to turn an opponent. One club night old Henry Myrtle arrived at the club crippled with arthritis and walking with a stick. I found I was being marked by him and although he could not use his legs, he could always take the ball from me. Never sink me, just pressing me down low enough that I couldn't get my shoulder clear of the water. After this experience I had to learn to show the referee that I was being fouled or turn and kick myself free. On the Montague baths closing in 1926 the only water polo was at Nairn or when we went to regattas at Invergordon and Findhorn, and I remember well when I played for an Inverness and Nairn select against Perth amateurs and select. By then I had learnt you have to keep trying when you have been fouled as after being sunk in front of goal I pushed up from the bottom at the deep end and found the ball in front of me and by throwing it over my shoulder I managed to score the winning goal. However there was ten years before Inverness swimming club was reformed when Inverness pool (Glebe Street) was opened on 1 July 1936. Only four of the old team remained active, Jock Sutherland the goal keeper, Gordon Myrtle, Dan Davison and myself, who both worked in the pool; but now being professionals we could only play in practice games. After a couple of weeks the LMS Club had started and Dan Davison was appointed coach to the amateurs and I coach to the LMS.

The new swimming baths in Inverness are great – they are what was badly needed. I wasn't disappointed to see the Glebe Street baths close as they were never a good pool. They copied Glasgow when they were built instead of going to see the latest built pools. They copied the old pools. They were behind the times when they were built and they spent one and a third millions to refurbish them in the 80's and really spoilt them. Not improved. The only thing I would like to see now if they could build a diving pit which could be used as a 'swim-down' for swimmers preparing for races at the Galas. Inverness used to have diving champions, Brian Davidson and Morris Campbell, who dominated Scottish diving for ten years. They dived at the Commonwealth Games – they were good.

Some more well-known names who worked and swam at the Glebe Street Pool –

Ian MacBean
Rod Dyce
Alex C. MacGillivray
Bill Morrison
Peter MacGillivray
Rod Geddes
Peter Shore
George Fallon
Roddy Munro
Ian Black
Sandra Whyte
Elizabeth MacKenzie

Working Life

I got my first job in the New Inverness Laundry in Telford Street. My two sisters already worked there – one in the packing room and one in the checking room. I started in the place where the bed and table linen was folded and finished. We called it the big roller room, the linen was fed through big rollers and we folded it at the other end. Then I moved to the hand ironing room and I liked the work there. When they saw I was good at this I was moved to the finery ironing. I worked on fine stuff like shirts and ladies' garments. We used gas heated irons which hung down from above. When things like the Northern Meeting was on we got clothes from all the shooting lodges.

It was a long day, we started at 8 am and finished at 6 pm. We got a few minutes break for a cup of tea and in the middle of the day I walked home to Friars Street for my dinner. It was very tiring standing in the same place all day but we were quite happy. The two bosses would take turns to look in at starting and stopping time just to see we were in on time and didn't leave early.

There were four of us in the ironing room and the work had to be done properly. The clothes would be wrapped up damp for us to iron. They were very fussy and if the manageress wasn't pleased we would have to do it all again. We worked on a Saturday morning until noon and after stopping work we had to wash and scrub the workplace and wash and starch our white aprons. The aprons were hung up to dry ready for Monday morning. Sometimes when we were busy at the height of the season we had to work till 8 o'clock at night and for that week our pay was ten shillings.

After the laundry, I was in service in a house in Island Bank Road where I lived in. It was very hard work and a long day. First job was at 6 am to scrub the front steps. After that all the shoes and boots had to be cleaned and polished. Then I had to clean and black-lead the big range in the kitchen. It was like being a slave and after a year my mother came and took me away from there.

I left school in 1916 when I was fourteen. I went to the Labour Exchange and they sent me to three places – the Dochfour Estate Office at 62 Academy Street, A J MacKenzie the Solicitors, and Gilbert Ross the Ironmongers for interviews. That evening was awfully wet and I was drying clothes round the fire and there was a knock on the door. There was Mr A.J. and Mrs MacKenzie, they had walked all the way from Old Edinburgh Road in the pouring rain to tell me I could start work. They sat there and got warm and he said, "You can start anytime. We usually pay 3/6 a week but since we know your grandma so well we'll give you 5/-". So I got 5/- a week with a shilling off – 19/- a month.

When I was seventeen I left and went to Dalneigh Farm to work in service. That was jolly hard work – I had the housework and I had the dairy at 5.30 am. All the things had to be scrubbed outside no matter what the weather was like. There was another girl as well, the two of us and Mrs Fraser herself. She wouldn't ask you to do what she wouldn't do herself – she was fair that way.

I left the High School (Crown) when I was fifteen (1930) and my first job was in the office at Holm Mills but after six months I left, but at that time, if you left your job voluntarily you didn't get any unemployment money for six weeks. However you could sit at a tribunal and explain your reasons for leaving which I did at that early age. I faced the head of the Labour Exchange and a few councillors who were there as a committee to hear your reasons. Of course at that age you were in tears overawed by these men and with no support, you were just sitting on your own. Inevitably the judgement went against me and I had to wait six weeks with no money but I got another job before the six weeks were up working with Wm Munro, Wholesalers, in Falcon Square.

It was a very busy square in those days and there was a trial you had to go through – we went through the back station to work where Wordie's lorries and their horses were and many a time we had to dodge these horses because they weren't really broken in for that job. You would get your jacket sleeve bitten when you were passing if you weren't careful.

Once there was a wages dispute. My boss Mr Munro paid his lorry driver £2 per week, that was all he got. There was no such thing as overtime in those days. It was from 8 am till we got finished, that was what I was told when I asked what my hours would be. Anyway, Baillie G (another employer) paid his men £2.5/- a week and my boss got on to him because he said it would make all the other firms' drivers want more wages. But Baillie G said he still paid his drivers £2 a week, but he paid them 5/- a week more for honesty.

My first job was with what was called County Benefit, an insurance society that I think originated in York House (Church Street). They used to pay insurance for your eyes and teeth treatment. We paid out the money and I used to go with the cheques to the dentists and opticians. They got so much for spectacles and teeth. There were other benefit places in town, it depended on who you were insured with. I got 2/6 a week to start with for wages and then it went up to 7/6 – I thought I was a millionaire.

You used to be issued with a pen-nib for doing printing work on drawings and heaven help you if you came back for another nib within two months. It was inspected and checked and it was pointed out that you hadn't kept it wiped and cleaned and filled with a quill. You had to fill it with a quill. You were not allowed to dip it in the ink- pot because you might spoil the point.

There was a variety of goods we handled and believe me it was in all weathers. I'd have all the men standing by on the quay for the boats to come in but missing the tide through bad weather. All the transport had to be sent away and the men were sent home. It used to break my heart. I had my own regulars there but I employed a lot of casual labour as well. There was never any shortage of that especially before the war. You could get any amount of men. I used to have some good men who knew who to get and they would go round all the doors and pubs and the barmen would say, "Right you, report to the harbour at such and such a time for a job".

We used to work up at the canal, up at the top lock, that was for Langlands, they used to do general traffic right through Loch Ness and down the West to Glasgow about every ten days and we did a lot of work at Muirtown basin for the distilleries – heavy, heavy work that was, and we did the slates for the builders. Then we had the Thornbush for general cargo and bricks, a lot of bricks and at the harbour as well. I can remember when we had all four places going at the same time. Mind you, the boats we were getting then were much smaller than you get now. The channel wasn't deep enough to take the bigger boats.

It was all manual loading and unloading then – until the early 60's when we got one small crane. The whole lot (workforce) pre-war, if you took in the canal top lock, Muirtown, Thornbush and the Inverness harbour would be about 400, and they moved about all over the place. Times have changed, they don't know what hard work is these days. My God it was hard work, working on cement boats at three in the morning till ten at night every day except Saturdays when we worked till three in the afternoon, handling hundredweight cement bags and you would never hear a word of complaint from them.

In the late 40's I think it was, they were putting in new cables because we were all on DC electricity supply and it was being changed on to AC. We were working on the new cables which were going down in the main street and in Church Street in front of the Old High Church we started digging bones up – human bones. All we could do was put them back carefully as we were closing up the site and it was done with great feeling.

One of the first housing developments after the war was my old firm Norman Smart the builders. They built Glenburn Drive and some houses on Culduthel Road, and Lodge Avenue. I know they were only allowed to charge £1,450.00 per house. It was the Board of Trade that set the price, so the result was if two people came to buy a house then they'd to toss a coin as to who got it. You couldn't get a higher offer and that was a bad start. The Board of Trade also controlled all the timber. Most of the timber used in building was foreign, most of it from the Scandinavian countries and some from Canada. During the war it was all bought in by Civil Servants. They might have gone across to the Scandinavian countries with a slogan saying, "You can sell me any rubbish at the highest price". Then a new man, Harold Wilson, came to the Board of Trade and he scrapped the old system of timber control in a week. Then we started getting decent timber and started building.

My father was a traveller for A B Chalmers in the back station and his journeys covered as far south as Aviemore, then Nairn, Forres and so on. In these days the journey was about 40 miles and it would take him all day to call at these places and then return home. He would get his tea and then away back to work again to make up the orders so that they could be delivered to the customers the next day, it was a pretty hard life. Coming back from Nairn one night when I was with him, the headlights of the car gave out and we had to creep home on sidelights and I recall that about five cars passed us coming in the opposite direction. This was about 1932 – there were so few cars in those days.

When I was working on a voluntary basis at the farm, one of the jobs I used to do was cut the grass with a tractor and horse and the 'gang' mowers down at the Longman Golf Course. That was quite a hazardous affair because the sheep were grazing there as well and as you were cutting the grass you had to try and make sure you didn't hit any sheep. Also their droppings came flying off the board and hit you on the back of the head.

The other part of the mowing duties was once a year at the cemetery. We used to cut acres and acres of grass there, but now it's all filled in. We used what was called a 'gang' mower, like an ordinary push mower. Three of these in line were all hooked up to the tractor and pulled along behind the tractor. As you were cutting the grass everything hit you on the back of the neck, there was no protection. This was at Tomnahurich Farm.

I was on the Stone of Destiny story. My press colleague and I had a brand new Morris Minor which belonged to the company and we were told to follow the Scotland Yard boys who were in a Jaguar and up from London. We could see the locals were winding them up so we gave up following the Jag. It was a Saturday night when the story broke and I found Kay Matheson in the Plockton Hotel and got a quote from her. In those days the telephone lines were all shared and my conversation was overheard by a woman in another hotel. That night I disappeared and everyone was looking for me but the following Friday the circulation manager of the People's Journal came into the office in Baron Taylor's Street and left a letter. It was from the D.C. Thomson organisation thanking me for my loyalty and enclosing a cheque for £25.

When I left school I served my time as a pharmacist in W & D Fraser on Eastgate. At that time there were thirteen chemists in Inverness. I can well remember when Boots the Chemist came into Inverness in 1928. They were situated at the corner of Inglis Street and High Street where Forbes the Draper was. At that time if you were working in a chemist's, your hours were normally 8.30 am until 7 pm and it was 9 pm on a Saturday night before you closed. Every third Wednesday you had to go back because the shop opened for an hour on Wednesday evenings. It also opened for an hour in the morning and an hour in the evening on Sundays, they worked long hours in those days. I can remember starting off my apprenticeship by getting 7/6 a week. I recall how thrilled I was when after a year I got an increase of half a crown which brought it up to 10/- a week.

Before I left school I was working part-time in a chemist's shop as an errand boy at Hendry the Chemist on High Street. There were three chemists on High Street at the time – Hendry, MacNair's which was at the corner of one of the lanes on High Street and MacKenzie the Chemist. I used to work every night from 5 o'clock till 8 o'clock but it would be about 9 pm before they got cleared up and got everything straight, then it would be a dash to the pub to get a dram before they closed. The pubs closed at 9 pm in the winter and it was 9.30 pm in the summer.

It was just the way of life. All the shops were open and Saturday night was a great night in Inverness for the people doing their shopping, the streets were just packed with people. You see, most workers were paid on a Saturday and that was when the wives, the women had to go and get their shopping done. The holidays were two days at New Year and one day at Christmas and the odd one-day holiday.

When I did leave school I was working for Urquhart the Seedsman on Union Street. They had a shop on the corner of Union Street and Academy Street. I used to work from 9 am until six or seven at night with a half-day Saturday. We were lucky we closed half day on a Saturday so I could go to the football match. I suppose they closed because they weren't getting business on a Saturday afternoon. My wage was 10/- a week to start with and it went up to 12/6 after a couple of years.

I also worked in a pub part-time, the Eagle Bar. A Mr MacGregor was the proprietor and he had one hand. I used to work for 7/6 a week part-time. We used to work on Friday night and all day Saturday, right up until 10 pm. They closed at 9.30 pm but by the time you'd washed all the glasses and swept the floors it was getting on for 10 pm. It was the same when I worked in the chemists, by the time the shop closed at 8 pm we'd all the cleaning up to do. One of the jobs we had to do was clean the medicine bottles that people brought back. You'd to wash them and pour some sort of acid into the bottle to burn all the sediment out. If it got on to your clothes it would burn them as well. We got no gloves or aprons, nothing but bare hands. The bottoms of my trousers were all little holes with the acid.

I started the milk round early in the morning, and again after school. My pay was 3/6 (three shillings and sixpence), and a pint of milk. I remember one interesting ploy that we used. The milkman was really responsible, but away up at the top of Fairfield Road, on the left hand side, was Dalneigh Farm. Just beside the road was a horse trough, an old bath filled with dirty water. At 7 o'clock in the morning when nobody's around, the milkman would say to me, "Jock, away in there". He would give me two quart bottles and I filled them out of this dirty trough. I filled two quart bottles of water and handed them to him. He would take the top of the can of milk and pour it into the milk. Now the funny thing is, of course, we all survived in those days. If it happened today I don't know what would happen. My job later on was in a laboratory, I went on to be testing the milk, and my mind often went back to the time when here was me busy contaminating the milk as hard as I could.

It's a wonder they didn't have typhoid or cholera or something.

Now where was Dalneigh Farm? That is where they started building Hawthorn Drive and that became the Dalneigh Estate. There wasn't a house there. There was one or two bungalows going up on the left hand side after Lochalsh Road, and a couple of bungalows as far as I can remember. It was a lot of big houses, I think, when Gossip the Dentist was there, and they all had maids and all that sort of thing. I used to go in and see the maids when I was delivering the milk. Then I think Dalneigh started just after the war. Up until then it was farmland.

I left when I was fourteen and a half years old. I started work on the milk cart at the age of eleven, at the Farmer's Dairy. It was quite a hard routine because I started at 6.30 am and I finished at 8.30 am. Very often I was late and sometimes I would be soaking wet. I would run home maybe from Fairfield

Road, get my breakfast and get some dry clothes on. Go down to the High School by 9 am and very often I was late. So I used to get the strap. I couldn't say what I was doing because you weren't supposed to be working you see. So I had to fall for getting thumped a few times. But then I was on the milk cart again at 4.30 pm and the work didn't finish until 6.30 or 7 pm. So it was quite a long day. The result was the lessons inevitably suffered. So instead of going to the Academy, which I think I could have done, I was quite glad to leave school. I thought to myself if I start work I won't have such a long day, you see. I'll cut my hours by leaving school.

So I started with Eddie MacGillvray the Butcher on Chapel Street. There was butcher's bikes and you delivered the meat. There was old man MacGillvray and Eddie, and he was great. He was a captain with the 5th Company Boys Brigade. Behind the butcher's shop which was on Chapel Street was the Mortuary. I remember the other boys would pull my leg when I would go out and meet them. "Oh look at him, it's not butcher's meat he's got, it's the bodies he's using. That's what they're selling!"

We used to have some old worthies at the Gas Works. The Gas Works was a place, if a bloke got time locally, thirty days inside or that, if he was local the Gas Works belonged to the Town so the first place they gave him a job was the Gas Works. You used to get all types in with some worthies amongst them. Remember Willie – he was very important and we were talking away to him one day and he says "I was on the phone to a friend of mine". "Oh", I says "Willie you've got the phone now?" "Aye" he says, "I bought it second hand in Perth". Remember the time the two of them were left on the shift. They were that drunk on wine. There was an old worthy there, he was a fine man really, a gem of a man, 'Big Dan'. He lived in Bridge Street. Dan used to like a 'bucket' and when the fires were out in the Gas Works' furnaces, Dan used to go and have a sleep there. They nearly lit the fire when he was in there and one of them was chasing up this bloke wondering where he was, and the bloke (Dan) jumped over the Chapel Yard wall and he fell into an open grave they were getting ready for the next day.

I remember once, it was April Fool's Day and I was only a boy, started in there (Gas Works) and they used to catch you with this April Fool business. They asked me to take this big hurly down to Cruikshanks, the old blacksmith down the Glebe, to get this machine. I'm going down with this hurly down the cobbles on Chapel Street and stotting. I could hardly hold it and I gets down to Cruikshanks and here the machine was this size (very small) and here's a big hurly to take it back. I took my time over it and took an hour off and when I got back it was "What was keeping you?" "Oh it was heavy for me", I says.

Trade and Industry

I started with the Rose Street Foundry the day after war broke out. Having served my apprenticeship I worked in the test depot and eventually became head of the test and experimental depot. Hunter-Gordon asked me to go down to Birmingham and start an office there and after a while I became manager of field operations. I was responsible for the servicing of our equipment, commissioning and sales. With the head office still being in Inverness I was coming up five or six times a year and we used to come up in the summer for our holidays and at Christmas. One thing that always did impress me if I'd been coming up on the overnight sleeper, was coming out of the station in the morning and looking at the Royal Hotel, and how clear the air was and how fresh everything was compared to the Midlands. Coming up to Inverness there was a different light – a different clarity.

My husband worked in the Foundry, he worked for fifty years in the Foundry and he was a journeyman. Our wages were £2.10/- a week. You could get a pair of shoes for ten bob (ten shillings) and a nice dress for £1; it was 3½d for a loaf and you could get a pennyworth of skimmed milk. When he retired he never got a pension, he was too old to go into the pension. The older men – they were given a bonus of

£5 a month but my husband died on the Thursday and I never got it. When he started his trade he got half a crown and they had to sign an affidavit to say they couldn't break the contract – his father had to sign it. He got two years off to go to the war (WW1) then he got back to the Foundry to finish his time - and after fifty years – no pension – just a nice letter.

At midday, and in the evenings, Innes Street would be thronged with 'black spots' moving three and four abreast down the street and making for over the Black Bridge. They were men in dungarees going home from work at the Foundry or the railway workshops. What cheery fellows they seemed to be in those days of long hours, hard work, no work's canteen and low wages. They never passed us without a word of greeting or giving us a cigarette card of our favourite film stars.

There was a lot of military work going on and I got a job in the Foundry. It was mostly maintenance work on the Foundry houses. There were one or two round about the Foundry in Rose Street and a big one in Auldcastle Road, one or two houses up that way and one of the London managers had one over in Ballifeary.

I did a lot of pattern work, machine guns and various gun engine parts. They were done to machine drawings and had to be very accurate. The draughtsman checked the pattern was right and took it down to the moulding shop. They used a special sand to make these moulds to pour the molten metal in. You just poured the metal in and you added various things to it, different types of metal, and when it set after an hour or two the fettlers just took a hammer and chisel, knocked the sand away and cut off the bit you made to pour the metal into and you were left with the casting.

The river was an attraction flowing right down through the bottom of the Capel Inch but up the side of Gilbert Street that's where the Tannery was. I used to go down and watch them washing the sheepskins out of the Tannery in the river. There was steps leading down and the skinners used to clean the skins in the river.

The Tannery on Gilbert Street had steps going down to the river where the skins of the sheep were washed and laid out to dry on the railings and then the skins went back to the factory. The Tannery provided employment for a lot of local folk.

Before going to school we would go to the Gasworks with a bogey and stand in a queue to get a ticket for a bag of cinders and then take it home and go to school.

The Gasworks – I well remember the manager. He was a big fellow called Dunk MacLeod and he had a big family. I was in school with one of his sons, George, and I used to go round there every Saturday morning because one of my jobs was to collect a quarter of coal and a quarter of cinders (quarter hundredweight) – a small baggie - and that did us for the week. That was eight pence for our fuel costs. You had to queue up of course. There was a wee office and you got a ticket for whatever amount you wanted. You had to have your own bag and you gave your ticket to a man who had a big weighing machine and he would shovel the stuff in and say, "Hold your bag open – that's your quarter". Then into your bogey with a couple of pram wheels on it and you hurled it home. There would be hundreds of boys there, from the Ferry, Merkinch, Innes Street, Church Street, all over the town because it was a cheap source of fuel.

We used to go in and play football there because 'Big Dunk' was the foreman. You went down Chapel Street and about fifty yards to the right - that was Manse Place. There were still a few houses there, three on each side, tenements, and up there, that was the Gasworks. There was a big sort of square, a lot of pipes and a terrible smell and steam coming out all over the place.

The Gasworks worked twenty-four hours a day making gas. It was all gaslights in the town, and in the houses and the streets. I remember the noise of the steam engine - it was a large steam engine which went up and down. Mr Campbell took it up and down to the Longman and they used the cinders refuse from the gas processing on the roads. It was a very noisy place to live. When I went to live in the country years later I couldn't get to sleep at nights because I missed the noise of the Gasworks and the Foundry. The Gasworks had a squeak; a particular squeak in the mechanism and that squeak was there for years. It was from some sort of hopper and we liked that squeak. We lived in the shadow of the gasometer and people used to say it smelt of gas and we'd all be ill, but we're still here to tell the tale.

I remember one time there was an explosion down at the Gasworks and my boss in the Town Hall told me to phone down but I couldn't get through. Everybody was phoning and he was quite annoyed. That was about 1947/48 but I don't think there was any injuries. I think it was round at the Manse Place side of the Gasworks.

Another place where we amused ourselves was the Gasworks. You could walk through from George Street to either Chapel Street or Rose Street. On Saturday one of our chores was to go for a tuppenny bag of cinders – about a hundredweight. I found that if I made a barrow I could carry three or four bags and make a profit going for the neighbours and getting a penny tip. I could make sixpence or seven pence which was a fortune for a young lad in those days.

At the bottom of the Longman Bridge, that's where the 'round' timber going into John Oaks' sawmill on the far side of the Longman Bridge went. They came in on horse-drawn pole lorries and at the shop at the top of Rose Street they put two horses onto the one lorry to get it up this hill. They would take a run at the hill and it was great to see them. That's where the Gasworks steam engine came back and fore from the coal depot at the back of the railway. The tar lorry came up onto the top of the Bridge and poured the tar down into the wagons going south. The tar was produced in the Gasworks.

I had a bogey – a two-wheeled bogey – my father made it for me because I started going over to the Gasworks on a Saturday morning. It must have been about 1922/23 and it went on till the 1926 strike. Coal was going up in price, then there was coal shortages, but I was going over to the Gasworks and getting two bags of coke cinders for my mother because the fire was kept going all day with cinders. Oh aye, when they would see me with the bogey and cinders the baker's wife would shout "Will you get cinders for me". I would get up at 7 am on a Saturday morning and over at the Gasworks by 8 am. My barrow would take four bags of coke and it was all right till I came to the Greig Street Bridge. I would stand there and some men would be passing and as sure as anything one of them would say "Do you want a lift up?", then they would say, "Well you can take two bags off and we'll give you a lift". But then they would go back and get the other two bags, and if I hurried they would give me a lift down the steps on the other side.

The Harbour was a hive of industry and boats were forever coming in and out. There were coal boats, cement boats, batten boats and once a year a sailing boat from Norway with ice. I can't remember how many masts she had, I think it was three or four, but she was a beautiful sight sailing in and out of the Firth with her masts up. When the batten boats came in, all the wood was piled up on the Harbour and Walkers Sawmill laid out their railway which carted the wood into the sawmill. We had a fine time getting a ride on the wagons and in and around the woodpiles. I remember the harbour being extended for the Coast Lines and the petrol tankers.

At 5o'clock, if you wanted to get up at 5 o'clock, say in November when the herring started and the boats started coming into the harbour, the Thornbush harbour, you could go down there and there would be men there and then you would see the boats coming in with their sail up, at the mouth of the river. They would drop their sail after a while and they would chug chug up to the wharf. And then down would go the baskets and they would come up full of herring.

There was a lot of firms at the harbour, the biggest was MacGruther & Marshall then, they were principally coal merchants and general and builders' merchants. They were also agents for most of the cement for building the Hydro dams, that was in the 50's right up until the dams were completed. They were also agents for the steam coal which was supplied to the Royal Northern Infirmary, the Inverness destructor and the Inverness Asylum (Craig Dunain Hospital).

MacDonald and Morrison were the next biggest. They were also builders' merchants for coal, lime and bricks. The bricks came in from Irvine's in Ayrshire right round by the Pentland Firth. MacDonald & Morrison were also agents for war-damaged trees. The trees that we got were from Germany, the Ruhr valley and they were riddled with shrapnel, we had to be careful when we were handling these. We also discharged all the Swedish houses which were built in Dalneigh.

The other firms were J & W Henderson and Whiteheads of Aberdeen. They were basically cement and builders' merchants. Then there was Robert Taylor's, John MacPherson and the Co-operative who all handled coal only. There was James Walker who became Inverness Sawmills and William Gray who handled all the timber.

Coast Line Seaways were general cargo and they had a big shed down at the bottom of the harbour, their cargoes used to come in every week. One boat came from Leith and the other came in from Liverpool. Outgoing, we exported an awful lot of whisky and food from a firm in Telford Street (Calindus). Then there was the SAI (Scottish Agricultural Industries) that was barley, phosphates and stuff for Orkney, cattle feed and barley. Then in December we discharged all the salt for the roads and for stockpiling.

Scotlog was a comparatively new firm and they started exporting whole trees and wood pulp to Sweden, Germany and Holland. Then there was Fishline, started by a Norwegian, exporting frozen fish, barrelled cargoes and cured fish to Germany, Poland, Norway and Sweden.

The British Aluminium Works at Fort William and Invergordon imported raw materials for the processing of aluminium, then we exported out ingots of rolled bars, blocks of aluminium (some of them up to a weight of 12 tons) to Holland. The strange thing was that Holland took all the exports from British Aluminium at Invergordon and stockpiled them up and the bottom fell out of the aluminium trade in this country.

We sent very, very heavy pieces of aircraft hangars from the airport at Dalcross, they went to Germany and we had some hair-raising times loading that. We also handled sand, gravel, tar etc for Orkney County Council. Also slates for the housing which came from Wales via the canal. We sent a lot of pit props to England, and bricks, sand and cement and other building materials for building the Rocket Range at Benbecula.

Then when MacDermotts started at Ardersier we came into the really heavy stuff.

It was a common sight on the day of the cattle and sheep sales to see the drovers take the herds along Eastgate, down Hamilton Street, Academy Street,

Chapel Street and then Shore Street to the slaughterhouse. I and a few others used to help the drovers, and keep the animals from running up the side streets. Many a time some ran away and I know of one house which had a bull in its living room. As they neared the slaughterhouse they seemed to get wilder and by the time they were in the yard they were really mad and many a time I leapt the fence in double quick time. If the truant officer knew, he could have picked up a lot of truants sitting by the sale ring watching the sales at Hamilton's Mart. Many a time I watched a killing in the slaughterhouse. The killing in those days was not so humane as today and I always think that seeing the brutal way it was done then has given me the compassion for my fellow man and God's creatures.

The slaughterhouse at that time would be about 150 yards past the Cromwell clock, so I got into the habit of, when the men would go away and the other boys would go off, getting to know the 'killers', as they were called then. There was 'Cabby' MacIntosh – I think he had been a cabman but then he went down to the slaughterhouse, I don't know – but his name was 'Cabby' anyway. He would say to me, "What's doing? How's your Dad?" He knew my father. And I got to know the others. There were three 'killers' in the first pens for the sheep, so I would see the sheep being killed. And he said to me one time, "Would you like some tripe?" And I said, "Yes, but I would prefer some liver," and he laughed and said "Oh, forget about the liver, we'll give you some tripe". And so he said, "It should be tuppence each". And I said, "Well, I need a penny for myself". So he said, "Well, tuppence. Now if you come down here every Tuesday night, you can have tripe, oh, maybe 4 lbs of tripe for four pence". That was two bags, two sheep's bags. Perhaps I shouldn't talk about sheep's bags on here for the faint hearted, the faint stomached people. But nevertheless that was how it was. And that was fair enough. Now they would partly clean them for me and say "Right, now keep running them under the tap". I had a basket I would put them into. They were damned heavy because instead of 4 lbs there would be about 6 or 8 lbs of tripe because I told them I could give them to so and so, and so and so, who were very poor, which I did, and that was fair enough. So within a week or two, I would find that a bit of liver was there and sweetbreads would be there and there would be one or two steaklets, mutton chops or something like that. That was alright, that was all for my own family. Then the tripe, my Dad would take them to whoever needed them. He knew people who were every bit as badly off as we were. So we had tripe to make soup, excellent soup and we got hot tripe and then we had pressed tripe which you could slice and have with potatoes and turnips and onion and, what not. You could have a lot of things with the cold tripe, beautiful stuff, and healthy.

We never starved you know, it was tripe and onions. Someone would go to the slaughterhouse and collect the tripe 'sheep bags'. They used to clean it – it was all clean ready and we used to collect it there, they used to have straw baskets to go and collect their tripe.

In those days the railway had its own workshop and the workmen clocked in and out at the last house on Railway Terrace. When these works clocked out Innes Street and Rose Street was a mass of people. As youngsters my friends and I could collect a set of cigarette cards in about a week. The younger railway workers often used to kick our ball up and down the street with us trying to retrieve it. They also broke a window and we got the blame – when the owner came out they had disappeared into the crowd.

Farms and Dairies

There were three farms down the Longman – Citadel Farm, Seafield and Millburn Farms. Every night after milking, the milk cart from the Citadel came round selling milk. There were no bottles but everyone had a milk-can to be filled from the churn. The Farmer's Dairy on Waterloo place used to sell cheap milk after the rounds were over and my friends and I were often sent there. We dallied on the swings at the Maggot Green and were often in trouble for swinging the milk cans over our heads trying not to spill it – but accidents will happen.

There were fields here up until then and the fields attached to 'Lethington' extended down from Annfield Road to Damfield Road and along to Walker Park, up to Leys Drive and down to Darnaway Road. At the top of the avenue there was a five-barred gate and the cattle were grazed in the field and twice a day they were moved from here to the Eldad Dairy in Argyle Street. I think they also had fields on what is now Old Mill Road. There was an iron gate for traffic or taking in a vehicle and there was also a 'kiss and tell' pedestrian gate (also known locally as a 'whirly-birly'. Before Harris Road was built, the fields there belonged to MacDonald and Fraser the livestock auctioneers, and the sheep and cattle were brought there from the country till the sales the following day.

When I was a small boy, when the men were working in the fields they came home at mid-day for a meal. I used to sit on the horse and they would take me over to Hilton Farm and I'd walk back on my own. Just at the burn on Burn Road there was a croft run by Bob MacFarlane, he used to go round selling the milk. There was also a laundry on Burn Road run by the MacKintosh family and they used to have dances in the laundry. They probably had an accordion or a melodeon and they were a great feature.

There was also a dairy on Lodge Road owned by a Mr Beaton, and then where Delnies Road is now, there was a piggery belonging to a Mr MacDonald who also had a market garden and a stall in the Market where he sold fruit and vegetables and he had the pigs just beside the burn. There was another man who had a market garden there called Ben Barclay.

In Bruce Gardens in those days in front of our house was the nurseries where the flats are now and behind us was Central Park. There was one or two houses further up Bruce Gardens and then there was the farm. Then the next one was Tomnahurich Farm and further down was Dalneigh Farm. In those days the High School wasn't there and Dalneigh Farm was virtually right down to Tomnahurich Street.

Where the retirement flats are now (Hanover Housing, Argyle Street) the lower half was a market garden, a mannie MacDonald had it and grew potatoes and vegetables. There was the Eldad dairy and a byre there as well. The country started at Kingsmills Road back in the 30's. All the sheep and cattle from outside the town were driven along Kingsmills Road and down Stephen's Brae to the mart. They usually ended up in the shops and the school playground and everybody chasing them all over the place.

The old Hilton Village was from the Poorhouse (Hilton Hospital) to Hilton Avenue, there were no other houses in the area at all at that time. On the left hand side of Old Edinburgh Road were open fields which belonged to MacDonald Fraser the Auction Mart. The five fields were used for grazing and when sheep and cattle came in from out of town they were put there until the sales. There was a little croft at the end of the lane and they had hens and four or five cows and a little dairy. In our young days we spent most of our time at Hilton Farm – that's where the Hilton houses are now. The grieve's cottage was the only house on the road between Hilton Village and Hilton Farm. Then there was the piggery owned by Roddy Fraser. We went to see Roddy Fraser on Sundays and chased the rats in the piggery and then we'd be up at Hilton Farm lifting tatties and turnips. We'd also go up to Druid Temple where Ian Rose was, he was a brother of Davy Rose who had Hilton Farm.

On Burn Road my father had a two and a half acre field (now Burnside Home) and he used to rent fields, two at Drummond House (now Oak Avenue). I used to herd the cows from there. He also had fields down on Drummond Circus and one or two paddocks on Culduthel Road (between No 94 and Drummond Stores). Where Delnies Road is now was a market garden owned by Ben Barclay. Next door to our place on Burn Road was a field belonging to Dan Beaton. He had a small dairy on Lodge Road and across from that was a market garden, which before that had been a small farm.

Transport

My father was a chauffeur with MacRae & Dick – he did the private hires. He had great tales of visiting Prime Ministers, but his masterpiece year after year until the man died was Randolph Scott, the cowboy actor. He came over here every year and he was my father's regular hire and asked for him specially.

The traffic in the town then, well, we were under the impression it was quite busy, but not like nowadays. When we were seven or eight, just before the war, it was nearly all horse-drawn then that changed to motorised vehicles. When I was in school it was nearly all horses and carts on the cobbled streets, the milkman, the coalman, the vegetable man, but there was a big change just before the war.

Dr MacKay lived at the bottom of Bridge Street and he had a brougham (horse-drawn carriage) which he used to visit patients. The first to have a car was Dr England-Kerr, and then Dr Helen MacDonald who lived at 52 High Street, her car had paraffin lamps on the mudguards, but she went back to using a bicycle as most of the doctors did. Dr MacFarlane Jnr used a moped, he was a familiar sight, he had a big moustache, used to smoke a pipe and wore a battered trilby.

Greig's buses were our first transport into town. I remember the first double-decker to come up the Leachkin. What excitement. Many's the winter I've helped push one up the old canal brae.

I left school when I was fourteen and my first regular job was with Willie Greig on the buses. He started the first bus service in the town, the Leachkin service. It started from the market, just opposite the station. The first bus in the morning was 7.30 am, the workers' bus. They were still working on the new hall at Craig Dunain and also started work on the Nurses' Home, so the service was more or less run to suit the nurses and workers. But they also ran the bus service all over the town. The fare from the town to the Leachkin was fourpence single and sixpence return. From the town to the cemetery gate was tuppence single, in those days they were quite hefty fares. There weren't many cars then but a lot of people used the buses. They used them to get to work in the morning for tuppence and back at night for tuppence.

I was a conductor, I rode horses in the summer and came back to Greig in the winter to get a job as a conductor. In those days you could also get a job as a washer or helping the mechanics at night. There was Greig himself and his main man Roddie Chisholm, they used to run about in a little Austin 7 checking that nobody was doing a fiddle with the fares.

In those days there were no starters on buses, the driver had to 'swing' the bus every time to start it. It was a heavy job. We started with the first bus at 7.30 am and we worked on until 11 pm at night with one night off a week. You took your 'piece' with you of course, enough for two meals. Later on they brought in shifts but even they were long, 7.30 am – 6 pm, maybe two hours off in the afternoon. I've seen us work all day and when you'd finished about 6 pm one of them would say, "There's a dance on at Kiltarlity tonight, you'll have to take a bus out". So you came off your shift, got the bus out to the dance at Kiltarlity and got back about three in the morning. The wages were 12/6 a week for a conductor and a driver got £2.10/-.

Greig's used to run tours in the summer round all the interesting places like Culloden and the Boar Stone at Culduthel. They had the driver and an old fellow MacVinish as the courier. They had picked up Americans at the station and took them on tour in an old bus – I remember it had a soft top and if the weather was good they took down the top. When they got to the Boar Stone old MacVinish was giving his spiel about the stone being carved '2000' years ago when one of the Americans said, "Yes boy, and I reckon this is the bus that took them to do the carving".

If you were on the Culduthel run on a Saturday night, all the people from Culduthel and Leys, all the farming people and the girls from the Castle, the blacksmiths from Culduthel Smithy – there were about half a dozen MacDonald brothers from the Smithy - and the people from Culduthel Hospital were on the last bus run at 9.30 pm. The

324

pubs closed at 9 pm. You knew who you'd taken down to town on the 6 pm run so before you took the last bus out you checked the numbers. You'd see that 'Jock' wasn't on the bus so you'd go and look for him and find him outside 'The Plough' or somewhere like that, but you never left without your load. I've seen me in the pubs shouting, "Come on, the bus is just leaving" and you'd get them aboard.

My father's family moved to Inverness about 1911-12. They had quite a number of lorries, about seven I think, and five of them were commandeered when the First World War broke out and were sent to France as ammunition carriers. I think three came back. I remember there were solid tyres on them, acetylene lamps, a canvas roof and half a glass open front.

When I was about twelve years old my first bicycle cost about £5. It was a 'Three Spires' model – the other makers then were Raleigh, Humber and BSA.

He was a driver with MacRae & Dick's horses and cabs in those days. There was a horse trough on Academy Street near the station where the horses could drink and another one at Waterloo, a big round one. Horses were the transport then. They used to have them going up to the canal to collect the people off the boats and going to the hotels. They all had their own brakes (coaches). They also had them going to Strathpeffer for people wanting to take the waters there. I drank them once, and by golly they're horrible. Some of the brakes had two horses pulling them, and some had only one. When we were kids we always used to get a scud on them. We used to go up to the boats at the canal – the Gondolier and the Glengarry – and we waited till all the passengers were away in the brakes and then we got a scud up to where the boats turned ready to go the next day up the loch.

There was the cabbies' hut and stance on Bank Street with a few at the Mercat Cross outside the Town Hall. One I remember was called 'Yochan' and the boys on the way home from school used to tease him but kept their distance from his whip. They used to sing this ditty –

"At the cross, at the cross
Where 'Yochan' lost his horse
And the wheels of his cart rolled away".

Do I remember the horse-drawn carriages – I remember running after them and sitting on the back. The 'May Queen' used to come out occasionally and oh it was lovely to see the horses, and the cabs in the

Station Square and the Exchange. Dr MacKay, his house was at the foot of Bridge Street, he had his own coachman. He used to be out there on Bridge Street with the horse waiting for him with his top hat and grey trousers. The only person who had a car then when I was little was Dr Paterson. There wasn't another car in sight. I think he had a carriage and had an accident. I think I heard a little tittle-tattle that his patients had to collect for him and bought his car.

The second car in the district, oh I can still hear it coming at the Muirtown Bridge – we would all stand there till it passed. Granny was quite frightened of the car.

A lot of men worked in the railway at that time just after the Great War. The railway was very busy because the rolling stock had gone down during the war and hadn't been replaced. My father was working in the carriage builders' workshop on the carpentry. He would work till about 9.30 pm along with all the other men and the families including myself and my sisters used to go up about 7 o'clock at night with a flagon, a blue enamel flagon, white on the inside – and it would be full of tea, and a lid on, and also sandwiches. That was the tea the menfolk had then, they had no time to come home at the normal time and they started work at 7.30 am.

Oh we had the trains just beside us, we had a railway station then. We got into Inverness from Clachnaharry for a penny halfpenny a mile. I spent my summer holidays watching the trains go by. The trains were a great attraction, standing up on the bridge and running away when the steam came up. We watched the Duke's train, the Duke of Sutherland. He had his own train and it came up in the autumn. They had all the people for the shooting and we always knew it and watched out for them all on the Duke's train, a little train it was.

Many a time I stood in Victoria Square and watched the railwaymen come from their work, hundreds of them, the place was black with them. There were hundreds worked on the railway then (1920's). My father worked on the railway, on the engines. It was quite a good job then, them and the Rose Street Foundry, they were the two main works.

I remember quite clearly as a small boy about six, we used to go down to Nairn and rent a house at the beach for a month and my father motored back and fore. We'd leave Inverness laden with budgies' cages and pails and spades. We passed a car round about Raigmore and father hooted the horn, waved and said, "That's Dr Campbell". We reached Gollanfield and another car passed, father hooted the horn, waved and said, "Oh, that's MacBean the farmer". We were just coming to Nairn, at Delnies, when a car passed. Father pulled on the handbrake, turned round and said, "Who the hell was that?" – changed days.

One of my earliest recollections of Inverness was standing beside an old lady when down the road came a vehicle apparently going on its own. The old lady shouted, "Hide – it must be the devil himself that's in it – it's going without horses". We had seen a motorcar for the first time – this car was driven by the late Dr Kerr who in wintertime would visit his patients by means of a horse-drawn sleigh complete with jingle bells.

There were very few cars around in those days, possibly the only ones who had cars would be doctors, and even some of the doctors came in cabs. They were just gradually getting cars and I think the first car in Inverness was owned by Dr Kerr. That was in the days when they walked with a red flag in front of it in case it went too fast.

He was driving this old Lagonda and we were on that straight between Muir of Ord and Beauly doing 70 or 80 miles an hour and he's feeling in his left pocket for his pipe and his right pocket for his matches at the same time – the number of times I grabbed that steering wheel. He was so used to an old open car, and the dirty old pipe. It was quite common for him to take the pipe out of his mouth and spit out of the window, but the window was shut now, so he would take his new coat sleeve and clean the window! It was an old racing Lagonda the boys had got and they put a racing clutch in it. It was a big black Lagonda and they put on a roof rack for carrying materials around for jobs.

The first car I had was in 1935, an A35 Austin, my father gave it to me as a birthday present. It cost £110 and I had it when the war broke out. Once during the war it was commandeered by the police. When I came home from the war my father said to me, "You'd better go up to the town, to Castle Wynd and see the Inspector about what's going to happen about your car. He told me to let him know when you came home".

They said to me, "Well we can either give you the present day (1946) price for the car, a second-hand car, or put the car down to the works at Rugby and have it completely rebuilt". So I got it back completely rebuilt and I had that car up until 1955/56.

There were a few garages, not many because in those days there wasn't many cars. There were a lot of chauffeurs for doctors. All the doctors had their cars and they all had a chauffeur, and most of the important people in the town had a car and chauffeur. I suppose it was cheap to employ people then. They had their garages and the cars were garaged. There was a lot of doctors in Ardross Street before the war, there must have been about fifteen of them. Some of them worked part-time at the Infirmary and had their own practices. They were the people with the cars. Nobody living in the town centre had a car – oh it was a great thing to have a car.

I believe the submarine submerged in Loch Ness very successfully, then it carried on to the West and back to its base. That would have been 1910/11. It had come from where it had been built and this was the test voyage. They had to test the way it would submerge and the depth of the water in Loch Ness seemed to be the satisfactory place so they chose Loch Ness. You see word went round that a submarine was coming and of course if there was anything special going on they came from all parts to see. I remember distinctly seeing it between the lock gates – this long cigar shaped sort of thing. My granny was interested in anything to do with shipping and some time later a dredger – a very beautiful dredger – came through. Word had gone round and she said, "We must go and see this". I can see it yet, newly painted and all those buckets going up very high, heading out to the open sea. Granny and I were just going in our gate looking back and she just shook her head and said, "That will never survive". Well it didn't. It was top heavy and when it got out into the open sea a storm got up and down it went. It capsized. I've seen dredgers but not like that, this one was terrifically high but it was a wonderful ship to look at.

The 'Gondolier' ran up and down the Loch to Fort William at that time and carried a lot of the 'Toffs' as we called them, with their luggage on the deck. We used to run up to Dochgarroch, two or three of us. I always did it because I knew fine I would get money and it was important to the family. So we'd run up to Dochgarroch and get on the boat there, on the locks coming through and the captain or one of the crew would yell at you. I would say, "I'm here to carry all the luggage to the cabs, I've got people here who want me to carry their luggage". So we'd drift down to Muirtown Locks and you'd go amongst them and say, "Can I carry your luggage to your hotel lorry?" It was lorries that carried the luggage to the hotels in those days. They would say, "Yes, we've got three cases here", or whatever and you would get three pence, or if it was one case, twopence. Then in came the Gondolier to the pier and there would be Stamford's lorries waiting. They had their place on Tomnahurich Street (Tesco's now).

During the summer months it was mostly tourists we had and it used to be a great night when the 'Gondolier' came in at the canal. It used to come up from Fort William three nights a week and it was really exciting the night the boat came in. Some of the larger hotels would have a bus there to meet the passengers and some of the others would have a taxi and porters would be all there meeting the boat. It was a very exciting event at that time.

It those days we enjoyed going up the canal on the 'Gondolier'. I had a grandfather, Kenny Munro, who was a Captain of the 'Gondolier' – a long, long time ago. I still have his photo and obituary in my possession. He stayed at Burnfoot, and the boat stayed at Burnfoot at night and went up the loch during the day. That was before the road was built, everything was delivered by boat up the loch, Foyers, Drumnadrochit, Lewiston, then they went up to Banavie and back down again. It took the whole day. He went home to Kilmuir on the Black Isle only at weekends, but there was no ferryboat then so they rowed themselves across the Firth.

I remember just before the 1914 war we were all taken out into the playground to see our first aeroplane (Bishop Girls' School).

There was an aerodrome down the Longman before the war and you could go round the town in an aeroplane for two shillings.

I had my Auntie who stayed on Longman Road and her back garden was right on to the aerodrome. All the planes were there, the 'Lysanders'.

Further down was the Longman Aerodrome. We saw some of our first planes there and they looked like paper and string.

I decided I would learn to fly so I joined this club at the Longman. It was interesting because if you couldn't get flying because there was no aircraft available you could always go and play golf because there was a 9-hole golf course there, except when the tide came in it was 7 holes – it flooded the fairways. In addition to the area which was used by Captain Fresson for his commercial flights, there was the area we used as a flying club and there was a third area for a gliding club. The gliding club had an old gentleman with a Rover car who towed the gliders at speed along the ground and then released them to make a circuit and come back down again. It wouldn't have been that great a speed because it was on grass. It probably got up to about 50 mph before he released the glider, you had to go with the wind but it was good fun.

Captain Fresson was flying his aeroplanes and there grew up the flying club. It developed into something called the Civil Air Guard which was partly supported by the Government to encourage people to learn to fly. It was fairly clear at that time that there was going to be a war and lots of young men were joining the TA. There was probably about twenty of us in the Flying Club but when the war became more and more obvious we were ordered to stop – but we were all simple, we thought we would be ordered to defend Inverness. Little did we know.

I would go and see Dr Kelly and he had a sleigh in those days. The sleigh was kept up at the top of Friars Street, there was a garage there for it. We used to go in there and he had a chauffeur. We always used to get a seat on this sleigh, there was more snow then than there is now. It was on runners and horse-drawn and that was how he went on his rounds. We never actually saw it in use by then but I remember sitting on it and we used to say, "Oh, this is great" pretending there was a horse there and using the whip.

Where Rossleigh's was (Tomnahurich Street), well there were stables in there. Stamfords had taxis later on when they became fashionable but then it was the cabs and horses and lorries. Maybe two or three of his horses and lorries would be at the pier waiting for the 'Gondolier' to come in. MacRae & Dick would have their horses and lorries too. They very often had their Blacks, the Belgian black horses, the funeral horses. Maybe sometimes they would be short of the other horses.

Stamfords would see me there and I would say the "Queensgate Hotel" or the "Columba Hotel" so the luggage would be taken off and loaded on these lorries, then you would climb up on the luggage which was easy enough but the horse would start at a trot and the luggage would go this way and that way. Although it was tied on firmly enough it would still waltz about and with the slippery cases you had to hang on for dear life. When you got to the hotel and got the luggage off you likely got tuppence or threepence.

There was a dramatic event involving the Heatherley girls from Allanfearn. One Sunday they were sitting in the trap waiting for the other members of the family to join them for the journey to church in Inverness. Whether the pony was startled or whether one of the girls said, "Gee up" but it took off with enthusiasm heading in the direction it knew well and dashed into town, turned right and galloped along Academy Street until it came to its usual parking place which was MacRae & Dick's garage. It turned in there but at that speed it failed to fully take the corner so that the left shaft of the trap hit the building and the two terrified girls were thrown out. They came to no great harm but the scar of the shaft was left on the cornerstone. There was little traffic in those days and practically none on the Sabbath, fortunately.

My father was the first Highland minister to own a motorcar – it was ST631, a Wolseley Tourer which was second hand. It was curious that, although the car could, if necessary, be turned into a sort of 'saloon' by putting up the hood and press-studding celluloid curtains along each side, we always travelled in the open air unless it was actually raining or snowing. My father had a fur cap with earflaps and matching gauntlet gloves and mother had a hat tethered by a scarf and a big foot-muff into which her shod feet could go. She enveloped herself in a big rug, either tartan wool or deerskin.

I can recall the heart-stopping speed of 30 mph downhill near Daviot. A lift to a pedestrian was often offered and accepted. You drove on the crown of the road and if another car was spotted approaching both drivers would ease their vehicles towards the left and very slowly pass each other. The ladies would bow their heads graciously and smile to each other while the men would raise their caps in greeting whether they knew each other nor not.

In snowy weather chains were put on all the wheels before setting off, the better to grip the slippery surface. In those days livestock went to market on the hoof causing some delay to a passing motorist, and even more delay to a car hoping to overtake the animals. We knew to leave early on market day to allow for delays.

Bowshers and Horses

Eventually when school days were over, in those days you put your name into some tradesman's for an apprenticeship and if you were lucky you got settled by the age of sixteen. If you left school at fourteen you had to take on the job of a 'bowsher' (message boy). At about 10.30 am till 11 am you would see all the boys pushing their message bikes up Stephen's Brae. What the bosses didn't know was that they all used to exchange messages to deliver and many a time I found myself delivering bread, butcher meat or vegetables all in the one street. It saved you delivering on three or four different streets. At sixteen you either got to work in the shop or started as an apprentice tradesman.

Most message boys had breeches, leather leggings and boots – guards against dogs – and took a pride in polishing them up and they really looked smart. Especially at the games or sports where they used to have the message boys' race with their message bikes. They also had a 'slow race' and some of these lads could sit still (static) on their bikes for ages.

The 'bowshers' used to go around on their message bikes with the baskets in front delivering people's messages (groceries). The used to have a congregating place at the top of Stephen's Brae. They used to exchange parcels – if somebody had a parcel for another part of town – like a message boys' sorting office. It would cut down on their time. My cousin was with a butcher and they used to get their 'scran' on a Friday night, all the bits and pieces of meat to take home for the weekend. I remember my granny making sheep's head broth and she always used to demand the eyes.

I worked as a 'bowsher' for Kings the bakers. I can remember they had an old Scotch oven with a semicircular opening and a big flat table where the bread was shoved in with a wooden 'peel' – a flat board on the end of a long pole because the oven was about twelve or fifteen feet deep and the fire was actually in the oven. It was hot, heavy work and all the ashes came out through a grate in the bottom. All the machines were driven by one big overhead shaft with great big slapping belts which were just inches above your head. When the war was on Kings used to supply huge quantities of rolls to various canteens in the town. I can remember they had big cardboard boxes to put in the carrier of the message bike. I had to cart it and I could hardly see over the top. I remember once on High Street when it was pouring rain, just pouring down, and I'd got this big cardboard box. I grabbed it and the box came up and left all the rolls standing up in a column on my bike for a second before they collapsed and vanished into the gutter.

A Wednesday afternoon and all the message boys had a half day then – the 'bowshers' – and they used to go down to the Citadel, the 'Ramparts' to play football and never came back till 5 o'clock.

All the 'bowshers' used to congregate on Stephen's Brae on a Saturday. If you went out with the Football Times on a Saturday night you got 1d a dozen, if you sold a dozen. We'd be outside the La Scala flogging the Football Times, then over for chips.

The Wool Fair was a very important event and people ran concerts. The Wool Fair was a kind of animal market down at the back of where the Caledonian Hotel is. There used to be rows of horses, Clydesdale and others. I have a bit in my scrapbook 9th July 1937 'Wool Fair Concert'.

Behind the 'Fluke' there used to be a hollow where the horse market was held. It's filled in now but this is where the horses were auctioned off and tinkers would buy them. They were probably working horses.

When we were kids we used to have great fun watching the 'MacAphees' we used to call them (MacPhees) – they were tinkers – especially when the Wool Fair or the horse sales were on the go. I don't know why but they always seemed to end up through the old village (Hilton) and the fields up the road. This night they were going up the road and there was an awful fight and we thought one of them was going to get killed. He got such a beating up but he just got up and shook himself and followed them up Old Edinburgh Road. But on the Monday morning when the man from the sale yard went to collect the sheep to go down to the mart he saw a bundle of rags lying under a bush in the field. When he had a look there was a body under it. A woman who followed them had been murdered. It was about a hundred yards or so down from the old Hilton Farm. MacPhee who murdered her got ten years – that was in 1934.

When I was two years old we moved down to Glebe Street where my grandfather had the Smithy. We stayed at No14 Glebe Street and Granny and Granda stayed at No13 and my two aunties at No10. It was a tenement and this was a great hoot because No10 Glebe Street was the address of the 'Broons' (Sunday Post). There were four houses and the Smithy.

On the south side of Duncraig Street was a blacksmith's smithy occupied by John MacBean who later moved to King Street.

There was a baker at No 4 Duncraig Street, Mr Pirie, and he used to leave his horse at the door. It was a wonderful horse, it used to eat out of a nosebag and we were kids at the time and we used to put our hands in the nosebag and pick out the locust beans. They were brown and sweet and we used to eat them and not once did the horse bite our fingers – it knew. We used to look in its mouth and count its teeth and lift up its hooves to see if it had its shoes on and the horse never touched us.

Then there was the Smithy, MacBean's Smithy, down on Duncraig Street and my young brother worked there. He was a blacksmith to trade. He used to make horseshoes and he loved horses. Sometimes the horses would go to sleep standing up when you were shoeing them and you'd have to give them a heave to waken up.

There was a Smithy at Culduthel in those days (1920's) – Simon MacDonald's and he had a great business. His sons were all blacksmiths, there were six of them and you'd hear the anvil going at four in the morning, out working making the horseshoes.

There were only ten houses there and Culduthel Smithy was next to us, that was owned by John MacDonald (1950's), we called him 'Jock the Smith'. The bus that came up from the town every hour went right up to the Smithy. My parents were having a party and all the neighbours were in. My father had been doing some drainage work in the front garden and 'Jock the Smith' left to go home from the party. It had been raining a terrific amount and the following morning we found his hat floating in the garden. There was great amusement – we thought he was actually in the hole – but he wasn't.

There was a passageway through from Deveron Street to Shore Street and there was a blacksmith's shop there. Many an hour was spent watching the horses being shod and I'm sure to this day I could fit a horse with a shoe though not nearly as neatly as these great craftsmen of the anvil.

There was another Smithy on Eastgate and after school we called in to watch these mighty men at work.

In Mary Ann Court there was a large stable where an old carter called Ned used to keep his horse and cart. During the day he was a haulage contractor and he had a great big Clydesdale horse. He used to unhitch the horse and feed it bran and treacle in a bucket as a reward for the day's work. Then he used to take it round to where Eden Court is now, there was a big market garden and just beyond that there was a large field and the horse used to graze there every night. He brought it round from Mary Ann Court along the riverside and if he was in a good mood he might let you ride on the horse's back. The girth of the Clydesdale was so colossal your legs stuck straight out.

On Haugh Road next door to 'The Tap' was a blacksmith – many horses were shod at this establishment.

Law and Order and the Firemen

My father was a fireman and he always had his bicycle pointing out ready to go, so when the fire alarm went off in the house I had to get the bike out in the street and he came belting out and away up to Castle Wynd. The Fire Station at Castle Wynd consisted of the Base and there were two fire engines in that Base which is now part of the Town House. Upstairs was a little office and that's where all the men would meet. In the Base with the fire engines were hooks all the way along with their uniforms on them and their fire boots. These were the kind of engines you sat on the side, hanging on. I got a shot on one once, a new vehicle they were trying out. The thing was all these men were retained firemen. They got a fee every half-year and the rest was for turning out for fires. If you got in the first engine you got 7/6, if it was the second one you got 5/-. So if you missed the first engine you missed out hence the need for speed to get to the Fire Station. The bike was ready to go. This was before the War in 1939.

There was a bell in the house which was very loud and then a box and buzzer thing on two sockets and the Deputy Firemaster's wife would ring this bell from their house above the Fire Station to call out the firemen.

My father was nearly killed in two fires although he never said much about it. There was one particular one in Drummond Street where he was trapped after stuff collapsed. It was at the Douglas Hotel, and I think it was drips of water coming down from the beam above, which kept him going till they got him out. Then in 1939 it became the National Fire Service and that was throughout the whole country.

In my early days the Fire Station was in Castle Wynd right opposite the Police Station. The Firemaster, Mr Treasurer, had to phone the railway where several of his men were working and get them to come to Castle Wynd. They had two horses to bring the fire engine to wherever the fire may be. They had to drive the horses very hard because sometimes the fire could be a good distance away. I can recall one or two accidents where firemen were thrown off the engine with the speed of the horses going round a bend.

The horses were well looked after, very fit and they didn't have much to do. When the horses were on the public roads they were alright but sometimes they had to go off onto rough country roads to say a farmhouse or cottages and it was very difficult not just for the horses but for the driver.

There were several serious fires, one in particular in what is now the Market, that was in my very early days. Some years later in Drummond Street there were three shops burnt to the ground and serious damage done to the back of what is now the Douglas Hotel, but there was no loss of life.

When I was eighteen I joined the Inverness Burgh Police in 1911. In those days you got sent out into the street with an older policeman and you got to know what your duties were. My weekly wage was 23/4. After fifteen years it would be 29/10, that was the maximum pay for a constable. The daily hours of duty were usually 11 hours – you were on duty from 5.45 am to 8.30 am, then 10 am to 2 pm and then from 5 pm to 9.14 pm. On the night shift it was from 8.30 pm till 6.15 am. Very long hours and we got one day off in twenty-one. If the man on the next beat was off on holiday or ill you had to forego your day off and you got no pay for it. For the first three years of service you only got eight days annual leave. During my first twenty years of service no officer was allowed a bike, you had to walk the beat. But for the last few years you could use a bicycle only in cases of emergency. You had to sign for it before taking it from the Police Station and then when you returned, show that it was in good order. In those days there was no Black Maria, so if you had to arrest a man you could well be a mile or so from the Police Station. It was a very severe struggle to arrest a man who was violent, as they often were in those days.

There were twenty-three men in the Burgh Police when I joined, including the Chief Constable.

The main crimes then in the Burgh were theft and breach of the peace and assaults, not the violence we have now and of course there was the drunk and incapable and housebreaking. There was quite a lot of housebreaking going on and the CID were kept pretty busy.

The Chief Constable's room was down in the front of the building and opposite that the Inspector's room. Upstairs the CID room and you had to go upstairs to the court. Opposite the CID room was the witnesses' room for the court, there was the odd trial went on in the court but mostly they were minor things.

The County Police Station was a house in Culcabock Avenue beside the old Stewart's Mill. It was one half the house and the other the Police Station. The policeman had a motorbike and sidecar in those days and how they managed to get them under arrest and take them back with a sidecar I don't know.

There never seemed to be anything desperately criminal then – petty crime and men getting drunk on a Friday night and coming home and their wives getting the worst of it. You would hear some screams and shouts but that was all. It was never taken to court.

The police were on the beat in the streets when war broke out and they were rounding up Italians who were in Inverness at the time. I know one of them was really frightened and they chased him right up the stairs in Academy Street past the office door and right up to the top of the building. He was frightened because he didn't know what was happening.

Because of lack of traffic then we were quite safe playing on the road. I recall someone would say, "The Ferret's on his way" and this would be the old policeman who would cycle very, very slowly up Bruce Gardens. All the kids would disappear and hide behind the fence until he was gone.

The police used to go round then, there used to be notices on the main corners of Church Street, High Street, Academy Street and Inglis Street saying, "No Loitering" and if the kids hung around at these corners the police would come along and say, "Move on boys" and that was it – they were chased.

I can't remember anyone talking about crime when I was young. There was plenty of pinching apples and I was caught a couple of times coming out of the skating rink because it backed onto Kenneth Street where a minister lived and he had a great garden of apples. I remember climbing over the fence with a jersey full of apples and getting caught by Mr Lumsden (local policeman). He gave me a kick up the tail end and told me to get lost. He didn't tell my father because I might have got another belt on the ear for being caught – not for pinching the apples.

On 10th September 1923 I joined the Police up at the Castle. My first posting was to Kingussie on the 4th March 1924 but before going there I was doing relief duty at Ardersier and I came back by train. No buses then, I got a train from Ardersier to Gollanfield then you had to change over and into Inverness. There was a terrific snowstorm, a real blizzard, and I went into Inverness and up to the Castle and was told I was being posted to Kingussie on the Tuesday. My folks lived out at Dores then and I was getting the weekend off and going out to Dores on the Saturday but the roads were blocked and I couldn't get out, the bus wasn't running. I had to walk up to Muirtown and get on the steamer out to Aldourie Pier and had to walk from there – about a mile or so to Dores.

On the way in to the Police Station that morning, it was the day of the Nairn Games, I was on a racing push bike coming in Island Bank Road and they were making the tennis courts at Bellfield Park and I took my eyes off and looked up. My hands were resting lightly on the handlebars and there was a stone on the road. They'd been carting stones for this tennis court and the front wheel got it and I went flat on my behind – cuts and bruises. It was wooden rims I had on the bike, and they were split all round.

I went into MacKenzie the Chemist on High Street and got bandaged up, then I went up to the Castle and Inspector Robert MacKay was there talking and there was a bit of a snigger. They said they were looking out for a man with a bandage on his hand.

I recall the arrival of the first police car in Inverness, it was a Triumph Dolomite, a long sleek car and the most unlikely thing for a police car. They didn't have any local drivers so the Chief took someone up from the South to teach them. However, this car was not at this stage ready to chase other vehicles so they used to chase boys on bikes – not like the bicycles of today, there was no gears on them, and they had a carrier on the front. You could have up to a hundredweight on it (these were message boys' bikes). The boys would be about fourteen or fifteen and they would have to push them up Castle Street Brae. At the top where the brae branched off to Gordon Terrace, Old Edinburgh Road and Culduthel Road there would be up to a dozen boys there first thing in the morning and it would sometimes be reported to the Chief Constable that the boys were holding up the traffic and the police car would be sent up.

One day a police officer caught me when I was riding my new bike – I got a new bike for going to the Academy – I think it cost 12/6. I was cycling it over the Greig Street Bridge and who came out of a licensed premises but a policeman and he caught me and gave me a right 'durrach' on the lug. When I went home I said nothing but the following week when I got home on the Thursday I got a right hammering. I wondered what it was for but my father had got a summons for me to appear at the Juvenile Court on the Saturday for cycling on the Greig Street Bridge. So I had to report to a Mr Masson at 10 am on the Saturday and sit in this room with a bunch of delinquents. I couldn't even get to the football. I had to sit for an hour every Saturday for a whole month and I thought it was all over when I got the 'durrach' on the lug. My father belted me – a terrible thing, my mother and father knowing their son was up in court. I never did it again. I think it did me a lot of good – it made sure I never did it again.

The gas lamps – well we used to find we were in darkness occasionally and we used to ask our parents why we were in darkness, because the man used to come with the wooden pole and turn them on at night. Then we discovered that he was a member of the Fire Service and he couldn't be in two places at the one time. Then eventually about 9 or 10 in the evening he would reappear and they would go on. He was doubling up. I remember them going out of the old Fire Station up behind the Town House.

The Riot Act of 1919

When the Yanks were here there was a riot in town, up in High Street. We were young then and we didn't bother, but the Yanks were chased out of town and they were kept at a base at the Carse. Jack, my husband, was living in Castle Wynd at the time and it happened in High Street, they saw it all.

I remember about 1918/19 being taken to Bridge Street. There was a milling crowd of Cameron Highlanders and American sailors – a riot – when our soldiers, on returning from the war, found their girlfriends had been pinched by the American sailors.

There was a big number of Americans employed at the Carse making mines for the Navy at that time and they had a patrol came through the town – eighteen men and a patrol leader. They were on duty in the town every evening. On this particular occasion one of the Police Constables on duty had to stick close to the patrol leader because he was under the influence of liquor and he became very abusive. The result was he had to be arrested. The eighteen men plus several hundred other Americans came up to the Police Station demanding the release of the patrol leader and I and all the other constables available were called in. We had to draw batons and charge and fight them down to High Street. At this particular time there were hundreds of ex-servicemen come home. The war was over and they were delighted to get the opportunity of attacking the Americans because they claimed that during the war these Americans who were in this area went away with their girlfriends.

A real battle took place on Bridge Street. Bridge Street from top to bottom was blocked with people. We were spoken to by many ex-servicemen saying we were doing our duty very well locking up the patrol leader and giving a rough time to all these Americans who were employed in Inverness at that time.

Note – It is believed that the Riot Act was read from the Town Hall steps to quell the riot and the Americans were shipped out the next day.

The Worthies and Wanderers

Oh Yes – 'Cappy Eppie' She used to play the melodeon and 'Forty Pockets' another old man who used to go about the Town – very tall in a long black coat and an old fashioned hard hat and he always had a pocket full of 'smokies' (sweets). He always gave us one or two and then we'd dodge round the corner and meet him again and he'd give us one or two more – he was a nice gentleman.

One of the best-known characters the (20's & 30's) was 'Sugar Legs' so called because he was very rarely sober and walked on wobbly legs. One of the jobs he held down for at least a month was as a general dogsbody at the nursery on Telford Street. He was told to take a hurly of manure to a house on Crown Drive. The wifie was a snob and when she came to the door 'Sugar Legs' said to her "Mrs Shaw?" "No" she said, "Mrs Sh-haw". "Oh well," he said, "in that case I've a load of sh*-** at the door for you".

Another character was 'Rory paint the siskin' and that's what he did. He used to catch the siskins on the shore at South Kessock and paint them yellow and sell them as canaries in a wee cardboard box for 1/6d.

There was another chap called 'Cheerio'. I remember him when I was a young boy. In the 1930's there used to be a policeman on point duty at the junction of Church Street and Queensgate from 5.15 pm till 5.45 pm at the end of the working day. 'Cheerio' would wait until the policeman disappeared then he would don a pair of white gloves, pull down his cap at a rakish angle and direct the rest of the evening traffic from the middle of the street.

We used to have a regular visit from 'Cappy Eppie' who used to come over the Black Bridge and down Grant Street. She always ate raw mince and seemed to be quite happy with her pipe in her mouth and the mince in a paper in her hand.

There was another man, George Stewart, 'Geordie the Dude'. He was beautifully dressed but a bit retarded but what attracted me was he had a beautiful gold tooth in the front and I couldn't take my eyes off this. He used to walk up and down the pavements talking aloud and shouting out.

Jock Gellon had a horse and cart with a big tank of paraffin at the back and he would go around Grant Street selling the paraffin for the lamps. The boys would turn on the taps and tell him his tank was leaking. He would go round the area shouting "Paraffeen" and the local youngsters would ask, "What do you feed your horse on?" and "Paraffeen" would be the shout.

We had a lot of characters – there was 'Cheerio' and Annie Bobo and a wifie with an accordion she couldn't play. On the foot of the Market Brae steps at the top of Inglis Street there was a black man called Joe who used to sell newspapers. There was a story about 'Cheerio'. Seemingly some woman said to him "If you ever see an old pram I could do with it". It was probably to carry coal or cinders. The story goes that he stole a pram from a close off Bridge Street when a woman carried her child into MacDonald's the ironmongers leaving the pram in the close. 'Cheerio' then sold the pram to the wifie who'd asked him to find her one.

There was the case of the 'Sutherland Lass' a coal boat owned by a chap from Brora. It had ceased to function and make money so they decided to scuttle it. Capt Gunn was skipper when they scuttled it out on the Firth. There was a big court case and 'Cheerio' who was in the crew was asked in court "Where were you when the boat was sinking?" "I was down in the bowels of the boat with a hammer and chisel getting the water in quicker," he said.

There was Black Lil's cottage and pond. We all thought she was a witch. She went to town on pension day with an old pram and dressed all in black and came home much inebriated.

We were pretty afraid of 'Forty Pockets'. He lived sometimes in the 'Model' down Chapel Street. There were often fights there. Some of them would play the mouth organ and one of them would play the spoons on his knees. There was another one 'Geordie the Dude' there. Today they would be sleeping rough I think.

There was 'Forty Pockets' that would be in the 30's and 40's. Then there was the man at the Greig Street Bridge who had a hurdy-gurdy – like an old gramophone, that was 'Clayack'. Then there was 'Cappy Eppie', she used to wear a bonnet pulled down over her face, she was a bent sort of wifie but she was a harmless soul. Some people called her 'Cacky Eppie' but it was 'Cappy Eppie'.

There was a mannie Craig who played a melodeon at the Greig Street Bridge and Wattie Clark who had an old pram with a gramophone with a horn on the top and stood and played the same tune all the time at the Clach Park.

There was another old character who stayed further down in what was a little road which runs through the Golf Course now (Torvean GC) Mile-End Cottage. It was a little black cottage with a flat black corrugated tarred roof. We used to call her 'Black Lil' because she lived in this little house. She was a bit fond of a dram and she would be coming home at night muttering to herself and we were dead scared of her, we thought she was a witch and we'd run into the house and say we'd seen 'Black Lil coming'.

Like all towns we had our 'worthies'. One I particularly remember was 'Joe Hoe'. He wore a top hat and opera cloak and went around reciting verses from Shakespeare. There was the 'Maggot Poet' who wore a 'cheese-cutter' hat and sold his poems for a penny and there was a coloured man with lovely eyes who sold newspapers in the street in all weathers.

We had regular beggars called after their line of patter or their appearances like 'Spare a Copper' or 'Forty Pockets'. There was music in the streets too by some of these buskers who wandered around looking for money. There was one old couple who regularly toured the streets, him with an orange box which his wife (or daughter) sat on while he sang 'Rock of Ages' or 'In the Good Old Summertime'.

Another old worthy that used to be in the town was 'Forty Pockets'. He used to wear three or four pairs of trousers and all rags. They called him 'Forty Pockets', he'd about six or seven coats on – he lived rough, of course, he was a right vagrant. But we used to be scared of him all right, when I was a kid. He used to wander about and when you saw him you used to get out of the way. He was a wild character. I don't know what he was – was he foreign or not? I've a kind of memory he was foreign from the First World War who just went on the walk. Quite a lot of First World War people took to the road.

There was another mannie, Old Gullon – the paraffin man – he had a carty like a chariot selling paraffin – calling "Paraffeen, Paraffeen". "What do you feed your horse on?" "Paraffeen". He used to go round the doors selling it.

The other worthy – she used to sing in the street 'Rock of Ages'. I think it was her father that was with her – an old mannie, that's what she sang 'Rock of Ages', that's all she sang. I think she teamed up with the guy that used to do the tap dancing after that. Something happened to the old mannie, I think. She teamed up with that bloke – Davy something the name was – he didn't belong to Inverness, I don't know where he came from.

     The other worthy that used to shout in the street was 'Geordie the Dude'. He was respectable. Oh aye – he was from the Stewart's. Crossing the Black Bridge he used to jump out in the middle of the road with something strapped to his wrist and shout and bawl and he would go into the station and he used to look at all the ads and shout them out. But he was in the First World War, he was in the Navy and he was shell-shocked. Oh he was always smart. He used to go down to the Thornbush and get a box of herring and go round the doors with the hurly and the herring and this wifie down in Madras Street, somewhere down there, she says to him, "What's the matter with your herring, they're no very fresh Geordie?" and he lifted the whole box of herring and put it over the wifie.

The other guy was 'Clayuck', he used to play the melodeon at Greig Street Bridge as well. He used to go into the graveyard and take the white heather off the graves and flog it on Chapel Street.

'MUSIC IN THE AIR'
GREIG STREET BRIDGE
(BW.

The other guy that used to knock around there, I think its Davy they called him, he used to tap dance in the street. He had a board and used to go along the street with the board and tap dance and sing. They all lived in the Model – a lot of them.

There was three Model Lodging houses, there was one in Chapel Street, one in Grant Street and one in Dunabban Road. There used to be a mannie with one arm and his stand was at the back door of 'Woolies', in front of the old Savings Bank and he used to draw with chalk on the pavement. He used to sit cross-legged there. I don't know what his name was. He used to have cardboards drawings as well and Chapel Street was another place he went. Of course they all lived in the Model – most of them anyway. There was another chap – what was his name? Remember he worked in the Gas Works for a while, he used to be at the back of Dunk's House, yonder when he used to take the coke out – the ashes. A great Caley man. Was it Wilson?

Oh the wee fellow – he lived in the Model too. They had a name for him – Ebbie Wilson. He lived in there a while too. He was making a bit of money then taking the coke and putting it into bags – 3d a bag – he was making a fortune at that time. He stayed at the Model. This other bloke, he used to look after the rooms for them or something and he was the cook.

Several other 'Worthies' of that era whose names didn't get a mention are 'Aleckie Duff' who would follow any band or procession through the streets. He was particularly fond of the British Legion Pipe Band. He was a simple soul but totally harmless and people enjoyed watching his antics as much as they enjoyed the music.

'Tubbac or Tubbac Lil' – a lady who had some deformity and frequented the Market although she did not seem to beg, but no doubt was given the odd copper or two.

Gaelic

Education was one of my father's great interests and he became a good linguist. He was able to learn Gaelic and to speak it reasonably fluently. He was certainly able to address the Inverness Gaelic Society of which he was Chief.

I don't mind (remember) if there was much Gaelic spoken in Inverness in the early days. My husband's mother and father, they belonged to Stratherrick and they both spoke Gaelic, they spoke Gaelic among themselves. They never taught the bairns to speak it. Any anything they wanted to say between themselves, well they spoke to each other in Gaelic.

My grandfather wasn't local, he belonged to Nigg in Easter Ross. He was a Gaelic speaker and he could read, write and speak the Gaelic. My maternal grandmother, who I didn't really know because she died in the middle of the first World War, she could speak some Gaelic. She came from Lentran on the outskirts of the Town.

Politics

My wife was a suffragette in the early 1900's and she was supported by Provost Alexander MacEwan whose wife was even more supportive.

I remember vividly the only time the British Cabinet met outside London, and that was in the Town House of Inverness in September 1921. I was on duty that particular day at the Station and met five Cabinet Ministers and had my photograph taken with them. Lloyd George, the Prime Minister was in Wester Ross on holiday at the time as Parliament was in recess and three of his Cabinet Ministers were up in Sutherland. The Irish question was so serious at that time that Lloyd George decided to call a Cabinet Meeting in Inverness. I can recall meeting Churchill on the Exchange as they were going into the Town Hall. He said he was very happy to be in such a lovely town and I quite agreed with him.

My father's time as Provost was generally regarded as being of quite a standing and he was particularly interested in public (Council) housing. He was a pioneer in the field of public housing. This was before the first World War. He was also keenly interested in the development of Hydro Electricity and at that time there was a relatively minor Hydro Scheme over at the Bught.

My grandfather was Joseph MacLeod and he was on the Council for many years. He would always be holding meetings here and there. He was always topping the poll, and when he got a good vote he would say "A vote like that is a plumper". He covered the Crown area as his ward. He used to live in Ardconnel Terrace and then he moved to 41 Crown Drive and that's where he stayed till he died. He was also Sir Murdoch MacDonald's political agent. He had an office in the High Street yonder, round about where the Maypole would have been.

I don't know how many people have heard of the Guildry Corporation. What was it? Who were they? Does it still exist? The ancient Corporation of Trades and Traders of Inverness goes back a long way. First mentioned in the charter of James V1 in 1591, it was originally formed for the purpose of establishing a fund which could be used to help members, their families or employees. I'm sure at that time outsiders would have considered Highlanders a wild bunch, the wood still damp under their oxters and still using square wheels. Not so! Cynics might say that it was more of a protection racket, a closed shop or an early trade union. Perhaps it was, just a little, but the formation of it so long ago, showed an amazing awareness of the needs of its citizens. Through the years the purpose of the Guildry has changed and latterly or perhaps I should say that until comparatively recently, its main duty was to pay annuities to deserving native born Invernessians. The bye-laws of the Incorporation were sanctioned by the Scottish Court of Session in July 1887 and at that time, entry was restricted to members, their sons and grandsons, with an annual fee of £1. Eventually other prospective members could be admitted, with approval, on an entry fee of £5, annual subscription of £1. The rules under the modified bye-laws stipulated that the sons of prior members must carry on a business as traders or merchants in Inverness or the surrounding districts, but these provisions have always been interpreted reasonably loosely in accordance with the wishes and guidance from the Dean and Council of the Incorporation.

I was admitted as a member in 1969, my father having been a member many years before that. In fact, in a Minute of 1859, the attendance of Alexander Kelly is recorded as Hatter. That's when the business was in Queensgate. I noted that on becoming a member, the membership showed that all were prominent members of the business community, shopkeepers, manufacturers, wholesalers and even the odd landowner. They were the doers of the community, those who risked their own capital, arranged their own loans and employed and cared for staff, whether clerical or manual workers. There were no Boards then. Readiness, enterprise, imagination and sound common sense were the ingredients of the day, and still is true today – putting your money where your mouth is they call it.

As I'd previously mentioned, the Court of Session of 1887 ratified the bye-laws and also confirmed that the first official Dean of the Guild was appointed 1649, this being taken from the Town Council records which state that the Dean was appointed 'on the application of the merchants'. However, no Minute book was kept until 1696 when an Alexander Duff of Drummore was noted as the Dean and the body of that time contained a list of 70 members which showed that it was certainly flourishing in those days. Also considering the economic climate in the population at that time, it shows remarkable awareness of the public spirit and a commendable co-operation between various factors in business. Indeed was it not a very early Chamber of Commerce or perhaps a more parochial CBI?

To come back to the funding, in those earlier days the funds were composed of entry money paid by new members, annual contributions, fines for non-attendance and pew rents for sitting in the Parish Church (that would be the Old High). An additional income which came later, in the 19th century was from feu duties from properties purchased in Inverness and believe it or not, in Aberdeen. This would have been seen as the nearest centre of commerce in addition to Inverness of course. The revenues of the Guildry were primarily applied for the benefit of older members for the relief of the poor and the crippled and for the widows and children of past members. Grants were also made from the said funds 'in aid of various pious uses and charitable and public purposes intending to promote the good of the Guildry and the community of Inverness'. Furthermore, it just goes to show the involvement of the Guildry. Funds were used 'for the paving and the watching of the streets, for building bridges over the Ness and the erection of the Courthouse'. It's a wonder they ever needed a Town Council at all in those days. One other thing, funds were used for the encouragement of the linen trade in the town, this industry being one of the main sources of labour for a considerable number of years and the export of which led to the further expansion of the harbour. A snippet regarding the funds – in 1883 the funds of the Guildry were recorded as being £3000, no small sum in those days. In the same year the Burgh Reform Act was passed by which the management of the Guildry was formally separated from the affairs of the Town Council. There must have been a fair degree of overlapping leading up to that.

This is where politics enter the arena. The format stipulated that previous privileges of the Guildry were withdrawn by statute, so that 'it should be lawful for any person to carry on or deal in merchandise'. This was the beginning of the end for the local Mafia – sorry the local Guildry – and thereafter it was basically a philanthropic organisation. Maybe it should have been the Town

Council that lost its powers, leaving the good, honest traders to run the town.

In the last 60 years or more, the Guildry has carried out its duties, not so much under a cloak of secrecy, as some people say, but rather with a degree of anonymity in keeping with the natural humility of citizens who decry the need of kudos and status, seemingly essential on today's public stage. It was nevertheless considered a great privilege and sign of approval to be asked to join the Guildry and I personally viewed my membership in that way. It was made virtually redundant by the welfare state and all its trappings but I was very proud of its origin.

Finally one little story of Inverness, which illustrates that nothing has really changed. In the Minute book of 1902, the Dean remarked on the poor attendance at the previous four meetings. He put forward a motion, passed unanimously that members should get an attendance allowance of 10/6 forthwith. It is interesting but not surprising that the following meeting had an attendance of twenty-three, an all time record.

Anecdotes

The stories which follow, come under no particular heading. They are simply reminiscences, funny, sad or interesting and too good to be left out. They are passed on to you as they were told to the interviewer.

Rat's Tail

"There were a lot of families in Church Street then. Above all the shops there were flats which are still there and also families in Manse Place and Bow Court. A friend of mine got married and had a house in the bottom of Bow Court with two rooms. One Saturday night him and the wife were in the front room and he heard a buaraching in the wall. He said "that's a B-rat" and he stood up and looked at the fireplace and there was a wee gap between the fireplace and the wall. All of a sudden a big rat's tail comes through it so he grabbed a hold of it. He says "what'll I do now?" as he couldn't get at it, so he took up the poker and says "you'll remember me you B...." and he had the rat's tail. He heard a squeal and the rat disappeared. There was a lot of rats around in these days as there was so many food shops."

Shepherds

"The sheep sales started on a Monday afternoon and continued all day Tuesday. When you would see a shepherd bidding for sheep you'd say "Do you want a hand with the sheep through the town?" He'd say "Yes – can you get another two boys – I've 40 or 50 sheep". Once he got them out on to Eastgate you turned right and went down Inglis Street. You had to block off Hamilton Street and High Street – that's what he wanted the two boys for – to keep the sheep on Academy Street. Then you'd to block off Station Square and Union Street, Queensgate and Strothers Lane. You went right down past the Cemetery and Chapel Street and he would give you threepence each."

Tripe

"We'd a chap that used to work in the gas works with us. He had one leg off from the hip and had a wooden leg. He loved tripe and every time my mother made tripe he always got a bowl. He says "I'll get my own tripe and cook it". So he got the tripe and I went up to see what he was doing with it and here he is sitting with the raw tripe cutting it up with scissors."

Plane Park

"A lot of strange things happened during the war. I recall something that happened in Farraline Park. The RAF decided to put all the wrecked aircraft from the North of Scotland in a great pile in the middle of this area where the buses are nowadays. I can remember it was a storage dump stacked high in the air. They were practically all British aircraft but there was the odd Nazi one among it. It did seem a very strange location."

For Sale

"I remember Fraser's Auction Rooms in Baron Taylor's Lane where the back of Arnotts is now. They always used to hang out a flag 'Auction Sale Today' – a red flag. One night they forgot to take it in and the next morning it was found at MacAvoys (next to the Playhouse) and it was stuck in the hand of the soldier who stood on the steps. (Note – this was a full size model soldier)."

Milko

"I remember when the milkman's horse used to bolt and ten gallon milk cans would fly into the air spilling their contents all over the streets. The cats and dogs came from here, there and everywhere and had the time of their lives. Eventually some brave Galahad would stop the horse."

Hot Dripping

"We used to go to the grocers for a halfpenny bag of broken biscuits. Burnetts used to do that – we used to go in for a penny bag and a box of cakes for sixpence. If you were very rich you could buy a hot pie for 1½d or a hot fruit cake for a penny. I remember the hot dripping from Burnetts – I used to buy it and put it on toast."

Jazz Fans

"There were funny incidents at the Northern Meeting Rooms. Two old ladies from Old Edinburgh Road, when they saw in the papers that Johnny Dankworth and Cleo Laine were on, used to take a box in the Meeting Rooms which was never otherwise open to the public. They were sisters about seventy years of age and we used to open up the box and they used to have the use of the toilet which was kept specially for Princess Margaret with a velvet seat on it."

Man Overboard

"Down at the Thornbush there was a boat in and we were about to start discharging cement about three in the morning – we used to start regularly at 3 am until 10 o'clock at night. The gangway had been put ashore from the ship and it was at an angle. I didn't realise the ship must have moved slightly, with the result that there was nothing holding the gangway aboard the ship where I was going on board. The gangway capsized and I went straight down. I went down head first in the mud. A few of the boys were about and they got a rope, got down on a ladder and dragged me up."

Drammies

"We had a lot of marriages from the West Coast and Stornoway in the Royal Hotel. Then when the Mod was on we had a terrific week – whisky was flowing like water. We were working until three and four in the morning, a long day and then back to work at 10 am. There was one thing about the West Coast people, they could fairly hold their drink but there was never any rows. On the Friday night, the last night, we had six serving in the bar and six doing the glasses. But you should have seen the lounge after four in the morning – it was like a football pitch."

Monkey Trick

"There was a girl from the village (Clachnaharry) and her father before her. They were all sea-faring people. Her father took home a monkey as a pet but it was banished because it used to go up the chimney and drop things down. It was banished to the town but it used to go up the spire on the Catholic Church and tie 'clooties' to it. So it was banished again but I don't know where it went to."

The 'Borrower'

"We had a rabbit man, we had rabbits delivered for many years and he came from Arpafeelie on the Black Isle, beautiful rabbits trapped there. He came at 10 am and sold my mother a pair of rabbits. Then at 5 pm he came back to borrow a shilling because he'd been to local hostelries and all the money he'd made was gone and he didn't have money for the Kessock Ferry Boat to take him home. Come the next week the rabbit man duly arrived with his rabbits and the shilling was repaid. This went on week after week – the shilling paid out one week and repaid the next – so in the end I think my mother must have lost the shilling because the rabbit man disappeared and we never saw him again."

Looking Up

"On Saturday night the shop didn't shut until 8 pm and we worked until 9 pm. One of us would come out still in our working whites, go into the middle of the street and call the others. Two of them would be in the close and one would come out, he would point up to the Steeple and they would shake their heads, and call the third one out. After another pointing session and before you knew it, you'd have fifty people in the middle of High Street all looking at the Steeple and pointing. We would do this about once a month as there were a lot of people from the country in town on a Saturday night. The Chief Constable came in to see the boss and said "This will have to stop – you're holding up the traffic on High Street on a Saturday night". The boss was as good at this game as the boys and he said "Away and chase yourself – one cab and horse on High Street at that time of night – where's the traffic?" The Chief Constable went away."

Feeding the Animals

"When I lived in Church Street there were all sorts of functions took place – the Empire Theatre – they actually held a circus there. As a child I remember lions roaring at the back of our house. They kept some of the animals at the back of the Theatre. Amongst them was a poor little elephant which they couldn't get into our close so they took it into the next close and the poor elephant got stuck. They had to chip away the stones to get it out. I remember looking out one day and there was a big bear walking along. We got quite pally with the bear because the baker's shop next door used to have little cup cakes which had jam in them and the old bear used to come up and eat the jam off them."

L-Plates

"There was one old boy who had a Baby Austin, he was a farmer, a big tall farmer and he was going down High Street towards the junction with Inglis Street and he was learning to drive. There was a Bobby on point duty at the corner and the farmer put his head out of the Baby Austin, which had a sunroof and shouted "Get oot o' ma road. Do you no see I'm coming". The Bobby waved him on."

Shut that Door

"I was standing on High Street – this would be the 60's I think and there was one or two closes which are blocked off now. But I was standing speaking to a chap and I was facing this close and behind the line of shops there was this little paved courtyard with old houses on each side. I was looking at this, at the two outside doors and the one on the right flew open and there was a man sitting on the toilet! That was in the middle of High Street in the 1960's."

Up the Close

"On Bridge Street there was one little bit where you went through into this close where there was a street lamp. There was a chap MacPherson who had an optician's shop there. He wasn't a qualified optician but he sold spectacles and things. His brother had a small antique shop on Castle Street. He would buy things in Fraser's Auctions and sell them for a few pounds more in his shop."

Upper Classes

"We were at the top of the trade and we used to attract people from all over. We had Royalty coming in during August and September. A Maharajah came in one day – before my time – and in those days there used to be lots of things hanging above the counters. The Maharajah pulled things down, looked at them and threw them on the counter. The assistant walked up to the Maharajah, poked him in the stomach and said "Hey you, put all these things back where you b***** well got them". The owner was mortified."

Penny Crossing

"I was the last one that crossed the bridge. It was on the back of a motor bike. I got a penny from a wifie that was standing in the crowd. Jack was a Councillor and he says to me "Come on Nan, on to the back of the bike". We were the last two that crossed. It was at night after they closed it (to traffic). I've still got the penny. They pulled down most of Bridge Street, Queen Mary's House and Castle Tolmie."

'Feek'

"This fellow used to live in Abban Place, MacDonald was his name but they called him 'Buckie'. He was an awful man for the drink – it was the methylated spirits, 'feek', he was drinking. We were in the terrace and the rhone pipe of his house ran along our garden where there was a dyke. He was a tall man and he used to plank his bottles in the rhone pipe. We used to take them out and clean our windows with it. He died young – it was a shame, he was nice."

Lights Out

"For the travellers who used the hotel in the war years it was lights out at 11 pm. One poor chap who was a traveller for distilleries had a night light on in his room trying to finish a chapter in his book. There was a bang on his door and a roar to get the light out. Another guest arrived late back at the hotel at 11.15 pm and rang the bell – he gave his room number and shortly after his suitcase was thrown out of the window for coming back late.

One day the lady was cleaning the front door when a young 'stirk' broke ranks and ran into the hotel. Through the front door, down a passage to the bar where it was too narrow for it to turn. It had to be escorted to the function room to get it turned and back to the street."

Pig in a Poke

"By 1939 it was all built up (Kessock). The ferry boat was running and there was a big traffic on the boat. You'd get farmers at night. You'd get to the station and there would be a bloke standing with a calf in a bag, the bag.tied at the calf's neck. He would put the bag in the luggage compartment at the back of the bus, down to the ferry and take the calf over on the boat. There were pigs taken on the bus as well."

Turning a Blind Eye

"One of my first jobs was for the old Saxone Shoe Co. When you look at that building (no longer there) on High Street you don't realise it goes right back to the Raining Stairs. Well, we had to put on a new roof, so we took down the old roof and had it stacked till Wednesday afternoon, half day in town and got a big lorry from Robertsons. The lorry driver went off for his dinner and my boys and the slater's boys were carting the stuff out when along came a young 'Bobby'. "Who's lorry's that?" he says, "You'll have to move it". Then along comes Sergeant Watson, he'd spotted this on his way down Castle Wynd. He never let on he knew me and says to the young

Constable "Are you having a problem?" – "Yes Sergeant" – "Well" says Sgt Watson, "Where does your beat extend to along there?" and he pointed along High Street towards Eastgate. "Oh along as far as Lochgorm Sergeant". "Well" says Sergeant Watson "if you go along there slow enough and come back slow enough, by the time you come back this'll all be gone". Then he turned on his heel and went back up Castle Wynd."

The Veteran

"If you go down Drummond Road where the Aultnaskiach burn comes through, there was an old man from the Poor House used to sit on the stone wall of the bridge. He was a veteran from the famous long march from Kabul to Kandahar sometime in the 1880's when they were fighting in India. He used to take birds in his hand – they knew him so well he had them tamed, they would sit on his finger and he would give them crumbs. He was a nice old man, a most unfortunate end for a man like that."

The Auctioneer

"He was an auctioneer and he knew everybody. When he had a sale on the women used to book their seats to come in and hear him. We also had another sale, my father was involved too, and they sold produce, butter, eggs, hens, whatever, and we used to bring them in live and you could buy a hen for a shilling. We would say 'alive or dead' – he would just pull its neck there and then."

Camping

"Willie went into the saleroom this day and found a paraffin stove, he took it home and put on a little kettle but he found it took four hours to boil it. He and his mate went camping so they set the alarm for 4 am. The other fellow woke up and lit the stove then went back to sleep. They woke up hours later and found it had a smoke leak. He said to Willie, "My God – Paul Robeson". They were as black as the devil."

Public Convenience

"Most of the Councillors were businessmen or landowners but this particular year one of the first Socialists gained a seat. The discussion was on whether the Council should sanction the building of a lavatory beside the suspension bridge. The Provost asked the opinion of all the Councillors but realised he had left out the new member "Sorry Councillor M" he said, "What do you think about building a urinal on Bridge Street?" 'M' stuck his fingers in his braces and said, "Yes Mr Provost, I think we should build a urinal, but I think we should have an 'arsenal' as well"."

Queensgate Grazing

"I remember my father telling me when he was a young man he remembered sheep in a field on Queensgate. He remembered that when Mafeking was relieved all the youths of the town went round searching for hurlies and took them to Queensgate and had a huge bonfire. The Police could do nothing about it there were so many of them."

The Bear

"The auctioneers were given the job of selling the contents of a shooting lodge in Sutherland after the death of the owner who had spent most of his life in India. One of the items was a 6ft Himalayan bear standing on its hind legs with arms outstretched and fangs bared.

Willie Michie started off "Who will give me £20 – nobody, well £10" – no offers. "What about a fiver" – again no offers. So Willie rapped his desk and said, "Right. I'll take it myself for £2".

"A BEAR RAISING INCIDENT AT DAVIOT"

G.W.

He had a friend, a minister at Daviot, so he said to the van driver "Next time you're going south, would you put this bear off at the Manse and hand him this card". A week later the driver arrived at the Manse, took the bear off the van, put it on the doorstep and rang the bell. The minister came out and was handed the card which said "From a grateful parishioner". The minister was flummoxed and he put the thing in his garage.

Six months later he put the bear down into Fraser's saleroom on Church Street. Along comes Willie Michie – up comes the bear "Who'll give me £20 for it" – nobody. "A fiver"– no, "Och well" he said, "I'll have it myself for £2". So what did he do? He said "Next time the van's going to Daviot will you put this off at the Manse and give him this card". The driver delivered the bear and handed the card to the minister. It read, "I heard you had one so I thought you'd like a pair"."

Christmas

"I remember crying at Christmas time. My mother was a widow and went out to work for 10/- a week. That was four of us existing on 10/- a week. So there wasn't much money for Christmas. So what we got was always an apple and an orange and much to my disgust I either got a jersey or a pair of boots – and that was the last thing I wanted for Christmas. I remember the lot of us were down in the dumps because that's all we got – that would be about 1926."

The Cabbie's Door

"When I returned from the war in February 1919 I was put into the Railway Station because at that time the Station had the Burgh Police, it was still the Highland Railway. The LMS (London, Midland & Scottish) Railway didn't come to Inverness until 1924. On one occasion I was in Station Square and a lady visitor to town complained she was being abused by a drunk man. I spoke to the man and he was very abusive so I attempted to arrest him. I went and spoke to a cabbie to ask if he would give me a hand but he said he wasn't a strong man. However I managed to get the drunk man into the cab and said "Drive me to the Police Station on Castle Wynd".

We struggled in the cab up Inglis Street and along High Street and at the foot of Castle Street the door and a part of the side of the cab gave way and we both fell out on to the street at the very foot of Castle Street. By now the cabman was at the foot of Castle Wynd unaware that part of his cab was lying in the street, but when he stopped he came back and I asked him to go up to the Police Station, get assistance and a warder and constable came down and eventually he was arrested. It turned out that he was a soldier from Northern Ireland and at that time he was a champion boxer there."

The Witch

"My great-grandfather was a master tailor and he was making a suit for a wedding and just the night before the wedding the trousers disappeared and they couldn't find them anywhere. Eventually in desperation they went to this woman, she lived upstairs, but before she got up the stairs she shouted "If you're wanting Mr Urquhart's trousers they're in Kirsty's kist" and she went and found that the girl who was working cleaning the house – had pinched them for her boyfriend. This old woman was blind but she had the second sight – or so they claimed, that was in Church Street."

Farraline Park

"Farraline Park where the Library is now, I can remember there was soup kitchens there as well. Two friends and I, we managed to get into the rafters above and we were looking down on to the soup kitchen – I think we managed to prevent one of them from dropping a dead mouse into one of the soup pans."

Pot Luck

"There was a Mrs Urquhart who lived across the landing from us when we first got married and she was nearly blind – very little sight. She had taken an enormous stock of tins in (beginning of the war) but the trouble was she couldn't read the labels and half the labels had got damp and fallen off anyway. At the most awkward times she'd come to the door just when you were dashing off and say "Read out and tell me what's on that labels", then of course she had trouble remembering which was which."

Landslide

"The path behind our house started to crack right to the gates of the Castle. My old grandfather who was a stonemason told the authorities they should see to it, so they poured concrete into the crevice. I was playing at a dance that night and when I got home at 3 in the morning I took my dog round the Castle Hill for a walk. I just got into bed when I heard this terrible noise and rushing of water. We all ran out and the houses had collapsed. The night before in the hall, which had just been built, there had been about two hundred youngsters. I remember thinking how lucky the children were when the landslide happened only hours afterwards, but no one was badly hurt. I went round to the back of the Castle after the landslide and you could see the people in their houses as if a wall had been sliced off. When the calamity happened my grandfather was very angry at the 'powers that be', shaking his stick at them, but a policeman came and took him away from the scene – he was so angry at them."

Piggies

Dunbar Hospital on Church Street had little rooms upstairs with very, very low windows, which are still there, and very low ceilings. I remember my father telling us that in those days there were so many animals kept alive up in the attic spaces. They were keeping pigs up there and they used to open the windows to give them a breath of fresh air and on one occasion one of the little pigs fell out on to the pavement and was killed. It just goes to show you what the conditions were like and what the smell would have been like.

'Halifax'

We had two wintering yards. One was in George Street, but a bigger one was in Muirtown Street. It was big enough to hold all our goods and chattels and our horse. We had a big stable to keep the horse and we also had a donkey before the circus disbanded. This donkey was called 'Halifax' and it stayed on the right hand side of the stables, and we had outside toilets at the side of the stables. Poor 'Halifax' took ill and the vet told us he was very ill, but a donkey never died in front of anybody, it waited until it was on its own before it died. We didn't believe this, but my brothers and uncles took hour about to stay up all night with 'Halifax' and the donkey just lay there and they would be patting it, it had been a really good servant to us. My uncle got up from the stable and went out to the toilet, he was only seconds away, but when he came back in, poor 'Halifax' was dead. He got a very good burial.

The Haymakers

I remember when I was about seven or eight and Urquhart the Seedsman had a place, it's where Drummond School is now, but it was a nursery then. I was up there with Billy Urquhart helping to make up the hay and when he had finished raking it up he still had the graip in his hand and he stuck it into the ground but it went through my foot.

We pulled it out and fortunately his father arrived at that moment and took me home and Dr Kerr came and fixed me up. He took a steel thing and put it through the hole and he said, "You watch and you'll see it coming through the other side" and then he said, "If you're walking in a week's time I'll give you a sixpence". I got the sixpence.

Two Old Friends Reminisce

He was a great boy, great on the physical stuff – only one leg but he would tackle anything. He got a fishing rod and waders and he went fishing in the river, wading with one leg off from here. So he's out there casting at the Friars Shott thonder, suddenly the leg went floating up and he's standing in the middle of the river with the fishing rod on one leg trying to push the wooden leg down. It went up with the current, the current pushed it up you see. So eventually he managed to turn round and the current pulled it down again.

He lost his leg with the Gas Works' big heavy wagon. It was actually an engine that used to take the coal from the siding in the Railway in Longman Road. He used to drive it from the siding up to the Gas Works – it was all taken by rail then, the coal for the Gas Works. When he got his leg off he cycled with just one leg. Before he got the artificial leg I remembered him with a crutch. He had this bike, just an ordinary bike with one pedal off and he used to cycle to Glasgow from Inverness in the summer holiday, home to his people in Glasgow. When I was a boy he got a new bike and he gave me the bike with the one pedal, just before the war that was. I had the bike for a long time.

I'll tell you a laugh about the bloke with the bicycle. New Year's morning I was up seeing him and he was going to Glasgow on the early train. He says, "I'll take the bike over" and I says, "I'll go over with you and take the bike back". Right so we gets over to the station and gets him on the train and I'm coming back with the bike and gets up on to the bridge and there's two blokes coming with a good shot. "By God, says one, you must have had it hard in the war". I says, "Aye, El Alamein".

Aye he used to go home to Glasgow on New Year's morning, that's when the trains ran then. We

395

went back to his house, and started making our breakfast. We made the porridge and bacon and eggs. I don't think we were home for three days.

Kessock Ferry Song

(To the tune of Galway Bay)

Have you ever been across the Kessock Ferry
To gather brambles on a holiday
Have you ever boiled a kettle near the
lighthouse
And watched the Avochies in Munlochy Bay

Just to hear again the landlord shout 'last
orders'
In that Hotel beside the Kessock Pier
Or to wash your sweaty feet in cool clear
water
Is a luxury that working men hold dear

How the breezes blowing over from the
Longman
Are not heather perfumed that is so
And the woman waiting at the Ferry bus stop
Speaks a language only Irish navvies know

To a stranger they will just say what they're
thinking
In no uncertain manner that I know

And before he even bats an eye
Or even starts blinking
They'll soon tell that same stranger where to
go

Now if it's trouble or a fight you're after
Take this bit of good advice from me
Catch a Highland bus outside Charlie's snack
bar
And get as far away as you can be

Anon

The Scaffy Man

(To the tune of John Brown's Body)

Now folks I think you know my job
A scaffy all my days
Its not as quite an easy job
As everybody says
I've shifted nearly everything
From beds to wifie's stays
In the back of my Corporation Cart

Chorus

Rubbish, Rubbish. All the rubbish of the day
Pots and Pans and Jeely jars
And hens that widnae lay
Herring bones and sausages
You could smell five miles away
In the back of my Corporation Cart

I've shifted nearly everything from chanty
pots to pails
I've sorted out a lot of stuff from rags to rusty
nails
I've shifted nearly everything out of Fraser's
sales
In the back of my Corporation Cart

Chorus

A wifie phoned to tell me
That she lost her bottom teeth
She lost the head and fainted till she heard
with great relief
We found them at the Longman
In a chunk of bully beef
In the back of my Corporation Cart

Anon

The End